GREAT BRITAIN AND
UNITED STATES EXPANSION:
1898–1900

Great Britain and United States Expansion: 1898-1900

by

R. G. Neale

MICHIGAN STATE UNIVERSITY PRESS

1966

Manufactured in the United States of America

Preface

IN THE STUDY of the early development of the rapprochement between Britain and the United States which began in the nineties of the last century, much importance has been attached in the past to the Spanish-American War and to Britain's attempts during and after the war to encourage the United States in imperialist adventures—adventures which would best serve Britain's attempts to preserve China from partition and British trade from exclusion. The purpose of this monograph is to examine the realities of the relationship between British diplomacy and American imperialism during and immediately after the Spanish-American War.

Most of the existing literature dealing with the Spanish-American War has been based upon surveys of public opinion, the memoirs and biographies of the personalities involved, the public records of the Spanish government and the United States State Department, the British parliamentary papers, and the German documents collected in *Die Grosse Politik der Europäischen Kabinette 1871-1914*. The result has been that investigations of some aspects of the war have been thorough and definitive while others have been strictly limited by the lack of adequate sources. In this way, studies of Spanish-American relations have been quite complete and Germany's attitude has been plainly revealed. American opinion concerning the war has been thoroughly analysed and German-American relations have been clarified beyond dispute. However, the standard studies of the one field to which most importance has been attached by English writers, that is, diplomatic relations between England and America during the war, have been very limited.

This limitation has been imposed by the unavailability of the relevant records in the British Foreign Office. As a consequence most investigations have been within the field of public opinion where the necessary materials have been available. The published results of research in this field have established conclusively the importance of the Spanish-American War in the development of English opinion concerning America, and they have analysed thoroughly the pressures within America which finally led to the annexation of the Philippines. For that reason no attempt has been made in this essay to examine public opinion except in so far as was necessary to the main purpose of the work. For the same reason it was thought unnecessary in chapters three and four to restate the conclusions of the excellent analyses, particularly that by C. S. Campbell, Jr., of the domestic pressures upon the American executive in favour of annexation. My task in this case was to clarify Britain's role in this particular phase of American imperialist expansion.

On the other hand, the lack of English diplomatic sources has had some unfortunate results. Where English diplomacy has been examined, reliance has been placed upon German and American sources supplemented by biographical material and by the carefully pre-selected publications of the British government, as well as the public opinion surveys already mentioned. The result has been that Britain's actual diplomatic policies have frequently been confused with what public opinion thought they were or should be. It is only since the Public Record Office has made available the relevant material that a re-examination of British policy has become possible. When the Public Record Office material and the Salisbury Papers became available, a division of opinion appeared among writers in the field. Some specialist articles challenged the conclusions of the older standard works concerning the role of the Spanish-American War in Anglo-American relations; but the new general works published, notably the brilliant *Anglo-American*

Understanding 1898-1903 by C. S. Campbell, Jr., upheld many of the earlier interpretations.

This work is an attempt to resolve this conflict in interpretation. It is an essay in diplomatic history confined within the limits of that discipline and designed to reconstruct accurately and to evaluate the real nature of Britain's diplomatic contacts with the United States concerning the Spanish-American War. Reliance has been placed predominantly upon the Salisbury Papers and the records of the British Foreign Office and Foreign Office Library supplemented by Colonial Office, War Office, Admiralty, and Customs Office documents, where the importance of the material concerned warranted their being brought to the notice of the Foreign Office. The activities of the Association of the British Chambers of Commerce were followed in the Letter Books and Minute Books of the Executive Council of the Association and in the correspondence between Sir Stafford Northcote, Lord Charles Beresford, and Lord Salisbury. Only secondary use has been made of *Die Grosse Politik* and of the United States Department of State records, for these have already been examined very thoroughly elsewhere. This applies particularly to the definitive studies of German policy by Professor T. A. Bailey and L. B. Shippee. In fact the brief section in chapter two dealing with the conflict in Manila Bay adds nothing to Professor Bailey's work and is included solely in order to complete the study of Britain's neutrality in the Far East. The French records of the period have not yet been made available but the Austrian documents have been used by J. A. S. Grenville of Nottingham University, and the Spanish archival material was used by Orestes Ferrara in his book *The Last Spanish War*.

The British records are particularly informative because in the period under examination the system still prevailed by which hand-written despatches and decoded telegrams were received in the Foreign Office and comments by under secretaries, secretaries, and ministers were minuted on the actual documents. This means that immediately contemporary and illuminating personal comment is supplied, so that reliance need not be placed too heavily upon biographical material selected, edited, and published long after the events with which the documents are concerned.

The method adopted has been to re-examine the conclusions accepted in previous writings by comparing them with the complete English records now available, concentrating almost entirely upon diplomatic action as distinct from public opinion. The purpose of the Introduction is merely to provide a starting point by briefly recalling to mind well known and established material relevant to the investigations contained in the four following chapters. Chapter one is an examination of the quality of British friendship for the United States before the outbreak of the war. It defines Britain's reaction to Spanish pressure for assistance against America as well as the response of the British ambassador to Washington and Foreign Office officials to European moves for intervention or mediation. It also attempts a realistic assessment of the extent to which the United Kingdom was responsible for the neutrality of the European powers. Chapter two examines the nature of British neutrality during the war, in particular the extent to which consideration for American as against Spanish interests determined cabinet policy. The varying attitudes of Chamberlain, Balfour, and Salisbury are examined in a variety of disputes from Gibraltar through Egypt and the Suez to Singapore, Hong Kong, and the Philippines. Chapter three, "Britain and the Peace," is concerned to analyse during this crucial period the extent to which the United Kingdom assisted or encouraged the United States in its Far Eastern expansion, and considers British policy in the Philippines in its proper context, that is, in close relation to the China situation. Chapter four is a re-assessment of the place of the Spanish-American War in the development of the Anglo-American entente after the peace. It deals with the effect of the war upon the settlement of outstanding disputes between the two countries and upon the diplomacy concerned with the open door notes. In this connection the Salisbury Papers finally solve the problem of Lord Charles Beresford's relations with cabinet and the Foreign Office. Each of the chapters can stand by itself and the conclusions thought to be warranted have in each case been stated explicitly at the end of each stage of the argument. For this reason, a conclusion involving an elaborate restatement was thought unnecessary, the whole work being concluded merely by a short note in retrospect.

The footnote references to the British Foreign Office documents give the volume numbers as they are listed in the index in the Public Record Office; the figures immediately following the letters refer to the country and those after the stroke refer to the volume in the series. Thus FO5/2571 refers to Foreign Office, United States, Volume 2571. (The code numbers of each country are listed in the Bibliography.) As all documents are arranged in chronological order, any document can readily be located by using the date and the despatch or telegram number.

The research upon which this work is based was made possible by most generous assistance from the Rockefeller Foundation in 1951 and from the British Council in 1959. Unpublished Crown copyright material in the Public Record Office, London, has been reproduced by permission of the Controller of Her Majesty's Stationery Office. The extracts from the papers of the Third Marquess of Salisbury are published with the kind permission of the present Marquess.

Brisbane 1963   R. G. Neale

Contents

Introduction

THROUGHOUT the history of the twentieth century the quality of Anglo-American co-operation has been of fundamental importance in determining the outcome of international conflicts and the quality and duration of international peace. In tracing the history of Anglo-American relations during this period it has been customary for diplomatic historians to attach great importance to the Spanish-American War. Their interpretations have been based upon research completed before the unpublished records of the British Foreign Office were made available to scholars. The purpose of this volume is to re-examine the nature of British-American relations during the Spanish-American War in the light of Foreign Office material which can now be used.

For such an examination certain preliminaries are desirable. As the British cabinet's attitude to America was an integral part of foreign policies determined by Britain's world-wide commitments, it is necessary to outline briefly the context of international events within which Anglo-American relations developed during the Spanish-American War. Secondly, in order to assess the importance of the war in the development of Anglo-American friendship, the nature of diplomatic negotiations between the two powers immediately preceding the war must be indicated. Finally, it is necessary briefly to recall to mind the known assumptions and convictions of those in the British cabinet and the American executive whose responsibility it was to determine the actual diplomatic relationship between the English-speaking nations.

In the international scene early in 1898 Britain was faced with two hostile combinations of powers: the Triple Alliance, dominated by Germany's ambitions, and the Dual Alliance, expressing, among other things, Russian and French jealousy of Britain's colonial supremacy in Africa and Asia. These alliances, although opposed one to the other, seemed at the time to be even more opposed to Britain. At the worst this could mean that Britain would not only be isolated, but would be in danger from a combination of powers agreed upon, if not united in, a conspiracy to despoil the British empire. At the very least it would mean that Britain would no longer be able to manipulate the balance of power, for that was possible only when the mutual antagonisms of the powers were greater than their rivalries with England. The reality of the danger was made clear to the British Foreign Office in a famous series of disputes.

The Kaiser's telegram to Kruger, sent after the failure of the Jameson Raid, made alarmingly clear to the English public the anti-British policy developed by Baron Von Holstein in Germany. This destroyed any lingering belief that France alone was the enemy and that Germany, whose Kaiser was Queen Victoria's grandson, was Great Britain's friend. It demonstrated clearly that Germany, as well as France, was England's imperial rival.

In West Africa, French colonial rivalry was equally obvious. Supported by the French Foreign Minister, M. Hanotaux, French colonial policy had been for large native forces commanded by French officers to occupy the West African hinterland, thus isolating the British coastal settlements which were based largely upon trade. Chamberlain's riposte was to supplement British trading activity by organizing a West African Frontier Force, under the command of Lord Frederick Lugard. While the Niger Conference attempted from 1897 to 1898 to decide by negotiation the division of West African territories, these rival military forces, in their endeavours to occupy as much territory as possible, were in danger of provoking an armed collision. It was not until June 1898 that the West African dispute was settled by an Anglo-French Convention.

This settlement, however, did not prevent the occurrence of the more famous Fashoda incident. As early as March 1895 Sir Edward Grey had announced publicly that the advance into the Nile Valley of a French expedition under secret instructions would be an unfriendly act and would be so viewed by England.[1] However, in 1896 French troops under Captain Marchand began their move from the south toward the Nile Valley and Sir Herbert Kitchener commenced his southern drive from Egypt in the north. The inevitable result was the meeting at Fashoda in September 1898 and for some months there was grave danger of war between Great Britain and France. It was not until February 1899 that Théophile Delcassé, who had replaced Hanotaux at the Foreign Office, agreed to modify French claims, and in March the Anglo-French Convention decided upon the boundary which was to limit French and British ambitions along the Nile and the Congo. It was not really until after this agreement and the appointment of M. Paul Cambon as French ambassador in London that Anglo-French relations moved toward that *bonne entente* which was finally achieved in 1904.

Meanwhile in South Africa a crisis in British-Boer relations was rapidly developing. Kruger continued his heavy import of armaments and was confirmed in power by the Transvaal presidential election of February 1898. Sir Alfred Milner's activities, together with Rhodes's recovery in April 1898 of the position Chamberlain had forced him to resign in 1896, and Britain's failure to acquire Delagoa Bay, all seemed to indicate the imminence of strife. In November came the shooting of an Englishman by a Boer policeman, who was tried, acquitted, and commended by the presiding judge. There followed a mass agitation and a huge petition to the Queen from her subjects on the Rand. This petition reached the Queen just after Milner's famous "Helots" despatch in April 1899. Then came the failure of the Bloemfontein Conference, after which war seemed inevitable.

In the Far East, as in Africa, British supremacy was also being challenged. Germany's policy of naval expansion, particularly as emphasized by the Naval Law of April 1898, was in itself a sufficient challenge to British naval strength and it became a very real threat when used to extend German influence in China. As early as 1896 Admiral Von Tirpitz had recommended that Kiaochow, dominating the province of Shantung, possessed the greatest potential for a military and economic base. The murder of German missionaries in August 1897 was the pretext under which Germany forced upon China a lease of Kiaochow for ninety-nine years, to date from January 1898. This demonstration of Germany's Far Eastern ambitions confirmed Russia and France in their determination to acquire additional territory and influence. There followed Russia's seizure of Port Arthur and Talienwan and the French acquisition at a later date of Kwangchowan. These Far Eastern activities of France and Germany and particularly of Russia were regarded by Britain as an imminent threat not only to the freedom of trade but also to the territorial and administrative integrity of China. Of this conclusive proof seemed to be provided by Russia's seizure of Port Arthur. The immediate response was a tremendous public outcry in England for stronger measures to protect British interests in the Far East.

In the face of hostile alliances, challenged in Africa and the Far East, and conscious of the threat implicit in Britain's isolation, cabinet had two alternatives: to endeavour to maintain the concert of Europe, or, if this proved impossible, to weaken either or both of the opposing alliances by seeking an agreement with one or more of the European powers. In pursuit of the first alternative, Salisbury made one last effort in 1897 and 1898 to maintain the concert of Europe; this was his attempt to reach a settlement of Near Eastern affairs. However, with the war between Turkey and Greece, followed by Germany's withdrawal from the concert in March 1898, his attempt failed.

In pursuit of the second alternative, Salisbury acquiesced in Chamberlain's two attempts in 1898 and 1899 to reach an agreement with Germany. The failure of both these attempts, and the increased antagonism which emerged from them, showed Salisbury's pessimism concerning Chamberlain's chances of success to have been justified. In January 1898, three months before Chamberlain's attempt with Germany, Salisbury himself had submitted to the Czar a detailed plan to settle all subjects of difference between Britain and Russia to the end that a full understanding might be achieved. This attempt was wrecked by Russia's seizure of Port Arthur, an action itself partly provoked by Germany's seizure of Kiaochow. The situation in March then was that Britain remained isolated, and all her attempts either to maintain the concert of Europe or to weaken the alliances opposed to her had failed.

This was the international environment in 1898 which so largely determined Britain's attitude to America during the Spanish-American War. To put an end to the dangers inherent in her isolation Britain was in search of allies.[2] Therefore, having failed with Russia and Germany and still being at odds with France, it was only logical that she should endeavour to win American support in international affairs, or, if this proved impossible, at least to ensure that American opposition to England should not be aroused.

These considerations had already guided British policy towards America since 1896. The astonishment and shock occasioned by the bitterness of Secretary of State Olney's ultimatum to Salisbury over the Venezuelan boundary dispute were followed in England by a widespread and powerfully supported demand that the dispute should be settled peacefully. At this crucial moment came the news of the Kruger telegram. This thrust German hostility into the forefront of British politics and converted into a cabinet decision the public desire for a peaceful settlement with America. The result is well known. Cabinet set out by arbitration and by diplomacy to settle Britain's outstanding disputes with the United States. Of these there were many. In addition to Venezuela, the most difficult were those concerning the seal fisheries in the Behring Sea, the revision of the Clayton-Bulwer Treaty as a prelude to the building of the isthmian canal, and the Canadian boundary. Although not all settled until 1909, a dramatic beginning was made when Salisbury agreed to submit the Venezuelan boundary to arbitration. The change in the tone of Anglo-American relations was emphasized by the attempt in 1897 by Secretary of State Olney and Ambassador Pauncefote to negotiate a rather innocuous arbitration treaty between the two countries. The object was to ensure the peaceful settlement of all future disputes. This treaty the United States Senate refused to ratify for two reasons—the assertion of its own predominance over the executive and the traditional antipathy to any entanglement with foreign powers which might limit America's freedom to determine its foreign policy. Despite this rebuff cabinet persisted in the attempt to reach an understanding, and inspired by the enthusiasm of Balfour and Chamberlain a secret formal approach was made to the President in March 1898 proposing that Britain and America should stand together to resist further territorial expansion in the Far East.

The cabinet whose responsibility it was to formulate English policy toward the Spanish-American War was formed in June 1895 and led by the Marquess of Salisbury as Premier and Foreign Secretary. A. J. Balfour was First Lord of the Treasury and deputized at the Foreign Office whenever, as was frequently the case, Salisbury was ill. Joseph Chamberlain as Colonial Secretary was perhaps the dominant figure in this cabinet, being permitted, if not demanding, "usually the power of a co-Premier and on some rare occasions more."[3] These three in particular determined the formation of Britain's foreign policy. On matters of defence they were advised by Lord Lansdowne as Secretary for War, and G. J. Goschen as First Lord of the Admiralty. In October 1900 Salisbury relinquished the Foreign Office to Lansdowne, and from this time on there was a marked increase in Lansdowne's influence upon foreign policy. Britain's ambassador at Washington was Sir Julian Pauncefote (raised to the peerage in August 1899), while Mr. John Hay was America's ambassador at the Court of St. James.

Salisbury, who was past his prime, was never as eager as were Chamberlain and Balfour to establish an Anglo-American entente. His rather cold and aristocratic temperament found American diplomatic manners most offensive. He threatened to resign rather than submit as tamely as Harcourt and the Opposition desired to American demands over Venezuela.[4] During the Spanish-American dispute, as it developed first in Cuba and then in the Philippines, his sympathy for Spain and his reluctance to see her humiliated were in accord with the attitude of the British court and aristocratic circles. Nevertheless his conception of Britain's security interests and his knowledge of America's potential strength enabled him to acquiesce in the attempts by Balfour and Chamberlain to establish an Anglo-American accord.

Balfour, however, was far more enthusiastic in his attitude toward America. He was a friend of Henry White[5] and was convinced that it was necessary to reach an agreement with America. This he made clear in his first important speech made in Manchester, January 1896, after the Prime Minister had approved its content. His theme was that "the idea of war with the United States carries with it some of the unnatural horror of a civil war. . . . The time will come, the time must come, when some statesman of authority, more fortunate even than President Monroe, will lay down the doctrine that between English-speaking peoples war is impossible."[6] It is very difficult to assess accurately the relative influence of Salisbury or Balfour in particular issues in March and April 1898, because of the facility with which Balfour moved in and out of the Foreign Office in order to ease the burden upon his ailing uncle.

There is no doubt that Chamberlain was the chief exponent of collaboration with America. He was married to a Bostonian and both he and his wife carried on a voluminous correspondence with American friends. He occasionally visited the United States as a private citizen and in this way came to know and to some extent understand the American scene. His Birmingham speech of January 1896 during the Venezuelan affair expressed a deeply felt conviction and was not mere oratory.

War between the two nations would be an absurdity as well as a crime . . . the two nations are allied and more closely allied in sentiment and in interest than any other nations on the face of the earth. While I should look with horror upon anything in the nature of a fratricidal strife I should look forward with pleasure to the possibility of the Stars and Stripes and the Union Jack floating together in defence of a common cause sanctioned by humanity and justice.[7]

At Washington, Britain was represented by Sir Julian Pauncefote, who had the very difficult task of succeeding Sir Lionel Sackville-West whose conduct before he was finally asked to depart the country had aroused a most bitter outburst of Anglophobia. Pauncefote disapproved of America's diplomatic manners, nevertheless from the time of his appointment in 1888 until his death in 1902 he skilfully conducted an uninterrupted campaign to achieve a lasting Anglo-American friendship. His task was not an easy one, for he had to deal with difficult people. President William McKinley lacked initiative in foreign affairs and was exceedingly sensitive to party considerations and business influences in his determination of foreign policy. Secretary of State John Sherman was senile and stubbornly isolationist, and prepared naïvely to accept Russian and German assurances. Nevertheless Pauncefote's tact and skill were such that he had succeeded by 1898 in establishing himself as the most trusted and popular ambassador at Washington. His task became much easier when John Hay became Secretary of State, and his position as *doyen* gave him added prestige and influence. Such was his popularity that even Theodore Roosevelt, so opposite in temperament to Pauncefote, could vote him "a damned good fellow."

Introduction

In London, as American ambassador, the British cabinet was most fortunate in having to deal with John Hay. His polished manners, his quiet humour, his social sensitivity, his patient courtesy, together with his skill as a host, won him a more general acceptance and popularity than the majority of ambassadors before or since have known. Even Queen Victoria approved of him. A renowned Anglophile, it was his constant task to supplement the efforts of Balfour, Chamberlain, and Pauncefote. The measure of his skill was that he could do this effectively without arousing more than the normal American criticism of any diplomatic action which could be interpreted as favouring England, America's traditional enemy. This same policy he continued as Secretary of State, publicly defining his intentions in these terms: "As long as I stay here [i.e. at the head of the State Department], no action shall be taken contrary to my conviction that the one indispensable feature of our foreign policy should be a friendly understanding with England, but an alliance must remain in the present state of things an unattainable dream."[8]

This brief sketch of the highlights of the diplomatic environment preceding the outbreak of the Spanish-American War would seem to suggest that cabinet's attitude to the conflict was almost determined for it. Unless they endangered Britain's security interests, Spain's difficulties with her colonies and her fear of American intervention would not be of great moment to the Foreign Office. The chief problems confronting those whose responsibility it was to determine Britain's international policies arose from the threats from Russia and Germany in the Far East, Africa, and Europe, the difficult arbitration with the United States, and the rivalry with France in Africa. In these circumstances, given the extent of Britain's commitments, the degree of hostility toward her, and the grouping of the personnel in the cabinet, it was most unlikely that cabinet would invite the hostility of the United States in the interests of Spain. Whether or not this was so will become apparent from an examination of the exact nature of the diplomatic relationship between Britain and America during the diplomatic preliminaries to the war.

Notes

1. R. C. K. Ensor, *England 1870-1914* (London: Oxford University Press, 1936), p. 244.

2. So much was this the topic of diplomatic planning that as early as December 1897 Chamberlain could begin one of his impetuous letters to Balfour: "Talking about allies, have you considered whether we might not draw closer to Japan?" After consideration it was decided not to attempt an alliance with Japan, but Chamberlain's letter is an excellent example of cabinet thinking at this time. J. L. Garvin, *The Life of Joseph Chamberlain* (London: Macmillan & Co., 1932-34), III, 249.

3. *Ibid.*, p. 7.

4. *Ibid.*, p. 160.

5. Henry White was first secretary in the United States embassy in London. B. E. C. Dugdale, *Arthur James Balfour* (London: Hutchinson & Co., 1936), I, 227.

6. *Ibid.*, p. 226.

7. Quoted S. F. Bemis, *A Diplomatic History of the United States* (3rd ed.; New York: Holt & Co., 1950), p. 421.

8. Quoted T. Dennett, *John Hay* (New York: Dodd Mead & Co., 1933), p. 221.

GREAT BRITAIN AND
UNITED STATES EXPANSION:
1898–1900

Diplomatic Prelude

I

UNTIL 1902 LITTLE DOUBT EXISTED that Great Britain had befriended the United States in 1898. This friendship, it was argued, was revealed by the manner in which the Foreign Office refrained from any action that would assist Spain and refused to participate in diplomatic procedures designed by some European friends of Spain to embarrass the United States. This inactivity might appear rather negative but, as England was the only naval power capable of enforcing international decisions, her inaction in certain circumstances could have been decisive. In 1898 the governments of Europe and the United States certainly believed that Britain's inertia was calculated policy designed to restrain any concerted European action and to permit the United States a free hand. This belief seemed to be corroborated by the public statements of British and American statesmen,[1] the reaction of the British, European, and United States press, and by British diplomatic action. McKinley and Theodore Roosevelt both testified to it and the Democrats even alleged the existence of a secret alliance between the

United States and the United Kingdom. This belief was so widespread and so dangerous to the government that Hay was forced publicly to deny the reality of any such written or unwritten agreement.[2] The Quai d'Orsai and German officials both made use of English expressions of goodwill towards the United States further to embitter Spanish relations with England.[3] In Vienna, Count Goluchowski, the Austrian Foreign Minister, condemned what he termed the criminal short-sightedness of England in encouraging the imperialist ambitions of the United States. In Spain at a later date the press claimed that Her Majesty's government had offered to impede any concerted European action in return for support from the United States in Britain's attempt to stabilize the Far East.[4] The Spanish Minister for Foreign Affairs believed England refrained from joint representations to the United States which would have prevented war. He questioned the British ambassador Sir Henry Drummond Wolff concerning this but accepted Salisbury's explanation that it was not so.[5]

This official belief was reflected in the continental press, which bitterly attacked the failure of the United Kingdom to take any action to prevent America's aggression against the interests of the monarchial principle as represented by Spain. In England, public statements by Balfour and Chamberlain[6] favouring co-operation between the United States and Britain were so pointed that questions were asked in parliament[7] as to the existence or otherwise of an alliance. Chamberlain desired an alliance and told the United States ambassador he would resign if the United Kingdom were to oppose the United States,[8] and Earl Grey was reported to have suggested to Hay that the United States should borrow the British fleet.[9] The pattern seemed complete when even Olney made his famous speech in which he spoke of "a patriotism of race as well as of country" and envisaged the possibility of Britain and America "standing together against any alien foe by whom either was menaced with destruction."[10]

To this impressive weight of evidence of British support for

2

the United States, diplomatic action seemed to lend an official seal. As early as June 1896, Salisbury had expressed to Henry White his opinion of the dispute: "It is no affair of ours, we are friendly to Spain and should be sorry to see her humiliated, but we do not consider that we have anything to say in the matter whatever may be the course the United States may decide to pursue."[11] This attitude governed the reaction to diplomatic reports from Spain and from the United States. Reports from Washington concerning the Cuban affair were merely routine until 24 September 1897, when the increased tension between Spain and the United States was reflected in an instruction from the Foreign Office to Mr. Frederick Adam (chargé d'affaires at Washington during Pauncefote's absence in London on leave) to telegraph any information as to the aims and intentions of the United States government. This instruction was prompted by a report from Drummond Wolff that the United States minister had warned Spain that "unless a satisfactory assurance can be given by 1st November that peace will be secured in Cuba, the United States will consider themselves free to take the steps necessary to this result with due regard to their own interests and general tranquillity."[12]

As State Department officials seemed reluctant to discuss the matter, Frederick Adam did not formally seek information from them, but forwarded a report of an interview with the Spanish ambassador, Dupuy de Lôme, which seemed to indicate no immediate prospect of conflict.[13] In contrast to Wolff's report from Madrid, Frederick Adam was assured that the United States note to which Wolff had referred was "unusually moderate and courteous . . . far more so than former communications," and that it was in fact an offer of the good offices of the United States in an effort to secure peace in Cuba. Reports that threatening language was used in the note were attributed to the indiscretion of the United States representative in Spain, Mr. W. L. Woodford, in particular to his "absolute inexperience and to his imprudent conduct in admitting certain newspaper correspondents into his confidence."[14] De Lôme held the view that the note was delivered at this time in an endeavour to settle the Cuban affair before the next session of Congress. He believed that the United States government "was not at all disposed to take any serious action on the Cuban question" because of the pressure from big business to keep the peace and permit the revival of trade. Despite these views expressed by De Lôme, Frederick Adam was more inclined to put his trust in the rumours current in Washington that the real purpose of the note and the request for an early reply was "to have a definite policy ready to lay before Congress, so as to be able to invite the co-operation of that body in a solution of the Cuban question, in the event of Spain's rejecting the good offices which have been offered to her."[15] This despatch was followed throughout October by others reporting the violent attack upon Spain that was developing throughout the United States press. These were received at the Foreign Office without comment, for Salisbury had once more reassured Hay as to Britain's attitude and Hay in turn reported to McKinley that the United States need not concern itself with any danger of British intervention.[16]

In January 1898 Pauncefote was back in Washington, and at first confirmed Adam's estimate of the situation. After a careful survey of the press and congressional feeling he reported that "there appears to be no ground for supposing that the present administration intend to take any active steps with regard to Cuba in the near future," though there were signs "significant of impending dangers."[17] However, February brought the publication of the Dupuy de Lôme letter, the sinking of the U.S.S. "Maine," and the outburst of journalistic and congessional jingoism which followed.[18] In February also the reports of the British consuls in the United States established clear evidence of active preparations for war. On 28 February Pauncefote reported that "there can be little doubt that preparations have been going on quietly for the last three months."[19] By 11 March, following the passage of a bill voting fifty million dollars for defence, Pauncefote summed up in these words: "It is now generally recognised that the intervention of the United States whether peaceable or otherwise, between Spain and the Cuban insurgents, can not be much longer deferred. Indeed I understood as much in conversation yesterday with the Secretary of State."[20]

Throughout all this period it will be noted that the Foreign Office had sent to the Washington embassy only one instruction concerning the dispute, namely to report all trustworthy information of America's aims and intentions. The explanation is threefold. In the first place, the United States did not raise the issue at the official level. Salisbury's early assurance to Henry White, the tone of the press in 1897 and 1898, and Mr. Hay's assurances to McKinley,[21] left the United States in no doubt as to England's attitude. Secondly, it is safe to assume that during Pauncefote's stay in London prior to January, the situation had been thoroughly discussed and the government's attitude made quite plain, so that Pauncefote needed no instructions provided that international complications did not arise. As will be shown, as soon as Spain and Austria sought to place the dispute on an international basis, the Foreign Office immediately sent further instructions. More important than either of these reasons, however, is the fact that, persuaded by Chamberlain's enthusiasm and Balfour's reasoned support, Salisbury acquiesced in a move to acquire America's active support in the Far East.[22] In the face of Russia's threat to the freedom of commerce in the Far East, the fate of Spain's colonies was a very minor matter. The attempt to persuade the United States to stand with Britain against further Russian encroachment was certainly not to be jeopardized by any gesture in favour of Spain.

Viewed only from the archives of the State Department and the Washington embassy, British policy appears as colourless inactivity which might well be taken to reflect a lack of interest rather than a carefully thought out policy. However, the Madrid records and the correspondence between Lord Salisbury and Sir Henry Drummond Wolff make clear the pressures brought to bear upon England in favour of Spain.

The Queen Regent's direct appeals to her aunt Queen Victoria are well known and became more frequent as the inevitability of war became more apparent to the court; but as early as March 1896 she endeavoured—and with marked success—to enlist the sympathies and support of Drummond Wolff who forwarded her appeals both to the Foreign Office and direct to Salisbury. He reported that the Queen had sent for him and begged him to seek Lord Salisbury's friendly counsel concerning Cuba. Believing that the President of the United States was friendly toward Spain it was her hope that Salisbury might be able to influence him not to act with precipitation.[23] The replies from both Balfour and Salisbury should have made clear to Wolff the uselessness of any further attempt to enlist more than their verbal sympathy for the Queen. Said Balfour: "We are not on good terms with the United States just now as a consequence of Venezuela and any interference of ours would be worse than useless."[24] Salisbury replied at greater length and with greater patience than he was to show towards Wolff for some time to come. "It is of course gratifying to us that the Spaniards should think so highly of England's moral support as they do but their preference is open to the interpretation that they want somebody to bell the cat." He advised Wolff that it was Britain's function "humbly to take a back seat and not at all to seek the front seat." He went on: "It should be added that we have no special fitness for the office: for any diplomatic movement in which we occupied the foremost position would be assured beforehand of the hostility of a powerful party in the United States." "Cuba," he said, "does not interest us at all except as a means of keeping the Queen Regent on the throne."[25] These replies in no way dampened Wolff's enthusiasm and in July he wrote again to Salisbury (who was in the south of France) begging him together with Lady Salisbury to come to San Sebastian to meet the Queen, of whom he wrote sentimentally, "You do not know what a charming woman she is nor the good she does."[26] To this as to every other appeal from or on behalf of the Queen Regent the British government returned a firm refusal to intervene in any way.

Drummond Wolff, however, remained a staunch advocate on behalf of Spain and the Queen and delivered to the Foreign Office and particularly to Salisbury a barrage of despatches, telegrams, and private letters[27] arguing the Spanish cause. He emphasized what he considered to be the value of Spain as a Mediterranean ally, hinting that it would be perfectly possible "that an arrangement could be made with Spain highly favourable to the position of both countries." He sought Salisbury's permission to follow this course of action and asked for an interview with the Prime Minister upon his return from the Riviera. When Salisbury refused to see him on this occasion, he telegraphed seeking permission to come to England to discuss the issue with the Prime Minister. He sought Salisbury's support for an attempt to persuade Austria to take the initiative in some form of joint action. He argued that such an action was most necessary to restrain the United States, for if war came the Spanish dynasty would be endangered. As he put it: "Both Carlists and Republicans who always fish conjointly in troubled waters will make the best capital they can out of the difficulties while France and Russia will get all they can in the Mediterranean."[28] This appeal for support in the interests of the dynastic principle (as it came to be known) was an attempt to build upon Salisbury's previously expressed opinion that Cuba did not interest England at all except as a means of keeping the Queen Regent on the throne.

To all these manoeuvres and appeals the Foreign Office and Salisbury turned a deaf ear—replying if at all with a brief and cold negative. The effect upon Wolff showed clearly in the plaintive note that crept into his letters as time went on. He concluded the letter quoted above in these terms: "I merely make these remarks in case they may be worth attention—but it is rather an uphill game to endeavour to elicit interest in

7

what many regard as a dead horse [*sic*] and gives the feeling of one crying in the wilderness."[29] Later in January 1897 he was still writing and complaining in a similar strain without receiving any reply. "I really do not know whether or not you approve of my writing to you so frequently. But I suppose that silence if not signifying consent signifies at least a polite acquiescence."[30]

Despite the clear indication of England's official attitude, Wolff's affection and admiration for the Queen, his solicitude for the fate of the dynasty, and his anachronistic belief in the value of Spain as a Mediterranean ally led him into actions which frequently brought him under the displeasure and suspicion of the Foreign Office as being at least unwisely pro-Spanish if not actively anti-American. This is shown very clearly in the diplomatic action and reaction following upon Spain's attempt to call into being a new concert of Europe. Her dual intention was to use it to neutralize any threat of direct action by the United States to solve the Cuban problem, and to coerce the United States into preventing aid from reaching the Cuban rebels.

President Cleveland's Secretary of State, Richard Olney of Venezuelan fame, made the first move early in 1896 by offering friendly but informal advice to the Spanish government through its ambassador Dupuy de Lôme, to the effect that it would be desirable for Spain to solve the Cuban problem by instituting reforms of such a nature that they would deprive the rebels of the moral support of the United States. This overture was ignored in Madrid, so Olney on 4 April took the logical next step and forwarded an official note to Spain suggesting that the good offices of the United States might be used in an attempt to reach a settlement on the basis of the retention of Spanish sovereignty combined with a grant of a reasonable degree of self-government to Cuba. This, in the opinion of the State Department, was the type of settlement which would prevent all thought of intervention by making it unnecessary. Despite the friendly tone, the threat was obvious.

Spain haughtily rejected the offer of mediation and in the Cortes, prior to the official reply to the United States, the Prime Minister promised a degree of reform but only after the pacification of Cuba had been completed.

Despite the tone of his rejection of it, the note seriously perturbed Prime Minister Canovas del Castillo and his Foreign Minister Carlos O'Donnell Y Abreu, and acting upon a suggestion by the Italian ambassador they sought to enlist the aid of the European heads of state in counteracting United States pressure. The project was initially discussed with the Spanish ministers and canvassed among the European ambassadors, all of whom supported it.[31] The plan was to activate Russia, and if not Russia then Austria, to initiate a move to unite the European powers in support of Spain's view of the Cuban-Spanish-American imbroglio and to lend the weight of their support to a series of extraordinary demands upon America. The design was to put an end to United States aid to the rebels, to ensure Spanish security from any American intervention, and thus to ensure Spanish success in putting down the rebellion and avoiding any internal threat to the Spanish throne.

Orestes Ferrara, from his investigation of the Spanish archives, has revealed that from the beginning there appeared a difference between the attitudes of Wolff and Lord Salisbury —a difference very puzzling to the Spanish Foreign Minister. In his letter of instruction[32] to the Spanish ambassador in London, O'Donnell pointed out "very confidentially" that as Wolff had kept Salisbury fully informed no difficulty should be encountered with Salisbury. The relevant portion of the document should be quoted:

I say to you in the strictest confidence, and for the purpose only of guiding you—begging, at the same time, that you dissimulate your knowledge of what I am about to tell you—that Salisbury has sent me, through Wolff, a verbal message, or rather a written message which Wolff brought with him from London and read to me, to the effect that although, because of the special circumstances in which the English Government finds itself in its relations with the United States, it is not possible for him to offer to take the initiative, he will nevertheless give us effective help if some other European Power will take the lead. This satisfactory declaration Wolff has made to me repeatedly, and I can tell you that he has not been hindmost among the envoys here, who have worked to get their colleagues to collaborate in this enterprise of ours.

In the light of Wolff's actions I am unable to understand the reserve which you say in your recent despatches that the Secretary of State for Foreign Affairs [Salisbury] has shown in his conversations with you; nor can I understand why he should speak as he did to the Austrian and French ambassadors, as described in your letter. It may be that he took this course in order to avoid committing himself in advance with those governments, before he had studied the Memorandum and before you, acting officially as my representative, had talked with him.

However, this contradiction can be left for time and your efforts at London to clarify.[33]

Given the cold reception by Balfour and Salisbury to Wolff's early appeal for support for the Spanish Queen, his continuing hope for British aid seems hard to understand. Through April to August, in terms that suggest very real support for O'Donnell's plan, he continued to urge Spain's cause upon the Foreign Office. In his opinion Austria was well fitted to take the initiative in "getting the powers to do something to help Spain." He pointed out that this opinion was shared by "the Papal Nuncio and everyone else who takes an interest in the country and the Queen Regent."[34] He made the important point that as Austria had neither navy nor colonies and certainly no colonial policy her advice would most evidently be disinterested. The number and the tone of these letters to Lord Salisbury entirely support Ferrara's belief that Wolff was an early and zealous supporter of O'Donnell's plan and shared his hopes.[35] However, O'Donnell's belief as to Salisbury's views as distinct from those of Wolff could only be explained by his inveterate optimism which led him to interpret Wolff's personal sympathy and support as the official policy of the United Kingdom.

The optimism with which O'Donnell set about his task very quickly received two sharp checks. The first was when Wolff withdrew his support, as did the French and several other ambassadors. This was probably due to the extremely offensive nature of the "Demands" accompanying the memorandum—demands which had not been formulated when the matter was first discussed. Wolff, knowing Salisbury's attitude, must have been horrified when on 7 August he saw the final formulation of the plan to which he had been sympathetic and to which he had lent his support. He must gladly have accepted Cleveland's neutrality declaration of 27 July as sufficient justification for not proceeding with the memorandum. This at least was the belief of Mr. Hannis Taylor, the United States ambassador.[36] The second check arose from the fact that before the Spanish ambassadors abroad had time to act upon their instructions, Spain's secret plans became known to the United States. The violent reaction of Mr. Taylor and the universal dismay on the part of Spain's representatives abroad when they saw the extreme and provocative nature of the "Demands" accompanying the note were sufficient to force O'Donnell and Canovas to issue instructions that the note should on no account be delivered. The curious thing is that O'Donnell always believed that Wolff was responsible for Taylor's discovery of Spain's plans.[37] The truth will perhaps never be known. There is no specific mention of the incident in Wolff's memoirs.[38] Taylor in his reports to the State Department implied that Wolff had been of assistance to him in discovering the contents of the note even if he had not been the first to make Taylor aware of its existence.

A suspicion of Wolff's support for O'Donnell's plan reached the Foreign Office in London at a time when Salisbury was in the south of France, and it was implied against him that he advocated that Britain should take the part of Spain against the United States.[39] The reaction was immediate and reveals the primacy of American over Spanish interests in British thinking. No pressure from Wolff, from Spain, or from Europe was sufficient to change the order of priority. Having confidence in Pauncefote's handling of the situation in Washington, the immediate concern of Foreign Office officials over the Madrid situation was to discover at once whether the United States could twist anything said or written by Wolff to show that Spain had been "put up" to the memorandum by Britain. In reply Wolff telegraphed that "in no way and on no occasion" did he hold out any hope to the Spanish government "more than . . . having full sympathy" with Spain in her trial. He strenuously denied having any part in the memorandum which he designated as "the spontaneous and unasked act of the Spanish Government."[40] His personal explanation to Salisbury of the discovery of the note by Mr. Taylor was that the United States ambassador overheard by chance the French ambassador telling a United States newspaperman of the memorandum. This enraged Mr. Taylor, hence his outburst about the affair when he called upon Wolff.[41]

After this event Wolff was almost studiously ignored by Salisbury. However, he continued to receive formal instructions from the Foreign Office interspersed with an occasional sharp query as to his actions in relation to America's representatives. A typical and revealing reply to such a query in February 1897 reads: "I am anxious to assure you at once that I have never said a word to the United States minister that can be construed into an opinion far less a policy. I have seen very little of him [Taylor] latterly and any discussion that might be going on is conducted altogether at Washington."[42]

This episode has been followed in some detail because it contrasts so clearly the sensitivity of the British Foreign Office to United States affairs with the continued support for Spanish interests by the British ambassador in Madrid. Even after this narrow escape from a grave diplomatic error Wolff continued to be sympathetic toward Spain and more particularly toward the Queen Regent. During the tense months of March and April 1898 when on leave in England (the embassy being left in the charge of Mr. G. H. Barclay), he approached Chamberlain "rather in the Spanish interest" but Chamberlain avoided discussion, giving him no opportunity to plead Spain's cause.[43] On the other hand he was received by Salisbury who took the opportunity to read him a lesson in the diplomatic facts of life. The theme of the lesson can be discerned in Wolff's reports to Salisbury after his return to Madrid. In May he wrote: "In the conversations I have had since my return I have carefully avoided any question of intervention or mediation,"[44] and again later in the same month: "The idea has gained ground that England is going to join the United States in the present war. Of this of course I know nothing, but from what you told me some time ago I know that Spain is regarded as a negligible factor."[45]

The universal reluctance on the part of the great powers to initiate any action on Spain's behalf did not dash completely the hopes of the Spanish government. And as tension increased renewed attempts were made to invoke the aid of European and British diplomacy in support of the Spanish effort to prevent American intervention.

When it was learned that McKinley intended to submit to Congress the report of the committee which investigated the "Maine" disaster, the Spanish government feared that such a step would lead to open conflict. An attempt was therefore made to obtain the "friendly offices" of England in order to induce the President "to keep within the jurisdiction of the executive anything referring to the difference with Spain with a view to an honourable settlement."[46] Cabinet's reply set the pattern for the response to every subsequent Spanish request for aid of any sort. "Her Majesty's Government would regard with regret any incident calculated unnecessarily to embitter the relations between Spain and the United States. But they cannot think that any useful end would be served by offering unasked advice to the United States Government on a subject so obviously within its competence as the time and method of communicating a report of its own officers to Congress." Her Majesty's ambassador at Washington would be informed "in case the latter should have an opportunity of informing the United States ministers of the conciliatory attitude of the Spanish Government."[47]

On 27 March Barclay informed the Foreign Office that Spain had formally requested "all the representatives of the Great Powers" to advise the United States government and Spain "to accept arbitration or some other means of settling the questions"[48] raised by Woodford's note of 23 March.[49] In London, the French government sought a definition of England's attitude to a suggestion that friendly representations should be made by all or some of the Great Powers, at Madrid and Washington simultaneously, "avoiding anything which might arouse the susceptibilities of the United States and based on grounds of humanity and on the common interests of the Powers in averting a conflict which might have deplorable consequences."[50]

These enquiries from Madrid and Paris were forwarded to Pauncefote in Washington, with a minute in Balfour's own hand that summarized the attitude and action decided upon. "We should be very much guided in our answer by the views of the United States Government. You might confidentially sound the opinion of the President."[51]

Pauncefote consulted both Hay and the President and on 30 March telegraphed a reply to the effect that at the present time the President "considers action proposed by the French Government to be premature. I was also given to understand that although your Lordship's message was fully appreciated, the proposals of the French Government would not in any case be acceptable."[52]

Barclay was then instructed that the Spanish ministers could be informed that the United States government had been sounded as to its attitude to an offer of Britain's good offices and had replied that such an offer would be premature and would have no useful effect. Her Majesty's government could therefore not encourage any such step. Obviously Her Majesty's government had no intention of initiating any move in the interests of Spain, and just as obviously approval would be sought in Washington before cabinet agreed to participate in any attempt at mediation by European powers.

There the matter rested until the issue was raised to the international level by Austria. The dynastic bonds between the Austrian and Spanish ruling houses were strong and Austria, under constant pressure from Spain, but after much hesitation, sought to organize the European powers in an effort to prevent any high-handed action by the United States. On 2 April the Austrian ambassador asked Balfour to join with the other great powers in a suggestion that their good offices might be used by the United States in the interests of peace. "I replied," wrote Balfour to Pauncefote, "that in my judgment an offer would do more harm than good unless the United States were desirous that it should be made. But I added that I was quite prepared to authorise you to consult with the President on the subject."[53] This Pauncefote did and the note was submitted by the powers on 6 April expressing the hope that if the United States intervened it would be in the interests of peace. This note had actually been framed by Pauncefote in collaboration with the Secretary of State and the President.[54] As Bülow and the Austrian minister agreed,[55] England valued United States friendship above that of Spain and without a united and energetic naval demonstration the gesture was avowedly platonic.

It would appear then that for the period up to 6 April 1898 no doubt can exist of the friendly attitude of the United Kingdom to the United States. However, in 1902 Germany publicly charged the United Kingdom with having proposed a second plan for mediation to the great powers in 1898, this time directed against the interests and policies of the United States.

The controversy arose in this way. The Kaiser had had a yacht built in the United States. Miss Alice Roosevelt was to launch it and Prince Henry of Germany was to be present at the ceremony. Both the German and the American press made much of Prince Henry's visit and of a growing friendship between the United States and Germany. Given the German, and in fact the European, hostility to British policy in Africa, and given the popular clamour in England for a closer liaison with the United States, it is not surprising that a counter campaign developed in the British press emphasizing the growing Anglo-American accord and its previous manifestations during the Spanish-American War. The incident which set off the controversy arose out of a reply to a question in the British parliament just after the announcement of Prince Henry's visit. On 20 January, apparently on his own initiative and without any prompting from the Government or the Foreign Office,[56] Mr. H. Norman (a member of the Opposition) questioned the Government concerning any British action to initiate, or to participate in, mediation between Spain and the United States in 1898. Lord Cranborne, Under Secretary for Foreign Affairs, replied that the Government had agreed to the first note (i.e. of 6 April) after ensuring that it was acceptable to the United States, but had declined to associate itself with other subsequent proposals "which seemed . . . open to objection as having the appearance of putting pressure on the Government of the United States and offering an opinion as to their attitude."[57]

This formal reply was correct, and of itself should not have given offence. However, in the atmosphere of competition between Germany and Britain for popularity in the United States, it appeared to contain a sinister innuendo that Britain's refusal prevented a united attempt by the European powers to restrain the United States. This aspect was emphasized by the United States press which reported the matter in sensational headlines. "Britain Blocked Effort to Coerce United States" was the heading of an article in the *New York Herald* that purported to give a report of an interview given by "a high official of the British Foreign Office." According to this official the Foreign Office had every reason to believe "that Austria was merely put forward as a sort of buffer in order to sound us, and that France, Germany and Russia were behind her and only waiting our assent formally to announce their own."[58] Furthermore, the definitive statement was made that the plan for collective action was dropped on account of cabinet's refusal to act, and because of this Britain incurred the enmity of the European powers.

Pauncefote reported to the Foreign Office that Cranborne's reply "had a most important and decisive effect on public opinion" in America and had baffled efforts made in "certain quarters to misrepresent the facts." He reported further that there was a strong conviction in the United States that Britain had rendered a great service in that momentous period, and enclosed cuttings to this effect from the *New York Post,* the *New York Herald* and the Washington *Evening Star.* These extracts, he concluded, "accurately reflect the sentiments of all but the Irish Party."[59]

A reply from the German press was inevitable. In an article in the *Kreuz Zeitung,*[60] two specific charges were made. The first of these was that on 14 April 1898 Great Britain, through her ambassador to the United States, had proposed a new collective note in which a declaration was to be made that the powers considered the United States intervention in Cuba unjustifiable. This attempt to censure the United States failed, it was argued, only because of Germany's refusal to participate. Secondly, it was charged that in June or July, when the United States was progressing victoriously in the Philippines, England tried to induce Spain to ask for peace in order to prevent the United States from acquiring territory in this area, for such action would be more annoying to England than to any other power. These charges provoked a particularly bitter controversy, further exacerbating British relations with Germany after the failure in 1901 to agree upon any form of alliance.

The first problem is most difficult.[61] Did Britain propose a second mediation which was designed to restrain the United States and which failed only because of German non-participation? The German government confirmed this section of the *Kreuz Zeitung* report and asserted that this was so; the British government categorically denied it.[62] A battle raged in the European and United States press. Germany alleged that the Associated Press accounts favouring the United Kingdom's view were inspired by the British Foreign Office and designed to embitter American-German relations. The French newspapers (to quote Monson, the British ambassador in France) "were so carried away by vindictiveness as to report with delight the declarations of the German press in their denunciation of what they are pleased to call British hypocrisy."[63] Most of the English and United States papers condemned the action as a clumsy attempt to mar the Anglo-American friendship which they believed to be stronger than ever. The *New York Tribune's* comment was typical. "No matter what any Power may or may not have done or desired to do, it was Great Britain that stood like a lion in the path of any European coalition against it."[64]

The explanation usually accepted to date is an account written by G. W. Smalley (the Washington correspondent of the London *Times*), a friend of Pauncefote and a supporter of Anglo-United States collaboration. According to Smalley,[65] the Austrian ambassador, at his government's direction, recommended that the great powers should send a further note to the United States suggesting that the last-minute concessions made by Spain in granting the insurgents a cease-fire and promising to Cuba a degree of autonomy provided a reasonable basis for peace. Pauncefote, acting solely as *doyen* of the diplomatic corps, and at the instance of some of his colleagues, called a meeting of ambassadors at the British embassy. Being a ready *rédacteur*, he made a rough draft of a statement embodying the sense of the meeting. This draft was taken by the French ambassador, M. Cambon, who translated it into French and changed the wording slightly. This change Pauncefote failed to notice. He signed the note as his own, and forwarded it to the Foreign Office for a decision, which when given was against any further action. This explanation was generally accepted by American and British newspapers of the time and has been accepted tentatively by historians.[66] However, it is merely an opinion, and has not in any way disposed of the basic contradiction between the published British and German documents which refer to the matter.

As this second note never reached the United States there is nothing in the files of the State Department to solve the problem. The published French documents do not refer to it, and the French government has not yet made available any others for the period. The private papers of Lord Pauncefote used by Mowat seem only to authenticate the account given by Smalley. There is no reference to the matter in the Salisbury Papers deposited in Christchurch College Library, Oxford. The brief notes in the collected papers of Sir Thomas Sanderson and Lord Lansdowne housed in the Foreign Office Library refer only to their attitude when the problem was first raised by Germany in 1902[67] and illustrate the complete bewilderment of officials in 1898. Sanderson, who was in the Foreign Office in London at the time, wrote to Lansdowne immediately the issue was raised, to say "if Baron Holleben reported that Pauncefote had urged the adoption of a fresh collective note on instructions from us he clearly misinformed his government." The publication of relevant documents in *Die Grosse Politik*[68] did not seem to clear up the diplomatic puzzle, but certainly lent weight to the German version.

Theodore Von Holleben, the German ambassador to the United States, cabled to Berlin in 1898 that the British government through Pauncefote initiated proposals for a second collective note and that Pauncefote drafted the note submitted. "Very surprisingly the English ambassador took the initiative for a new joint action of the representatives of the Great Powers in Washington. We believe that the Queen Regent is represented in this matter by the Queen of England."[69] According to Holleben the proposal was that a Spanish note of 9 April should be taken as a basis for a re-examination of the whole

question. If the powers shared this view it would be necessary
to dispel the erroneous belief current in the United States that
the civilized world believed armed intervention imperative.
Holleben added: "Personally I regard this demonstration
somewhat coldly." The Emperor agreed, adding, "I regard it
as completely futile and purposeless and therefore prejudicial.
I am against the step."[70] Holleben stated later in a letter to
Prince Hohenlohe,[71] the German Chancellor, that he was completely puzzled by the whole conduct of England, which oscil-
lated between encouragement of the United States and support
for the European powers favouring Spain.

To make matters more difficult, just as the German documents affirm the German account so the papers of Chamberlain
and Balfour and the British documents establish beyond a
doubt the veracity of the British government's official account
of its action. On 14 April 1898 Pauncefote telegraphed[72] the
Foreign Office in a form very different from Holleben's report
to Berlin. In his opinion the attitude of Congress left little hope
of a pacific solution. There was a belief generally current in
the United States that the military action proposed by the
United States was approved by the great powers, yet the Spanish memorandum afforded a reasonable basis for peace and removed all just grounds for hostile action. Having thus stated
his estimate of the situation Pauncefote went on to give a formal statement of the joint recommendation decided upon by
the representatives of the great powers at the meeting held at
the British embassy. "Should the Great Powers [sic] adopt the
above view it is evident that the moment has come to correct
the mistaken idea prevailing here that the proposed intervention has 'the support and approval of the civilized world.' "
This could be done most effectively by the Foreign Ministers of
the great powers delivering an identic note to the United
States representatives at foreign capitals "declaring their inability to approve an armed intervention the justice of which they
do not admit." This note should be given the widest publicity
"so as to relieve the civilized world from all moral responsibility

for an act of aggression which it is sought to support by an appeal to its authority."

The official reply to this was given by Balfour on his own initiative without consultation with any other cabinet member and before the attitude of any other power was known to him.[73] Lord Salisbury was in the south of France, Chamberlain was in the country, and Balfour instructed Pauncefote through the following telegram sent to Sir Thomas Sanderson, Permanent Under Secretary of State for Foreign Affairs:

I confess to be in great perplexity. The representatives of the powers at Washington and the Austrian ambassador in London appear to wish us to give the United States a lecture in international morality. If Pauncefote had not associated himself with this policy I should have rejected it at once, but he knows our views, he is on the spot, and he is a man of solid judgment. It seems a strong order to reject his advice. Will you telegraph him in this sense.

We are ready to join any representation agreed on by the other powers in favour of peace. We are also ready to make it quite clear that we have formed no adverse judgment to Spain as is assumed apparently by Congress, and to express the hope that the declaration of an armistice by Spain may afford an opportunity for a peaceful settlement. But it seems very doubtful whether we ought to commit ourselves to a judgment adverse to the United States and whether in the interests of peace, anything would be gained by doing so.[74]

With this instruction Chamberlain heartily agreed, telegraphing his approval of the action in terms which lauded Balfour's instinct above Pauncefote's experience. It would therefore appear that Britain rejected the proposed mediation before being aware of the German reply. The official attitude of the Foreign Office, even though it differed from Pauncefote's, was, as Balfour had earlier informed Hay, "completely formal, not to take any step not acceptable to the United States."[75]

There are obviously four parts to the problem, namely the attitudes of the British government and the British ambassador, and of the German government and the German ambassador. The British government's attitude is clearly revealed in the

Chamberlain-Balfour correspondence and in Foreign Office records. The German government's policy was just as clearly demonstrated in *Die Grosse Politik*. However, a comparison of British and German documents reveals both that the Kaiser and his advisers were misinformed about the attitude of the United Kingdom, and that the British Foreign Office was not fully informed of the tone and extent of Pauncefote's activity. It was out of this situation that the quarrel arose between Britain and Germany in 1902 over the British attitude to the United States in 1898.

A partial answer to the riddle of Pauncefote's action lies in an examination of correspondence between Pauncefote and the Foreign Office made available by the Record Office in 1951. These documents fall into two sections, namely the actual correspondence between Pauncefote and the Foreign Office in 1898, and the correspondence between Pauncefote and the Foreign Office initiated by the German charges in 1902 referring to the action taken in 1898. From these it appears that Pauncefote, in an attempt to preserve peace, went much further than his government would have approved and much further then he let his government know. Here is the story very briefly.

Up to 8 April 1898, Pauncefote was quite clearly instructed not to take any action unless previously assured that it would be agreeable to the United States. He knew the contents of the note delivered by the Spanish ambassador to the President on 10 April. On 11 April Pauncefote was informed by the Foreign Office that the Spanish government had agreed to an immediate suspension of hostilities and that they requested the United Kingdom to assist Spain in putting an end to American aid to the insurgents and in obtaining natural and just compensation for damages inflicted by the United States. "We must leave any action on this request to your discretion," wrote Balfour.[76] On 12 April, in reply to this last instruction, Pauncefote sent off a lengthy despatch[77] to Balfour outlining what he considered to be revived hopes for peace and his disapproval of President McKinley's action in not making clear to the nation

22

the extent of the Spanish concessions in the note of 10 April. These concessions were an agreement to an immediate cease-fire, a promise to grant to Cuba a form of government analogous to that in Canada, and the relief of the "reconcentrados." This in Pauncefote's opinion "disposed of the humanitarian question," and made "the more reasonable politicians disposed to think that there would remain no legitimate cause or pretext for war." He argued further that as the diplomatic correspondence had not been laid before Congress the public had been misled by the bellicose press, which ignored the Spanish memorandum and expressions of regret over the sinking of the "Maine." Having delayed his speech to Congress in order to consider the Spanish note, and in response (as Pauncefote believed) to pressure from great financial circles in New York who favoured peace, the President toned down certain aspects of his speech and notified Congress of the cessation of hostilities in Cuba. McKinley however did not "as specifically requested enlighten public opinion" as to the other concessions made by Spain. The newspapers announced that war was now delayed, that conflicting opinions were running riot in the capital, and that the Republican party was possibly divided on the question of hostile measures. The despatch concluded: "The action of Congress is therefore uncertain . . . and war is certainly less imminent."

To this enthusiastic despatch Pauncefote received no reply. His telegrams after this were entirely formal reports indicating that he realized the futility of attempting to move the Foreign Office from its firm intention not to interfere. Congress met on 13 April and it was apparent that the Senate was intent on war and bound to override McKinley. Apparently extending instructions to use his discretion, Pauncefote took a part in discussions leading to the suggestion by all six ambassadors that a second identic note be delivered by the Foreign Ministers in the European capitals to all the various ambassadors from the United States. Pauncefote did not indicate what action he personally had taken in these proceedings,[78] nor did he indicate from what quarter the initiative had come. He omitted this both in his original telegram informing the Foreign Office of the proposal, and in a later despatch in reply to a Foreign Office request for any observations his local knowledge of the situation might suggest. On both occasions, however, he was careful to state the reasons for the action with which he identified himself.

In consequence of the resolution passed by the House of Representatives the 13th . . . and the menacing attitude of the senate . . . the representatives of the Great Powers met . . . and resolved suggest a further note . . . for the purpose of controverting the statement made by the President and the impression which prevails in the United States, viz., . . . that the armed intervention of the United States in Cuba under existing circumstances . . . meets with the support and approval of the civilized world.[79]

Balfour's reply refusing to act has already been quoted,[80] and in response it brought a further statement from Pauncefote[81] agreeing with Balfour that it would be sufficient, in order to make clear to Congress that its violent action was not approved by the civilized world, to point out to the United States that the powers felt the Spanish armistice offered an opportunity for peace. The tone of this reply was a marked retreat from the support with which he had accompanied his previous recommendations. Again on 16 April Pauncefote advised delay on any proposed action by the powers until the President once more had the direction of affairs in his hands.[82] He believed that the President was most anxious to avert war. The next day he advised further delay because of the resentment expressed in advance by Congress at the possibility of European interference.[83] Balfour, fortified by his telegram from Chamberlain, put an end to further conjecture by Pauncefote in these terms. Given "the extreme improbability that unsought advice will do any good and the inexpediency of adopting any course which may suggest that we take sides in the matter, we shall at least for the moment, do nothing."[84]

There the matter rested until 1902 when it became a subject for lengthy debate between Germany and the United Kingdom.[85] The correspondence involved throws more light on Pauncefote's attitude and action. On 8 February 1902, the Foreign Office asked Pauncefote for any observations he might have to make concerning the German charges.[86] He replied:

The meeting was verbally convened at the request of some of my colleagues . . . it took place at the British Embassy only because I was *doyen*. There was a general discussion in which I made no proposal or took any initiative . . . the French ambassador drafted the telegram at the request of the meeting. No record was kept of the proceedings which were of an informal and conversational character.[87]

On 12 February, the German Emperor called on Sir Frank Lascelles and read to him Holleben's telegram of April 1898 and his own minutes on it referred to above.[88] On 13 February Pauncefote was sent a copy of Lascelles' report of this and asked for any observations.[89] Pauncefote in reply sent a rather different account from that previously transmitted. He denied that the telegram was sent at his request, but added,

With regard to your Lordship's question respecting any proposal or initiative by me, I desire to explain that I strongly advocated at the meeting an identic telegram . . . and even prepared a rough draft for consideration which . . . I handed over to my French colleague to assist him in framing the telegram ultimately adopted. That is the draft my German colleague pretends was originally submitted by me for transmission to the Governments of the Great Powers.[90]

When asked by the Foreign Office if he objected to any correspondence being published Pauncefote answered in the negative, but submitted a further "corrected" account mentioning the rough draft, stressing the unanimity of the decision, the rewriting of the draft by the French ambassador, and emphasizing his desire for peace.[91] As Lansdowne minuted on the decipher of the telegram, this was "a more adroit account of his action than that contained in his earlier telegram."

There is one other element to be considered. The popular refusal to believe the German account of Pauncefote's action was due to his great reputation as the arch-protagonist of Anglo-American friendship and to his great success in fostering this particular aim of British diplomacy. But it must be emphasized that there was much about American diplomats and diplomatic methods of which Pauncefote most heartily disapproved, and he long remained sceptical of American "friendship" for Britain. This reflects his aristocratic background and sympathies as well as the unpleasant bickering over the Venezuelan affair. His attitude had something of the disdain of the "Great Gentleman" for the gauche and bourgeois habits and manners of the *nouveau riche*. Some of his private comments[92] upon American diplomacy, if they had been made public (as was Dupuy de Lôme's letter criticizing the President), even if they did not wreck the growth of Anglo-American accord would at least have made Pauncefote as unpopular as his predecessor had been. This is an important and previously neglected aspect of Pauncefote's attitude, for it enables a proper appreciation to be made of the indignation underlying his letter of 12 April to Balfour criticizing the President, as well as his telegram giving his reasons for associating himself with the second note.

From this I think these conclusions follow. Pauncefote disapproved of the violent action of the United States and of McKinley's failure to make the best use of the last-minute Spanish capitulation. He believed that the President and other powerful financial interests were in favour of peace. He believed that the public had been misled by a partisan yellow press, and he believed that a clear statement by all the powers that they considered the Spanish capitulation a basis for a peaceful settlement would, as he put it, create a "great moral force in the interest of peace." So deeply was he convinced of this that on his own initiative and without advising the Foreign Office he gave his influential support to a last-minute effort to persuade the great powers to condemn the action contemplated by the United States. Moreover, he did this despite the reiterated reluctance of the cabinet to take any action not previously approved by the United States government.

This correspondence makes Pauncefote's personal estimate of the situation plain enough. The difficult question is to decide just who took the initiative. Holleben and the Kaiser stated bluntly that Pauncefote was responsible. The Foreign Office and Pauncefote just as bluntly denied it, claiming that the initiative in the matter was taken by Austria.[93] As the King minuted, "It seems a case of diamond cut diamond."[94] It would need a chapter in itself to analyse the lengthy debate and to weigh the mass of evidence as well as the variety of press reports produced by both sides in the rather bitter controversy between Germany and England over this matter.[95]

However, the most relevant points are these. Holleben, supported by Cambon, based his charge upon the manner in which the meeting was convened and conducted. As Holleben put it, "As his colleagues were not informed by Lord Pauncefote that it was at the request of some of them that he had called the meeting of ambassadors, and that [*sic*] as he himself had advocated an identic note, it was fair to infer that he had taken the initiative in proposing it and therefore that it was an English proposal."[96] Cambon added that Pauncefote brought the note to the meeting and presented it to the assembled ambassadors who discussed it, and a unanimous decision being arrived at, Cambon translated it into French, altering it to agree with the sense of the decision.[97] In these circumstances it seems that Cambon and Holleben were justified in their belief even though they were aware of the previous refusal by England to follow any course not previously approved in advance by the President. It was this aspect that so puzzled Holleben.[98]

The Foreign Office was worried over this question and ordered a review of all correspondence relative to it. When completed, a minute was appended to the effect that "there is nothing to show that Sir J. Pauncefote took any initiative with regard to this resolution."[99] Pauncefote's denial was accepted by the Foreign Office and after prolonged argument with Germany, the British charge that Austria was the prime mover in the matter was sheeted home by the production of a most pertinent piece of evidence.[100]

It is important to note that the Austro-Hungarian Government had received an independent suggestion from their Representative at Washington recommending strongly the course proposed in the identic telegram, without any reference to the opinion of his English colleague and that neither that Government nor the Government of France suggested that the telegram originated from British initiative.

Both the Austrian and French governments called their ambassadors in London,[101] and the French Minister for Foreign Affairs saw the British ambassador in Paris to discover what would be the attitude of the British Foreign Office. It could be of course that this action was taken in the belief that the projected intervention was initiated by Pauncefote without the backing of his government. However if this were so it would be highly improbable that the Austrian and French governments would have failed to mention to the Foreign Office Pauncefote's responsibility for the proposal.

The conclusive point is, however, the activity mentioned above of the Austrian officials, an activity which fits perfectly into the pattern of previous Austrian action in support of Spain. On 16 April, Count Deym (the Austrian ambassador to the Court of St. James) called at the Foreign Office to discover the British attitude to the proposed collective action. Count Deym forwarded to the Foreign Office[102] a note sent to him by Goluchowski in Vienna who had received it from the Austro-Hungarian ambassador in Washington, M. De Henglemüller.

This note was no formal statement of the situation in the tone of Pauncefote's report to the Foreign Office. Couched in the language of an enthusiast out to persuade his superiors, it contained forceful argument designed to convince the Austrian Foreign Minister of the desirability of the projected action. Beginning "If it were possible to induce the European powers to agree to a fresh collective note which should no longer be a friendly appeal but which should express disapprobation of the aggressive attitude at Washington," it went on to argue that such a declaration would be "a lasting service in the cause of peace," and "it would be a great advantage to Europe in the case of War." The "hypocritical manner" of the committee of the Senate in repeating assurances that armed intervention should take place only with the approval of the civilized world would sufficiently justify the denial by the powers of this approval. Being so convinced of the worth of the proposal, and seeking to convince his government, it is inconceivable that the Austrian ambassador would not have given added weight to his argument by reporting any British initiative as support for it. This is particularly so as it was Goluchowski who was convinced that any protest without British naval support would be worthless.[103] Goluchowski supported his ambassador and expressed disappointment at the "unpalatable" and "unwelcome" news of the British and German refusal to act.

I think it can be assumed then that the initiative was taken by the Austrian ambassador at Washington, acting without explicit instructions from Vienna. He could take this action in the certainty that it would be approved by his government, because it fitted so logically into the pattern of past action and instructions. Without reviewing all Austrian policy it is sufficient to point out that Austria took the initiative in seeking support for the first collective note.[104] Again on 11 April Goluchowski agreed to support a Spanish request for the withdrawal of United States naval forces from Cuba and the Philippines as a quid pro quo for the Spanish cease-fire. The

Spanish ambassador at Vienna and the Austro-Hungarian ambassador at Washington so informed Rumbold and Pauncefote respectively, adding that the representatives of other great powers would make similar representations.[105] Given the clearly expressed attitude of the British and Austrian governments, the Austrian ambassador could initiate the proposal for a second collective note, confident that he was acting in accordance with the wishes of Vienna. For Pauncefote to have initiated the same proposal would have been for him to act in direct defiance of the reiterated reluctance of his government to do anything which he was not previously assured would be acceptable to the United States.

II

The claim has been made that "in international affairs Anglo-American friendship first became a decisive factor during the Spanish-American War when the British Government, faithfully reflecting public opinion, manifested goodwill towards the United States and supported her growth as a colonial power."[106] It is therefore pertinent to endeavour to discover exactly how decisive British friendship for America was during the diplomatic prelude to the Spanish-American War. In this there are two problems. In the first place, how important was the action proposed by the ambassador at Washington but rejected by the European governments? Secondly, which power was responsible for the rejection?

In answering the first question, it is apparent that the most effective pressure that the powers could have applied to the United States in an endeavour to prevent war would have been, as Goluchowski pointed out,[107] a united naval demonstration. If this had been planned and England, the most powerful naval force, had refused to act, her attitude could indeed have been decisive. But, as has been shown, the action suggested by the ambassadors in Washington was merely a statement of disapproval; as Balfour put it, "the representatives of the powers at Washington and the Austrian ambassador in London appear to wish us to give the United States a lecture in international morality."[108] The intention was, in the phrase of the note, "to correct the mistaken idea prevailing here [the United States] that the proposed armed intervention in Cuba . . . has received, to quote the words of the President 'the support and approval of the civilized world.' "[109] No actual intervention of any sort other than this "moral" protest was planned. Therefore even if Britain's inaction was decisive, it was responsible for preventing no more than this rather academic gesture. There is no evidence to support the view of the Spanish Minister for Foreign Affairs that the action suggested would have prevented the war if England had co-operated.[110] The most that could have been hoped for would have been that such a gesture would have given McKinley the moral fibre to attempt to lead Congress away from the war upon which it was intent. As it was, in the face of the rabid warmongering of the press and of Congress, the President withheld from Congress news of Spain's final capitulation and surrendered the initiative to the expansionists of 1898.

The second question is this. Was it Germany or England or some other combination of powers or of circumstances that ensured the rejection by the powers of the action recommended to them? The Kaiser claimed that it was not England's but Germany's attitude that was decisive. With the confidence derived from a reading of Holleben's report of Pauncefote's initiative, the German Foreign Office confirmed the report in the *Kreuz Zeitung* and the *North German Gazette*.[111] This report stated that "when on April 14 England through her ambassador proposed a fresh joint note in which the Powers should declare that Europe did not regard the armed intervention of America in Cuba as justifiable, the rest of the ambassadors telegraphed to Europe for instructions, and in consequence of the decisive refusal of Germany this step was abandoned."[112]

The reply from England was to the effect that "Great Britain never proposed through Her Majesty's ambassador or otherwise any declaration adverse to the United States in regard to their intervention in Cuba. On the contrary, Her Majesty's Government declined to assent to any such proposal."[113] This it will be noted is a correct statement of the action taken by the Foreign Office, but does not make any rival claim as a counter to that in the *Kreuz Zeitung*. The counter claim was made by the press in England and America, namely that the projected note was dropped because of Britain's refusal to participate. In the light of Holleben's account, it is understandable that the Kaiser thought it "rather too strong that the exclusive merit of having prevented intervention should have been claimed for England."[114] Hence the "rectification" published in the *North German Gazette*. In view of these rival claims, it is necessary to decide whose attitude, if any, was decisive in preventing the presentation of the second note to the United States.

It is immediately obvious from the preceding analysis of England's policy that Balfour's decision not to take part in the proposed action did not in any way depend upon the attitude of Germany, nor indeed of any other power. In the Spanish-American dispute, cabinet had consistently refused to take any action which had not been previously concerted with the United States executive. That is why, without waiting to hear the response from any other power, and without seeking to consult any other member of the cabinet, Balfour could decide to refrain from the action proposed by all the European ambassadors at Washington. This decision to refrain from any interference had been made as early as 1896 and had been followed consistently since that time. England's decision, whether influential or not in other European capitals, was her own and was not influenced by Germany's attitude to that dispute, either at the time of the second note or at any time previously.

It is equally obvious that Germany's decision not to participate was made despite the fact that as far as Germany's information went it was the British ambassador who had initiated the move. It is not so certain, however, that Germany's attitude to the dispute previous to the Austrian suggestions for united action was not determined in part by her knowledge of Britain's determination not to become involved. Whether or not this is so should be made evident by an examination of German policy as it developed from the time when Spain made known to the European capitals the contents of Woodford's ultimatum (23 September 1897).

The Kaiser's immediate response to the news was a suggestion that some demonstration should be made in the interests of the Spanish court and monarchy in general.[115] Kaiser Wilhelm's initial enthusiasm ("in einer Aufwallung seines monarchischen Solidaritätsgefühls")[116] was not echoed in the Foreign Office[117] where grave doubts were expressed about the advisability of any action such as the Kaiser contemplated. The instruction finally sent to Count Eulenburg, the German ambassador at Vienna, outlined some of the considerations which made caution necessary. It was feared that England and France by not participating in any intervention would turn the situation to their own advantage and endeavour to involve Germany in disputes with the United States. Eulenburg was informed that some of the European press was already recalling the Kaiser's telegram to Kruger and its unfortunate international repercussions. If any action were contemplated an effort should be made to have Russia guarantee participation by France. If France and England did refrain from an action in which Germany joined, then serious political and economic disadvantages for her could follow. Germany was second only to England in exports and imports to and from the United States, and the new American tariff could be used to discriminate against nations whose policy was regarded unfavourably. The instruction was that any German action must be taken with great caution. It must not endanger friendly relations between Germany and America and it must include the co-operation of France, England, and Russia. Eulenburg was sceptical of the chances of inducing either France or England to participate and suggested that Austria should be advised to initiate the plan. Bülow and the Emperor approved Eulenburg's suggestion and instructions were sent to guide the conduct of Prince Lichnowsky (chargé d'affaires at Vienna). If the question of intervention were again raised, he was to advise the necessity for a united European stand, and to state that although Germany could not lead such an action, she would be prepared to support suitable plans from London or Paris, perhaps on Austrian initiation.[118] At this time even Goluchowski, the Austrian Foreign Minister, was reluctant to make any move because he feared the cabinet would not support him, despite the close dynastic ties between Austrian and Spanish royal families.[119]

Very early, then, it appeared that although the Kaiser favoured some action in Spanish interests, the considered opinion of the Foreign Office was that Germany could neither initiate nor lead any such move, and could participate only if all other European powers would co-operate, and provided that the move was of such a nature that it would not provoke any unfriendly reaction in Washington. This remained Germany's attitude throughout the period before the outbreak of war, the only change being that Bülow and the Kaiser became more and more circumspect in their replies to any suggestion for German action. They became certain that England certainly would not join such a move, and that France would be guided by Russia who was obviously intent upon winning American goodwill. This development is clear in the German reply to Spain's request in February 1898 that Germany should lead a demonstration on behalf of monarchy as against republican America. German leadership, replied Bülow, was not the most suitable method. It was doubtful whether France would be persuaded to any action in defence of monarchy, but if she could be moved to lead intervention because of her noted material and financial interests in Spain, then Germany would be prepared to lend her support.[120]

When Austria in March suggested once more that Germany should take the initiative, Bülow in a long despatch went over all the old ground, showing himself more pessimistic than ever. No more than a polite academic gesture could be hoped for. France was unwilling to act because Russia would not, and England had obviously declared in favour of the United States as against Spain. Therefore any move by Austria or Germany would be worse than useless. He regretted the plight in which the Queen Regent found herself and suggested papal mediation.[121] So convinced was the government of the uselessness of any action such as that first suggested by the Kaiser that Germany would not even make a move to unite the European powers with a view to advising both Spain and the United States to accept arbitration as a means of settlement.[122] Extreme caution guided the advice given Holleben when the first collective note was mooted. Only to the extent that all five ambassadors acted together was Holleben to participate—and this only because of Austria's request. Bülow stated that from the evident attitude of England, France, and Russia, the step would be ineffective, and that Germany "should join in the mediation of the powers only if all others take the lead and only in so far as is indispensable, in order not to awaken distrust from other powers and also in America."[123] Finally, without waiting to consult other powers or to learn their reaction, the Kaiser refused to participate in the second collective representation proposed, as he understood, by Pauncefote.

It is apparent that Germany's policy went through a minor transformation. The initial fervour of the Kaiser was tempered by advice from the Foreign Office, so that from the beginning no action was contemplated that might produce a hostile reaction in the United States. After some time, German willingness to support a move led by some other power was replaced by a reluctance to participate at all, and then by a flat refusal to do so in any circumstances. In this process, the knowledge that England would not participate had some influence, but apparently no more so than the views and actions of France and Russia. There was no suggestion at any time that Germany's action was dependent upon British policy alone. Russia, intent upon her Far Eastern ambitions, had nothing to gain and much to lose by antagonizing the United States in the service of Spain. The Czar's policy was to seek an amicable relationship with the United States, and Russia's attempts to achieve this occupied many of Pauncefote's despatches.[124] France, bound to Russia by alliance, fearful of Germany, and preoccupied in Africa, could see no profit in alienating a country which regarded her as a traditional friend. France however at least sought to know what Britain's attitude was toward Spain's requests,[125] but agreed entirely with the views expressed to her. It is true that Bülow suggested[126] that the hesitancy of Russia and France was perhaps induced by England's silence, but a more accurate description is that England's attitude merely confirmed France in a viewpoint decided by her Russian affiliations and her African ambitions. The evidence does not warrant the suggestion that England's refusal to countenance opposition to the United States was at this particular period decisive.

To argue what would have been the case *if* England had led any attempt at intervention must remain a profitless speculation. As it was, neither Germany, England, France, nor Russia was prepared to initiate any such move, and even Austria was reluctant. Given the alignment of the powers, and their rival ambitions, the determining factor was the consideration that it would be far more profitable not to offend the rising power of the United States than it would be to make a gesture in defence of a monarchy incapable of defending itself. America's freedom from European attempts to restrain her was due at least as much to the preoccupation of the powers with their own ambitions and rivalries as it was to British friendship.

Notes

1. E.g. John Hay's speech quoted in Dennett, *op. cit.*, pp. 188-89, concerning Chamberlain's visit to the United States. The Spanish ambassador received a series of telegrams from his government complaining bitterly of the reports of Mr. Chamberlain's language, which had appeared in the newspapers, and laying stress on the fact that no contradiction had appeared in the English press which had repeated statements of American journals. The ambassador said that the impression had been produced in Spain that Mr. Chamberlain had really gone over to persuade the United States to retain the Philippines. FO5/2364, Sanderson to Pauncefote, Private, 19 September 1898.

2. Dennett, *op. cit.*, p. 221.

3. FO72/2068, Wolff to F.O. [Foreign Office], Most Secret, 15 May 1898, No. 106. "The report of Mr. Chamberlain's speech has created a great turmoil as the papers believe an Anglo-American alliance to be directed against Spain. They are pointing out how Spain can assist the adversaries of England at Gibraltar and elsewhere." He said that feeling against England was already high, adding in explanation, "the Austrian, German and French Ambassadors having been in constant communication with the Court and Government and holding irritating language."

4. FO72/2065, Wolff to F.O., Despatch No. 322, 15 September 1898.

5. FO72/2068, Wolff to F.O., Telegram No. 131, 27 May 1898.

6. E.g. Chamberlain's Birmingham speech of 13 May, reported in the *Times* (London), 14 May 1898.

7. *Hansard, The Parliamentary Debates of the United Kingdom of Great Britain and Ireland* (London: 1898) [hereinafter *Hansard*], Fourth Series, 1898, LIV, 12 March, 1526.

8. S. Gwynn (ed.), *The Letters and Friendships of Sir Cecil Spring Rice: A Record* (London: Constable & Co. Ltd., 1930), I, 253, Spring Rice to Thayer, January 1898.

9. C. Olcott, *The Life of William McKinley* (New York: Houghton Mifflin & Co., 1916), II, 130, Hay to McKinley, 4 April 1898.

10. *Atlantic Monthly*, LXXXI, No. 487 (May 1898), 588, quoting Olney's speech on "The International Isolation of the United States," delivered at Harvard, 2 March 1898.

11. H. James, *Richard Olney and His Public Service* (Boston and New York: Houghton Mifflin & Co., 1923), p. 244, White to Olney, 17 June 1896.

12. FO5/2323, Salisbury to Frederick Adam, 24 September 1897. See also *Foreign Relations of the United States, 1898* (Washington: Government Printing Office, 1901), pp. 568-73.

13. FO5/2322, Frederick Adam to Salisbury, No. 267, 30 September 1897.

14. The reporters mentioned were from the *New York Journal*, the *Evening Standard* (London) and the French *Le Temps* (Paris). Frederick

Adam checked with the legal adviser to the Spanish legation, Mr. Calderon Carlisle, who confirmed the reports in the *Times* of Woodford's "indiscretion" with the press. *Ibid.*

15. *Ibid.*

16. Olcott, *op. cit.*, p. 129, Hay to McKinley, 6 October 1897.

17. FO5/2361, Pauncefote to F.O., Despatch No 14, 20 January 1898.

18. Accurate accounts of Spanish-American relations at this time appear in many standard texts such as Bemis, *op. cit.*

19. FO5/2361, Pauncefote to F.O., Despatch No. 44, 28 February 1898.

20. *Ibid.*, Despatch No. 58, 11 March 1898.

21. See p. 4.

22. The formal request to the United States to stand with Britain was made on 8 March 1898. See 117.

23. The Papers of the Third Marquess of Salisbury (MSS in Christchurch College Library, Oxford) [hereinafter Salisbury Papers], Vol. CXXXI, No. 34, Wolff to Salisbury, March 1896.

24. *Ibid.*, Vol. CXXXIV, No. 83, Balfour to Wolff, 2 March 1896.

25. *Ibid.*, No. 85, March 1896.

26. *Ibid.*, Vol. CXXXI, No. 56.

27. *Ibid.*, Nos. 35, 36, 39, 45, 46-51.

28. *Ibid.*

29. *Ibid.*, No. 35, 16 March 1896.

30. *Ibid.*, No. 97, 12 January 1897.

31. The Spanish archives covering this incident have been used exhaustively by Orestes Ferrara, LL.D., Ph.D., one-time Cuban ambassador to Washington. See his *The Last Spanish War,* translated by William E. Shea (London: Williams & Norgate, 1937).

32. *Ibid.*, pp. 22 ff.

33. *Ibid.*, pp. 22-23, quoting Spanish Archives Docket 35, 1896, No. 17.

34. Salisbury Papers, No. 45, 13 June 1896.

35. Ferrara, *op. cit.*, p. 21.

36. Taylor to Olney, 13 August 1896. Quoted in full Ferrara, *op. cit.*, pp. 56-57.

37. Ferrara, *op. cit.*, p. 52.

38. Henry Drummond Wolff, *Rambling Recollections* (London: Macmillan & Co., 1908).

39. Salisbury Papers, Vol. CXXXIV, No. 2, Wolff to Salisbury, 23 January 1899.

40. *Ibid.*, Vol. CXXXI, No. 63, 8 September 1896.

41. *Ibid.*, No. 66, 25 October 1896.

42. *Ibid.*, Vol. CXXXII, No. 11, 18 February 1897, in reply to Salisbury of the same date.

43. Garvin, *op cit.*, II, 297.

44. Salisbury Papers, Vol. CXXXIII, No. 8 of 7 May 1898.

45. *Ibid.*, No. 131, 17 May 1898.

46. FO72/2067, Telegram No. 5, F.O. to Barclay, and Telegram No. 31, F.O. to Pauncefote, 26 March 1898.

47. *Ibid.*

48. FO72/2068, Barclay to F.O., Telegram No. 16, 27 March 1898.

49. *Foreign Relations of the United States, 1898*, pp. 696-97. See below, p. 35.

50. FO5/2517, F.O. to Pauncefote, Telegram No. 36, Very Confidential, 28 March 1898.

51. *Ibid.* This, together with additional material quoted herein (p. 15), supplies the evidence to support Hay's despatch to Sherman of 6 April 1898 quoted by C. S. Campbell, Jr., *Anglo-American Understanding 1898-1903* (Baltimore: Johns Hopkins Press, 1957), p. 31, n. 20, evidence which Campbell suspected might have been given only verbally.

52. *Ibid.*, Pauncefote to F.O., Telegram No. 28, paraphrase, 30 March 1898.

53. *Ibid.* (Balfour's draft not numbered), Balfour to Pauncefote, 2 April 1898.

54. FO5/2365, Pauncefote to F.O., Telegram No. 29, 5 April 1898.
FO5/2517, Pauncefote to F.O., Despatch No. 100, 8 April 1898.

55. Johannes Lepsius *et. al.* (eds.), *Die Grosse Politik der Europäischen Kabinette 1871-1914* (Berlin: 1924) [hereinafter *Die Grosse Politik*], Band XV, Nr. 4124.

56. Statement to press. *Times* (London), 14 February 1902: "The initiative was entirely my own." See also a report of an interview with Norman in *New York Herald*, 21 June 1902.

57. *Hansard*, 1902, CI, 20 January, 311.

58. *New York Herald*, 21 January 1902.

59. FO5/2517, 31 January 1902.

60. Quoted in *Times* (London) of 6 February 1902, and *New York Times* of 7 February 1902.

61. The second charge is dealt with in chap. iii below.

62. FO5/2517, Lascelles to F.O., Telegram No. 12, 12 February 1902.

63. *Ibid.*, Monson to F.O., Telegram No. 57, 17 February 1902.

64. *New York Tribune*, 22 January 1902.

65. G. W. Smalley, *Anglo-American Memories* (2nd series; London: Duckworth & Co., 1912), pp. 178-85.

66. R. B. Mowat, *Life of Lord Pauncefote, First Ambassador to the United States* (London: Houghton, 1929).
L. M. Gelber, *The Rise of Anglo-American Friendship* (London and New York: Oxford University Press, 1938).
B. A. Reuter, *Anglo-American Relations During the Spanish-American War* (New York: Macmillan & Co., 1924).
L. B. Shippee, "Germany and the Spanish-American War," *American Historical Review*, XXX, No. 4 (July 1925), 754-77.

67. The Private Papers of Lord Lansdowne and Sir Thomas Sanderson 1898-1905 (MSS in the Foreign Office Library, London) [hereinafter Lansdowne Papers], General, Vol. XXXI.

68. Chiefly in Band XV of *Die Grosse Politik*.

69. Shippee, *op. cit.*, pp. 760-61, translating the despatch. *Die Grosse Politik*, Band XV, Nr. 4140.

70. Shippee, *op. cit.*, p. 761.

71. *Ibid.*, p. 762. *Die Grosse Politik*, Band XV, Nr. 4143.

72. FO5/2365, Pauncefote to F.O., paraphrase of Telegram No. 37 in FO5/2517, 14 April 1898.

73. Balfour-Chamberlain correspondence in Dugdale, *op. cit.*, pp. 262-63. The letter is also in the Foreign Office records in FO72/2084, apparently neglected by Dugdale.

74. Dugdale, *op. cit.*, pp. 262-63, and FO5/2517, Balfour to Pauncefote, Telegram No. 72, 15 April 1898.

75. A. L. P. Dennis, *Adventures in American Diplomacy 1896-1906* (New York: Dutton & Co., 1928), p. 72, quoting Hay to Sherman, 6 April 1898.

76. FO5/2364, F.O. to Pauncefote, Telegram No. 63, 11 April 1898.

77. FO5/2517, Pauncefote to F.O., Despatch No. 103, 12 April 1898.

78. This aspect worried Mr. F. Bertie, the senior official at the Foreign Office, when Balfour's reply to Pauncefote was received for transmission to Washington. Bertie was a friend of Pauncefote, and in a rather ingratiating letter to Balfour he gave it as his opinion that the ambassador "has as *doyen* made himself the mouthpiece of his colleagues, without giving what was, or ought to have been, his own view." FO72/2084, Bertie to Balfour, 17 April 1898. This however is an undocumented opinion for no record exists of the meeting in the British embassy. See an unnumbered Minute by Lansdowne to Sanderson in Lansdowne Papers, General, Vol. XXXI.

79. FO5/2365, Pauncefote to F.O., Telegram No. 37, 14 April 1898.

80. See above, Balfour to Sanderson in Balfour-Chamberlain correspondence.

81. FO5/2365, Pauncefote to F.O., Telegram No. 39, Confidential, 16 April 1898.

82. Pauncefote expected a conflict between the House of Representatives and the Senate over the constitutional powers of the President.

83. FO5/2365, Pauncefote to F.O., Telegram No. 40, 17 April 1898.

84. FO5/2517, Balfour to Pauncefote, Telegram No. 78, 17 April 1898.

85. For exhaustive examinations of this problem see R. G. Neale, "Anglo-American Relations During the Spanish-American War: Some Problems," *Historical Studies Australia and New Zealand*, VI, No. 21 (1953), 72-89 and Campbell, *op. cit.*, pp. 244-52.

86. FO5/2517, Private Telegram to Pauncefote sent 6 February 1902.

87. *Ibid.*, Private Telegram, Pauncefote to F.O., sent 7 February 1902.

88. *Ibid.*, Lascelles to F.O., Telegram No. 12, 12 February 1902. This was repeated to Washington and hence appears in file FO5.

89. *Ibid.*, F.O. to Pauncefote, Telegram No. 11, 13 February 1902.

90. *Ibid.*, Pauncefote to F.O., Private Telegram, 13 February 1902.

91. *Ibid.*, Pauncefote to F.O., Telegram No. 9, 14 February 1902.

92. Cf. Pauncefote to Salisbury, 26 June 1896, in Salisbury Papers, Vol. CXXXIX, No. 34, 1895-98. "I send you by this mail Mr. Olney's further note on the proposed general Treaty on Arbitration. It is quite in the style of the American journalist and I am sorry to have to transmit a document in such bad taste and in such bad form. I doubt whether Mr. Olney is responsible for more than the first and last pages. It was probably written by the President sitting in his shirt sleeves, between two bottles

of whisky, under which conditions he is reported to have penned his previous message about Venezuela." See p. 109.

93. FO5/2517, F.O. to Lascelles, Telegram No. 7.

94. *Ibid.*, Lascelles to F.O., Telegram No. 12, 12 February 1902.

95. Some of the relevant correspondence has been collected in Case Volume FO5/2517.

96. *Ibid.*, Lascelles to F.O., Berlin, 17 February 1902.

97. *Die Grosse Politik*, Band XV, Nr. 4144.

98. *Ibid.*, Nr. 4143. Letter of Hollenben to Hohenlohe of 23 April.

99. FO5/2517, Summary of Pauncefote's correspondence, dated 6 February 1902.

100. *Ibid.*, Memorandum printed for use of F.O., 8 March 1902, forwarded with Despatch No. 63 to Lascelles in Berlin, 10 March 1902.

101. *Ibid.*, F.O. to Sir Edward Monson in Paris, Telegram No. 99, 16 April; F.O. to Sir Horace Rumbold in Vienna, Telegram No 56, 16 April.

102. *Ibid.*, F.O. to Sir Horace Rumbold, Despatch No. 32, 16 April 1898.

103. Shippee, *op cit.*, p. 757. Austria's disappointment expressed here was corroborated by reports to London from Vienna. FO5/2517, Mr. R. Milbanke to F.O., Telegram No. 18, 19 April 1898.

104. Shippee, *op cit.*, p. 757; FO5/2517, Lascelles to F.O., 12 February 1902. The Kaiser referred to an Austrian proposal of 2 April 1898 as the beginning of the case.

105. FO5/2365, Telegram No. 34, Pauncefote to F.O., 11 April 1898.

106. Gelber, *op. cit.*, p. 17.

107. See above, n. 103.

108. Dugdale, *op. cit.*, pp. 262-63.

109. FO5/2517, Pauncefote to F.O., Telegram No. 37, 14 April 1898.

110. FO72/2068, Wolff to F.O., Telegram No. 131, Most Confidential, 27 May 1898. It was Wolff's opinion that Austria had convinced the Spanish court that England alone stood out from a joint move which would have prevented war and Pauncefote's peerage in 1899 was thought to be his reward for handling the affair. Salisbury Papers, Vol. CXXXIII, No. 15 of 31 May, Wolff to Salisbury, and Vol. CXXXIV, No 36, Wolff to Salisbury, 2 August 1899.

111. FO5/2517, Lascelles to F.O., Telegram No. 12, 12 February 1902.

112. *Times* (London), 6 February 1902, reporting from Berlin, 5 February, and quoting from the *Kreuz Zeitung*. The *North German Gazette* was used as the official medium for Foreign Office announcements. This was admitted by the Emperor. See FO5/2517, Lascelles to F.O., Telegram No. 12, 12 February 1902.

113. *Hansard*, 1902, CII, 11 February, 991. Cranborne's answer to a second question by Mr. Norman.

114. FO5/2517, Lascelles to F.O., Despatch No. 33, 14 February 1902.

115. *Die Grosse Politik*, Band XV, Nr. 4118.

116. *Ibid.*, footnote.

117. *Ibid.*, the last section of the footnote.

118. *Ibid.*, Nr. 4121.

119. Shippee, *op cit.*, p. 756.

120. *Die Grosse Politik*, Band XV, Nr. 4123.
121. *Ibid.*, Nr. 4125.
122. *Ibid.*
123. "und dass wir uns an der Mediation der Mächte nur dann beteiligen dürfen, wenn alle übrigen vorangehen, und nur so weit, als unerlässlich ist, um bei den anderen Mächten und auch in Amerika selbst nicht Misstrauen zu erwecken." *Ibid.*, Nr. 4137, 7 April.
124. FO5/2378, Memorandum from Balfour to F.O., 16 August 1898. FO5/2362, Pauncefote to F.O., Despatch No. 217, 22 June 1898, deals with the Russian press campaign in Washington.
125. See p. 14.
126. *Die Grosse Politik*, Band XV, Nr. 4133.

Problems of Neutrality

II

THE DECISION TO REMAIN NEUTRAL did not in the least reduce Britain's problem to an automatic administration of neutrality regulations. Cabinet policy was based upon three principles: to remain neutral and therefore to adhere to international agreements regulating neutrality; to protect British interests in those areas close to or involved in the conflict in any way; and to preserve and to cultivate that amicable relationship with the United States which was regarded as so fundamental to the future international security of Great Britain. These three principles were often incompatible one with the other, and frequently the first was modified or endangered to ensure the success of the remaining two. That this was so can be demonstrated by an examination of the methods by which were solved the problems of neutrality which arose in Canada, Gibraltar, Egypt and the Suez, Singapore, Hong Kong, and Manila. In these disputes, the pattern to which British officials constantly adhered was one of the accommodation of international law to suit the necessities of British security and British-American friendship.

I

On 11 April 1898, President McKinley sent his war message to Congress.[1] This surrender of the initiative by a President hitherto reluctant to seek war, to a jingoistic Congress inflamed by the campaigns of the yellow press[2] made war inevitable. The threat of war during March and early April was sufficient to alert British commercial interests and government departments to the necessity of defining Britain's neutrality policy, and of obtaining from the belligerents a clear statement of their intentions concerning the right of search, the capture of contraband of war, and the use of privateers. On 17 March Salisbury sent instructions to the Customs to maintain a strict watch on vessels being built for Japan and Chile, but rumoured to be destined for Spain and the United States. Any trustworthy information was to be sent immediately to the Foreign Office in case it became necessary to detain the ships in order to comply with the provisions of the Treaty of Washington (1871).[3]

On 28 March the British Admiralty sought from the Foreign Office a definition of contraband coal.[4] On 2 April the Foreign Office, again with the Treaty of Washington of 1871 in mind, instructed the Customs officials to keep a close watch on passenger ships of the Red Star Line which were known to have been built as auxiliary cruisers to be acquired by the United States government in time of war.[5] On 5 April the Colonial Office, at the instance of the governor of Jamaica, also sought a ruling on contraband coal.[6] On 6 April Lord Charles Beresford, the prominent champion of British Far Eastern interests, questioned the Attorney-General as to "whether in the event of war unfortunately breaking out between the United States and Spain (neither Spain nor the United States being signatory to the Declaration of Paris) either power would have the right to search for and capture enemies' property in all neutral vessels including the British." The reply was that "neither Spain nor the United States having acceded to the Declaration of Paris, their rights as belligerents are not affected thereby. The right of search for and capture of contraband of war would undoubtedly exist. Whether either Power would consider itself entitled to search for or capture goods not contraband of war on neutral ships is a question which it is not possible to answer."[7]

Given the predominance of the British merchant marine and the importance of United States wheat and cotton to England and Europe, this matter of search and contraband was vital to English shipping and commercial interests.[8] In these circumstances, newspapers and interested parties urged the government to make immediate decisions upon the questions of neutrality, privateering, and the right of search.[9] Given the strength of public opinion and the intent of both Government and Opposition to secure the friendship of the United States, and because of the most unpleasant past history of neutrality disputes between England and the United States, it is understandable that the Foreign Office quickly defined its own views and sought an indication of the policy intended by the United States.

By 14 April Sir Francis Villiers, under secretary in the Foreign Office, had edited a draft of a Proclamation of Neutrality modelled on the 1897 Proclamation referring to the Turko-Greek War. This was re-edited by Salisbury, Balfour, and the legal officers, in order to prevent any delay in proclaiming neutrality should war between Spain and the United States break out. The only variation from the 1897 precedent, which included references to the Declaration of Paris and the Foreign Enlistment Act, was, significantly enough, the specific mention of the United Kingdom's obligations under the three rules of the Treaty of Washington. These did not become part of international law until the second Hague Conference, 1907, but were accepted by Britain as binding during the Spanish-

American War.[10] The Proclamation of British Neutrality was signed by the Queen on 24 April 1898, and published in the official Gazette on 26 April. However, in view of the imminence of war, formal instructions concerning the observance of the laws of neutrality had been sent to all governors of colonies by Chamberlain on 22 April.[11]

On 23 April 1898, Pauncefote was able to telegraph the decision of the United States concerning the Declaration of Paris. This was to the effect that:

The following recognised rules of international law will be strictly observed:

1. The Neutral flag covers enemy's goods with the exception of contraband of war.
2. Neutral goods with the exception of contraband of war are not liable to capture under an enemy's flag.
3. Blockades in order to be binding must be effective, that is to say, maintained by a force sufficient really to prevent access to the coast of the enemy.[12]

These were the last three of the four rules of the Declaration of Paris, 1856, to which the United States was not a signatory because of its unwillingness to agree to the first rule which stated: "Privateering is and remains abolished."[13] The view of the United States government at the time was that Article 1 should be amended to abolish under all conditions the capture of private property other than contraband, by adding "and that the private property of subjects or citizens of a belligerent on the high seas shall be exempted from seizure by public armed vessels of the other belligerent except it be contraband."[14] This quite obviously was to protect the interests of a comparatively weak naval power such as the United States government felt itself to be in 1856. However, in 1898, when at war with Spain, the naval strength of the United States relative to that of Spain was such that the State Department informed Pauncefote that it would also be the policy of the United States government not to revert to privateering.[15]

Spain also agreed to abide by the last three rules of the Declaration of Paris, but naturally enough reserved the right to revert to privateering if circumstances demanded it.[16] In an endeavour to obtain Spain's adherence to the complete declaration, unofficial representations were made to Austria to urge this upon Spain. This the Austrian government was reluctant to do. As the Austrian officials informed the British ambassador in Vienna, Britain could not expect Spain to forgo the advantage of not being a party to the Declaration of Paris.[17]

Ever since the American Civil War, Britain had sought consistently to remove the threat to the security of a maritime power which was implicit in Palmerston's policy. The Liberal government in the United Kingdom had, during the American Civil War, condoned the building in British ports of armed cruisers destined for use by the rebellious South. A defence of this action, and a refusal to arbitrate the "Alabama" claims, amounted to the creation of a precedent which would permit weak naval powers to equip themselves with a navy built in neutral ports. A realization of this was behind the readiness of those British governments which succeeded Palmerston's to arbitrate the "Alabama" claims, and to agree to the principles embodied in the agreement with the United States concluded as the Treaty of Washington, 1871.[18]

Britain also endeavoured to use the Spanish-American War to extend the scope of international agreement against privateering. The attempt to secure Austrian pressure on Spain failed, but, undeterred, Balfour attempted to use the occasion to obtain German agreement to a principle favouring a sea power as against a land power. Through Lascelles, the British ambassador to Germany, Balfour made unofficial representations to the effect that "as it would be exceedingly adverse to the interests of neutrals it might become a question whether the signatories of the Declaration of Paris might not be well advised in endeavouring to check this rise of privateers by refusing the hospitality of their ports to all ships of war not in regular commission."[19] The German reply was a counter proposal that

Germany, France, and Great Britain should tell Washington and Madrid that they desired the abandonment of the right of belligerents to search neutrals, and if objections were raised to this, then the powers should put forward a compromise proposal that belligerents should be denied the right of search if a neutral captain produced a certificate of clearance from the harbour authorities from which the ship was cleared or from his consul at a foreign port.[20] This was of course refused, the ostensible reasons being that despatches (for instance) could easily be hidden from harbour authorities, and that there was no way for harbour authorities to determine such matters as the destination of a cargo of coal, which, according to law, was contraband or not according to its destination. Of course the real reason for cabinet's rejection of the very neat German riposte to Balfour's rather naïve suggestion was that it was so obviously in the interests of a land power such as Germany, which might possibly be the victim of blockade in war. The matter was not pursued further during the Spanish-American War.

Having thus defined the British position in international law, and achieved a clear statement of their policies from belligerents, the British government was then prepared to meet each neutrality problem as it arose.

II

In their handling of two problems which arose immediately upon the outbreak of war, both Chamberlain and Balfour indicated that they would be guided in their administration of neutrality disputes by the same concern for American reactions which had been so clearly demonstrated in their handling of the suggestion that Britain should participate in a great power mediation between Spain and the United States.

The first problem, dealt with by Balfour, was trivial in itself, but important for that very reason, as it indicates how minutely cabinet actions were scrutinized in the light of their possible effects upon British-American relations. The problem arose in this manner. A Spanish torpedo boat had suffered damage in a storm in the North Atlantic and had put into Cork for repairs. The chief preventive officer of the Cork Customs had reported the incident and asked for advice. In parliament on 21 April Mr. J. H. Dalziel asked that steps should be taken "to ensure that in the event of war being declared between the United States and Spain before the repairs are completed the gunboat in question will be detained." Balfour replied that "if as is understood, the vessel is a commissioned ship of the Spanish Navy, it would be contrary to international practice that she should be detained."[21] Later, Customs were instructed to let the ship go. However, a very clear indication as to Balfour's conception of where British interests lay appears in a Foreign Office minute, referring to Balfour's answer. It reads: "Mr. Balfour[22] cut down his answer as originally settled . . . when the time came for this reason:—It appears there are two or three U.S.A. war vessels now at Hong Kong and in as much as we may have to consider the circumstances of that case with the Spanish case, it was thought better to avoid giving any specific statement of the practice in connection with the Spanish case which would of course bind us in that of the U.S.A."[23] It was quite obvious as between Spain and the United States whose convenience should be considered.

Given Chamberlain's enthusiastic and sometimes defiant advocacy of a British-American understanding, it would not be at all surprising to find that matters concerning neutrality which came within his province as Her Majesty's Chief Secretary of State for Colonies were interpreted wherever possible to favour the United States. This was indeed the case, and the neatest summary of his attitude appeared in a minute arising out of the first problem of note with which Chamberlain had to deal.

The occasion was a request by the United States to use Canadian waterways to bring some revenue cutters to the Atlantic. Permission to do this had been sought and granted before the war broke out but the matter had been delayed. After the outbreak of war the United States again requested permission to carry on with the movement. This matter was referred by the governor-general of Canada to the Colonial Office and the advice to the Foreign Office tendered by Chamberlain was summed up in the following minute:

Mr. Chamberlain is extremely anxious at the present time to refrain from any action which might be regarded as an unfriendly enforcement of the laws of neutrality as against them (the United States). . . . He would be obliged if the Foreign Office would deal with the matter through H.M. Embassy at Washington, and if it is absolutely necessary to cancel the permission already given, that an endeavour should be made to get the United States to withdraw the application. . . . It would be most desirable that an undertaking should be obtained that they will go straight to a U.S. port without engaging in hostile operations.[24]

On this understanding permission was granted. Unfortunately the Spanish government came to hear of the presence of the United States ships in Canadian waters and requested that orders should be given to prevent their departure.[25] After being assured by the governor-general of Canada that the ships had adhered to the conditions set out by Chamberlain and that the delay had been caused only because of the necessity to shorten one of the vessels to enable it to negotiate the St. Lawrence canals, permission was once more given.

These incidents make it quite evident that Balfour at the Foreign Office and Chamberlain at the Colonial Office were both prepared from the outset to offer every possible favour to the United States. These early indications were strengthened and confirmed by later incidents which demonstrated just how far cabinet and particularly Chamberlain were prepared to go. Most instructive is the differential treatment meted out to United States and Spanish citizens engaged in forwarding information from British territory to their home governments.

Consider first the treatment of a Spaniard on British soil in the "Caranza Case," as it is known. Caranza, a former Spanish naval attaché, wrote a letter from Montreal, which was "acquired" by the United States secret service. In the letter Caranza referred to his activities in organizing espionage and mentioned the capture by the United States of two of his agents. The letter was embarrassing not so much for its contents as its implications, which were discussed in parliament.[26] Pauncefote was asked to investigate the matter, to seek information, and to make any necessary enquiries in Washington. He found the charges made by the United States government to be correct, although the United States agents had stolen the letter from Caranza's Canadian lodging. Caranza was ordered to leave Canada on the grounds that the organization of espionage in a neutral country was a breach of hospitality. No prosecution was made, because it could only be based upon confidential information given by the United States, and according to Salisbury, if this information became public knowledge, the United States could not again be expected to make confidential information available.[27] As no prosecution was possible in the circumstances, the matter could have been let drop without Britain or Canada committing any technical breach of neutrality. However, such an action would have been certain to have turned loose against England the vituperation of the yellow press in the United States, and would not have been conducive to the growth of a public opinion in favour of that Anglo-American accord which was Chamberlain's aim at the time. As it was, not only Caranza but other Spaniards also were asked to leave.[28]

Given this precedent Chamberlain's methods of dealing with espionage activities by American citizens in Gibraltar are most instructive, particularly in the light of the clear legal opinion given on the case by law officers of the Foreign Office as against those of the Colonial Office. Major-General Sir Robert Biddulph, governor of Gibraltar, on 1 July 1898 sent a despatch[29] to Chamberlain containing the following information. At the outbreak of war the United States consuls in southern Spain went to Gibraltar. Most of them went on to the United States, but two, Mr. Carroll, former consul at Cadiz, and Mr. Hall, former vice-consul at Xeres, remained. These two, said Biddulph, were

commonly reported to be kept here in order to keep the United States Government informed of the movement of ships and other warlike operations. . . . It is so far common knowledge that the United States Government receives special information through Gibraltar, that the telegrams from Washington which appeared in the London daily papers giving the details of Admiral Camara's squadron, were stated therein to be derived from information received from the State Department agent at Gibraltar. The agent referred to is believed to be Mr. Carroll whose intimate knowledge of affairs at Cadiz enables him to secure sources of information which could not be available to the United States Consul at Gibraltar.

Biddulph added that Carroll and Hall were resident in Gibraltar because they held visitors' permits expiring 12 July. As these permits were for bona fide purposes of private interests and not, he ventured to submit, "designed to allow the subjects of a belligerent power to use a neutral country as a port of observation" he proposed not to renew the permits. In his opinion the press news of the United States decision to send a fleet to the coast of Spain made it especially necessary to guard against any abuse of neutrality.

Chamberlain's reply was not an order to investigate and act in accordance with neutrality regulations, but was a curt telegram: "Have you any clear proof of persons named sending information as to military operations and drawing pay from United States Government."[30] Biddulph obtained information from the Eastern Telegraph Company, under conditions of secrecy, that Carroll had sent telegrams to the State Department, the last one on the day of the departure of Admiral Camara's squadron from Cadiz. In view of this, and Carroll's statement to friends that he was detained in Gibraltar by his government, despite his wish to return home to the United States, Buddulph proposed to take action under the Aliens Order in Council, and deport Carroll.[31]

At this stage Chamberlain referred the matter to the law officers of the Colonial Office, then forwarded the correspondence to the Foreign Office under a minute to the effect that he had consulted the law officers who gave the opinion that no action should be taken at present to terminate the residence of Mr. Carroll and Mr. Hall. Mr. Chamberlain intended (with the approval of Lord Salisbury) to instruct Biddulph not to take action under the Aliens Act. The instruction from Salisbury was brief—"an awkward case but concur."[32]

In order fully to appreciate Chamberlain's action, it is worth quoting in full the opinion of W. E. Davidson, the legal officer of the Foreign Office:

It is a very awkward case indeed, as it seems to me. I should have been disposed to think that we have enough before us to justify action under the Aliens Act, and that such action would have had a good effect as showing that we were determined to preserve the most scrupulous neutrality towards Spain and as giving us a practical proof to produce when allegations to the contrary effect were made by Spain or other foreign States.

But this is of course as much or more a question of policy—which is outside of my functions—as a matter of law. One cannot well judge of the Law Officers' opinion without knowing what exactly was referred to them, but as they have informed Mr. Chamberlain that they consider that no action should be taken at present, and as he [Mr. Chamberlain] agrees with that view, there seems no valid ground for not concurring in his proposal that the Governor should be instructed to take no action at present.

It is difficult however to overlook the fact that we have practically turned a Spanish spy out of Canada a short time since at the instance of the United States and that if the Spaniards should hereafter lay stress on our adverse action towards them in that case, and our friendly attitude towards the United States in this case, it would be not too easy to show that we have been entirely consistent.[33]

W.E.D. 23/7/1898.[34]

As Davidson so succinctly put it, this was "as much or more a question of policy . . . as a matter of law."

III

In British territories in the Far East the actions of the colonial administrative officials clearly reflected Chamberlain's partiality for the United States. In this there is no evidence whatever that they were acting under instruction. On the contrary it is certain that they acted on their own initiative and informed Chamberlain later. An excellent illustrative case is that arising out of the activities of the Philippine rebel leader, General Emilio Aguinaldo.[35]

On 19 May the Spanish consul at Singapore protested to the governor of the Straits Settlements against what he claimed was a breach of the Foreign Enlistment Act. The incidents from which the charge arose make an interesting story. The United States consul-general (Spencer-Pratt) and the United States consul at Singapore (Bray, a British subject) acted as intermediaries between General Aguinaldo and the American Admiral George Dewey. In fact, in Pratt's own words, "When six weeks ago I learned that General Aguinaldo had arrived incognito in Singapore, I immediately sought him out. An hour's interview assured me that he was the man for the occasion. Having communicated with Admiral Dewey I accordingly arranged for him to join the latter at Conte."[36] Aguinaldo and Bray (who collaborated with Spencer-Pratt) were friends of long standing, and Aguinaldo sought Bray's advice about the war in general and about the possibility of Philippine independence being granted in return for assistance to the United States forces. Dewey, being short of troops, was

54

quick to accept Aguinaldo's offer without promising anything about the future status of the islands. The Spanish consul claimed that Aguinaldo was transported to Hong Kong by the United States revenue cruiser, the "Hugh McCulloch," and that this was the first act in a series of breaches of the Foreign Enlistment Act; Bray and Spencer-Pratt, it was argued, were guilty of "inducing Aguinaldo to accept an engagement in the military service of the United States."[37] In reply, the acting Colonial Secretary of the Straits Settlements, C. W. S. Kynnersley, asked for proof other than press reports of the action charged, stated that he would seek legal opinion in the matter, then went over to the offensive by asking bluntly of the Spanish consul whether he knew that on 25 April the Spanish ship "Isla da Panay" left Singapore with soldiers for Spain and whether he knew on 25 April that a state of war existed.[38] The view held by W. M. Collyer, the Attorney-General of the Straits Settlements, was that Bray and Spencer-Pratt had induced Aguinaldo to co-operate with the United States without their being engaged in the military service of the United States. Collyer admitted that this opinion was based on the only evidence available, that is on accounts published in the press.[39] He concluded that there would probably be a different story if all telegraphic communications were made available.[40]

The scene then shifted to Hong Kong, where Aguinaldo had arrived in order to join the Americans who were stationed off the island. The story was taken up by Major-General Black, C.B., the administrator of Hong Kong.[41] On 16 May Senor Navarro, the Spanish consul in Hong Kong, requested the Colonial Secretary to intervene and prevent the departure of Aguinaldo and his rebels. They were known to be due to leave for Manila on the "Hugh McCulloch," which was anchored in Chinese waters off the mainland of China, in Mirs Bay, opposite Hong Kong. The Attorney-General counselled that there were insufficient grounds to enable the administrator to act as desired. Naturally the Spanish consul protested against this lack of action, which he claimed was favouring one of the belligerents to the detriment of the other.

This story reached the Colonial Office in two editions, and in each case it was referred to the Secretary of State for his information, rather than as a request for advice. Major-General Black sent his account forward on 20 May. Concerning his policy of refusing to prevent the departure of the rebels from Hong Kong the legal officers of the Colonial Office appended this minute:

It is possible that the action complained of might constitute an offence under Section 11 of the Foreign Enlistment Act of 1879 on the ground that a military expedition was being fitted out, but the facts before us are not sufficient to justify any action at present, or any further communication unless some further action is taken or further representation made by the Spanish consul.[42]

The whole file was then forwarded to the Foreign Office under a minute indicating Chamberlain's attitude to the administrator's policy. "Mr. Chamberlain proposes with the concurrence of the Marquess of Salisbury to acknowledge receipt but to express no opinion as to the action of the Colonial Government."[43]

There was no reaction from the Foreign Office until after 29 July, when Chamberlain forwarded the documents from the Straits Settlements giving the story of the incidents at Singapore. Sanderson (Permanent Under Secretary of State for Foreign Affairs) pointed out to Salisbury that the United States consul-general publicly avowed his negotiations with Aguinaldo on behalf of Dewey but that technically there was no breach of the Foreign Enlistment Act because of the lack of other evidence. Nevertheless he felt that Her Majesty's government should complain to the United States over the activities of Pratt at Singapore. This was done by Pauncefote in September,[44] the whole affair ending in an atmosphere of polite futility. Pauncefote presented the remonstrance of Her Majesty's government to Mr. Moore (acting for the Secretary of State). The reply was as could be expected, that Aguinaldo made no arrangements with Pratt and that press reports to that effect were incorrect. Nevertheless the United States government regretted that Her majesty's government had any cause to think a representative of the United States was wanting in the observance of conduct necessary to his position. There the matter ended.

From this rather complicated issue I think one thing clearly emerges to uphold the thesis of this chapter. It demonstrates the fact that colonial officials, acting entirely on their own initiative, and under no instruction other than the formal order to administer the neutrality regulations, were of the same mind as Chamberlain in that if possible they were concerned not to impede in any way the war effort of the United States. This was a clear reflection of that public opinion in favour of the United States cause so pointedly expressed in the period immediately prior to and during the war.[45] This public opinion has already been shown to reflect the close community of the United States' and the United Kingdom's economic and political interest on the Asiatic coast and in the islands of the Western Pacific. If either the governor of the Straits Settlements or the administrator of Hong Kong had desired to assist the Spanish cause and yet remain within the law, there were certainly ample grounds for detaining Aguinaldo until further investigations were made or at least until the advice of the Colonial Office had been received. This is obvious from the opinion of the legal officers and from the fact that Salisbury and Sanderson felt there were sufficient grounds either to warrant, or to make necessary, a formal remonstrance to the United States. This remonstrance might have been merely a face-saving precaution, or it might have been a reflection of the sympathies of Salisbury and Sanderson, but in either case they found sufficient grounds to complain, and the same grounds could have been made the occasion for administering neutrality regulations in favour of Spain rather than of the United States.

The case also reveals a difference between Chamberlain and Salisbury in their approach to the question of neutrality. Chamberlain was the enthusiastic supporter of action in favour of the United States during the early period of the war, and even after any hope of close co-operation in world policy with the United States had died (i.e. after March 1898) he was not prepared to make even a formal reproach against the United States. Not so Salisbury, whose sympathies and manner of approach to the problem are examined below.[46] Only when dealing with such matters as the export of arms to belligerents and the use of cables was Chamberlain's approach formally correct, and in both these matters the United States needed no assistance. Moreover, the formal administration of international law normally operated against Spain in these matters. In point of fact the export of arms to the Philippines had been banned since the outbreak of the insurrection there. When, on 14 May 1898, Chamberlain sought the opinion of the Foreign Office as to how to instruct the governors of Hong Kong, the Straits Settlements, and the North Borneo Company, the reply was that "consequent on the active disturbances there" all that was necessary was the renewal of the usual proclamation forbidding the export of arms to the Philippines.[47]

IV

As with Balfour and Chamberlain, Salisbury's attitude to problems arising out of the administration of Britain's neutrality reflected closely the motives governing his attitude to the war as a whole.[48] His prime concern was with the security of British interests, and where these were held to be involved in any particular dispute, Salisbury was prepared to take the measures necessary to preserve the British position. Although remaining unconvinced of the extreme danger of England's isolation, he was prepared to guard against any extension of it by fostering friendship with the United States, whose power he recognized and whose victory he believed certain. However, in any particular situation where British security was not directly involved, his lingering sympathy for Spain and for the difficult position of the Spanish Queen Regent found expression in a formal and legalistic attitude which fell far short of Chamberlain's eagerness to accommodate international law to the advantage of the United States. The latter attitude has already been indicated in the protest over the Aguinaldo affair. It is revealed quite clearly in his handling of neutrality problems involving Egypt.

It will be remembered that in 1898 Egypt, under her Khedive, was still legally a part of the Turkish empire. After the revolt of Arabi Pasha, Cairo had been occupied by British troops under General Lord Wolseley, the Egyptian armies were disbanded, and the British remained with a force sufficient to dominate any local government or to suppress any revolt. The Khedive and his government were accorded the help of British advisers, the chief of these being the consul-general, who could, when he considered it necessary, veto any financial measures of the Khedive.[49] The consul-general from 1883 to 1907 was Sir Evelyn Baring, later Lord Cromer, and he it was who brought before the Foreign Office the problem of administering Egypt's neutrality.

The detailed issues in the dispute were the amount of coal Spanish ships of war should be permitted to load, and the length of time Spanish ships should be allowed in port. The real point at issue was whether Britain would endeavour to facilitate, impede, or remain strictly neutral toward an attempt by Spain to reinforce her fleet and troops in the Philippines by sending a fleet of fifteen ships through the Mediterranean and the Suez Canal.

The issue arose on 23 June when, acting under instructions from his government, the acting United States consul-general in Cairo put the American view quite concisely. He asked Cromer's assistance to prevent any Spanish ships of war visiting Port Said or Suez from obtaining coal and other stores which would enable them to proceed to the Philippines.[50] It was to this end that all the consul's future actions concerning the passage of the fleet were directed. To the United States this was a matter of some moment and not just a technical legal point, for although Admiral Dewey had destroyed the Spanish fleet in Manila Bay on 1 May, he could not move against the Spanish land forces until reinforced. Extra ships, supplies, and men did not arrive until 30 June. The consul-general therefore endeavoured to persuade the Egyptian government to order the Spanish fleet to leave Egyptian ports at the conclusion of the twenty-four hours' stay permitted by international law, and he sought continually to prevent the Spanish admiral from loading any more coal than was necessary to enable his fleet to reach the nearest port of his own country or some nearer destination.[51]

If Spanish intentions had not been obvious enough to justify the American view, they were made quite apparent by the Spanish ambassador's request to the British Foreign Office to facilitate the coaling of the Spanish fleet at Aden, Colombo, and Singapore on the way to the Philippines.[52] This unnecessary official avowal of intentions seems to lend weight to the report from the British consul at Port Said, who informed Cromer that he had received information "that the Spaniards would in reality be rather glad to be delayed and hindered in their voyage, their present proceeding being merely a demonstration in order to satisfy public opinion."[53] When it became known in Madrid that Egypt would not offer any facilities other than those permitted by law, the Spanish government issued a protest which it surely could not have hoped to be effective except upon public opinion within Spain. The Spanish Minister for Foreign Affairs put his case to the British ambassador in these terms. Speaking "in much agitation" he argued that

the question is not one of neutrality between belligerents but of preventing Spain from sending [sic] to put down an insurrection in one of her own colonies where savages were likely to murder and torture Christians. The expedition had been sent not only against the American forces, but to preserve order in the provinces and the question of hours was important. His Excellency is immediately about to issue a circular on the subject holding the Egyptian Government responsible.[54]

To this Salisbury did not reply.

The attitude and action of the British Foreign Office in this Egyptian case provide an instructive contrast to Chamberlain's policy and the courses followed by colonial officers. In public, the Foreign Office was prepared to some extent to maintain the formal and legal authority of Egypt. Mr. M. Davitt in the Commons asked whose responsibility it was to administer the neutrality regulations. The answer given by Lord Curzon, written by Villiers of the Foreign Office on the advice of the legal officers, was that it was the primary responsibility of the Egyptian government and that Her Majesty's government assumed there were sufficient grounds for the action of the Egyptian government in permitting Spanish ships to overstay the twenty-four hour limit.[55] However, in fact no latitude whatever was given the Khedive to decide the matter according to his own sympathies. This limitation was necessary on the one hand because of the overriding importance to Britain of cordial British-American relations, and on the other because of the fact that Turkey had not made any declaration of her attitude to the dispute, nor had she declared her neutrality. In this situation the Khedive, if permitted freedom of action, could have permitted the coaling and repair of the Spanish fleet without any breach of international law. But of course, because of the known relationship between Egypt and Britain, the British Foreign Office would have been held responsible for any such action and this did not fit into the pattern of cabinet policy. This policy was known and acted upon by Foreign Office officials no matter where their sympathies lay.[56]

Upon receipt of the American consul-general's request to prevent the Spanish fleet from obtaining sufficient supplies to enable it to reinforce the Philippines, Lord Cromer telegraphed the Foreign Office suggesting that he should "advise the Egyptian Government" to adopt whatever practice had been adopted at British ports. As he was unsure of that practice in the case of coal he asked for instructions.[57] The sympathy for Spain which lingered among the more conservative officials, as among the court circles, showed out once more in a minute by Villiers. He commented: "The Turks have not issued any proclamation of neutrality. Any restrictions on the supply of coal at Port Said or Suez will in all probability operate to the disadvantage of the Spaniards only, but I suppose the advice suggested to Lord Cromer is right."[58] This decision was endorsed by the legal officer (Davidson), and Salisbury approved instructions in those terms to Cromer. There was no discussion as to whether the matter should be left in the hands of the Khedive, for, given the previous statements and instructions concerning British policy issued by Salisbury, Balfour, Chamberlain, and indeed by the Opposition, no such action was conceivable.

Once Egypt was committed to neutrality by the Foreign Office decision, the administration of the international laws regulating the conduct of neutrals revealed attitudes very different from those of Chamberlain and the Colonial Office officials. To Cromer, the matter remained essentially the question as to whether or not the Spanish were to be permitted to reinforce the Philippines. His original query as to coaling was replied to formally by the quotation of the rule that a Spanish ship of war was to be allowed "so much coal only as may be sufficient to carry such vessel to the nearest port of her own country or to some nearer destination."[59] In return, on 24 June Cromer cabled putting the problem as he saw it to the Foreign Office. "In the application of the rule, shall I be right in advising the Egyptian Government to refuse coal to Spanish ships of war or to transports flying the Spanish flag if they arrive from Spain and if their manifest intention is not to proceed to the nearest port of their own country but eastwards to the Philippine Islands."[60] To this Cromer received no reply until 28 June, for his question set off a prolonged legalistic examination of the rights and wrongs of the case. The issue was further complicated by the question as to whether or not the provisions of the Suez Canal Convention of 1888 had been invoked by the British government and were in operation.

Davidson's immediate reaction was minuted on Cromer's telegram: in his opinion rule three spoke for itself.

If therefore the manifest intention of the Spanish vessel is to proceed to the Philippine Islands (which is not the nearest port of her own country or some nearer destination) then if the Egyptian Government intend *mutatis mutandis* to apply our rule they will refuse to give a Spanish Man of War so much coal as may be sufficient to carry her to the Philippine Islands.[61]

Salisbury added his comment. "I do not follow the argument. The rule is that so much coal shall be sold to a belligerent as will take him back to his own country. But unless my memory deceives me—there is nothing about his intention to go there."[62] However it remained to Salisbury a legal matter, his final minute being a direction to ask the opinion of the legal officers.

In the meantime, despite repeated requests Cromer was left without a decision on what he regarded as the crux of the matter. The Spanish fleet arrived at Port Said on 25 June, and Cromer advised the Egyptian government to refuse coal for the present and again sought a decision from the Foreign Office.[63] Meanwhile he discussed the matter with the French and American consuls, reporting to the Foreign Office that the French consul agreed with the refusal to act until a further examination had been made. "He seems disposed to think that coal should be given in sufficient quantity to take the ships to the nearest port which is obviously Spain and that it is no business of a neutral power to enquire too closely as to the direction in which the ships then proceed. The American Consul-General naturally does not accept this view."[64]

In London the legal argument continued, Davidson holding

that the Spanish should not have coal "if Egypt is to be guided by our rules, without a definite and clear undertaking that they are going not to the Philippine Islands but to the nearest Spanish or nearer neutral port."[65] From Cairo on 27 June Cromer pointed out that the Spanish fleet had already over-stayed the twenty-four hours permitted a belligerent by international usage and again sought a decision.[66] The Spanish admiral required 6,000 tons of coal which, in addition to his present supplies, would be sufficient for a slow voyage to the Philippines. Nothing further had been heard from the law officers but a minute dated 28 June reads: "Lord Salisbury thinks that if the ships have enough coal to go to any Spanish port they should not be allowed a further supply. Telegram to this effect to Cromer."[67] On 29 June Cromer acted, reporting that "as there appears no reason to doubt that the Spanish ships are furnished with sufficient coal to take them to the nearest port of their own country, I have advised the Egyptian Government not to allow any further supply to be delivered in any Egyptian port." Again, on the same day, as the United States consul was about to point out to the Egyptian govern-ment that the twenty-four hour limit had been overstayed, Cromer, upon Foreign Office instructions, recommended to the Egyptian government that they should advise the immediate departure of the Spanish fleet, and that if Spanish ships could be shown to be without coal they were to be given enough to take them to the nearest port of their own country and a formal declaration to that effect was to be obtained from the Spanish consul.[68] These instructions received the approval of and were adhered to by the law officers who finally brought in a decision in line with the action already taken independently.[69] The fleet was prevented from coaling from Egyptian lighters outside the three mile limit of Port Said, and when the fleet reached Suez it was asked to leave within twenty-four hours. Here the ques-tion ceased to be of any importance, for the fleet was ordered to return to Spain because of the threat to the Spanish coast by the reported presence of a United States squadron.

This episode has been treated at some length because of the contrast it provides between Salisbury's formal, legalistic, even academic attitude to this particular question, and Chamberlain's eagerness on every possible occasion to make the law serve the ends of British policy as he conceived it. Salisbury's feeling for and sympathy with past loyalties were outweighed by Chamberlain's impatient effort to maintain that understanding with the United States which he felt to be the key to the future. Chamberlain and Salisbury were agreed on the principle that British interests were best served by neutrality. The difference between them was that Salisbury regarded British policy almost as a regrettable necessity and Chamberlain welcomed the war as a golden opportunity to foster future understanding.[70]

V

Once the neutrality decision had been taken, Salisbury could in the Egyptian question permit himself the luxury of formal legality because there were no issues involved which would complicate the formal administration of neutrality regulations. An expression in the form of legal argument of his lingering sympathy for Spain did not directly involve anything vital either to British security or British-American amity. Whereever these were involved, traditional ties and sympathy for royalty in distress never prevented him from participating in or initiating effective action to ensure the protection of British interests and increased co-operation with the United States. Two incidents now to be examined, one concerning Mirs Bay near Hong Kong and the other involving Gibraltar, illustrate these aspects of Salisbury's policy. The first reveals his willingness in the interests of Anglo-American accord to accommodate British action to the needs of the United States armed services. The second illustrates how patiently ruthless he could be when he held England's vital strategic interests to be challenged.

Salisbury, like Balfour, was prepared to consider the convenience of the American fleet operating on this occasion in Far Eastern waters. It must be appreciated that the American fleet under Admiral Dewey had no United States coaling facilities closer to the Philippines than Hawaii. When ordered to the Pacific command, it had been Dewey's first concern to have sufficient coal and ammunition forwarded to the Pacific to enable him to operate efficiently.[71] When war broke out the United States fleet was at Hong Kong, and in accordance with the laws of neutrality, British officials requested Dewey to leave the territorial waters of the colony by 25 April. The first day of May saw the battle of Manila Bay and Dewey's destruction of Spanish sea power in the Far East, but he still needed a forward land base, for Manila itself did not fall until 13 August.

He chose as his forward base Mirs Bay, opposite Hong Kong. It was there that supplies reached him, it was from there that he negotiated with Aguinaldo and his rebel leaders,[72] and it was from there that his ships moved to the battle area. In this situation, if Salisbury had not been prepared to accommodate British policy to the convenience of the United States, Dewey and his fleet would have been forced to seek some other anchorage and develop some other supply base. Successive administrators of Hong Kong and Sir Claude MacDonald (the United Kingdom's ambassador in China) had for some time been pressing for the acquisition of sufficient territory on the mainland to secure the waters near Hong Kong from any hostile operations and to remove Chinese sovereignty from the shores of the mainland opposite the island. Negotiations with the Tsungli Yamen to achieve this purpose had been tentative until France demanded and received from China the cession of Kwangchowan.[73] They were then pressed forward toward conclusion. In May, Major-General Wilson Black, the administrator of Hong Kong, pointed out to the Colonial Office that "the presence of the 'Hugh McCulloch'[74] in Chinese waters in the position already indicated[75] emphasizes the danger to which this colony may be exposed and the risk of international complication which may arise from the northern boundary of the Harbour belonging to a foreign state."[76] By 9 June a convention had been concluded by which China agreed to grant a ninety-nine year lease of the peninsula opposite Hong Kong, the boundary being a line joining the deepest points of Mirs Bay and Deep Bay.[77]

Sir Claude MacDonald pointed out to Salisbury that if the desired base were to be obtained from the Chinese and taken up formally by Britain, the Colonial Office would then be faced with the difficult situation of enforcing neutrality regulations against the United States, just as had been the case in Hong Kong.[78] This of course would have incommoded Dewey's operations against the Spanish land forces in Manila. Salisbury indicated a way out. "If we get an engagement formally we might find an excuse for postponing the date of the lease."[79] In the same minute there was a note to the effect that the Colonial Office desired a delay in order to make the arrangements which were necessary. Salisbury's suggestion became a direction sent to MacDonald, to the effect that it was not intended to take up the formal lease on 1 July because the necessary arrangements required delay. Then the real reason for the delay was made quite clear when the telegram changed to secret code for the last sentence: "Have Americans ceased altogether to make use of Mirs Bay as a naval base?"[80]

The value of this concession to the United States should be assessed against the background of the very difficult situation with which Admiral Dewey had to deal at this time, i.e. between the destruction of the Spanish fleet at the beginning of May and the fall of Manila on 13 August.

. . . he had to be on constant guard against possible mine or torpedo attacks from the surviving officers and men of the defeated squadron. In addition he knew that the Spanish government was preparing a superior fleet under Admiral Cámara. . . . To meet this threat Dewey had an inadequate force and a seriously depleted supply of ammunition; and despite his urgent appeals the Navy

Department seemed to be assembling reinforcements with great deliberation. The strain on Dewey's nerves was further increased by the absence of cable communication, for it normally took about a week to send a ship to Hong Kong and receive a telegraphic reply from Washington. Moreover, the Filipino insurgents under Aguinaldo, were attacking Manila, and it was necessary to keep them from getting out of hand. . . . As if this all were not enough, the danger of an epidemic of disease in the fleet was great. . . .[81]

In these circumstances it is easy to imagine his and his government's reaction to any British move which would have forced him to change his base on the Asiatic mainland.

It might be supposed that the Colonial Office officials were merely using as a convenient pretext the suggestion that more time was needed to complete the administrative arrangements for occupying the new territory. This does not necessarily follow, for the dilatory manner in which the Foreign Office conducted negotiations prior to the French lease of Kwang-chowan did not indicate to the Colonial Office that there was any urgency in the matter. Moreover, administrative arrangements could not have been completed until the extent of the territory and the fate of the population involved had been decided. It was Salisbury who first made the suggestion for delaying the occupation, and the need for it was first presented by the ambassador reporting to the Foreign Office. The Colonial Office desire for delay answered perfectly Salisbury's need for some excuse. Chamberlain on many occasions endeavoured if not to force Salisbury's hand at least to influence him directly to adopt policies favouring the United States, but on this occasion the need for such a policy was discerned first by a Foreign Office official (MacDonald) and the solution was devised by Salisbury himself.

From the Spanish and American points of view this action of Salisburys, if known, could have been construed as a deliberate effort to facilitate the final victory of the United States. Conversely his action could be interpreted merely as a cautious evasion of an issue. The first proposition is ruled out by Salisbury's often expressed reluctance to see Spain humiliated, and the second at first does not seem to apply, for Salisbury was never the man to evade an issue, unless for some sound reason. In this case there was such a reason. His action was not designed to hasten the Spanish defeat, but to avoid creating a situation which would force him to act in such a way as to endanger amicable relations between the United States and the United Kingdom in a region where the rest of the cabinet believed England to be in need of allies. The United States had in March refused to stand with Britain against the Russian and German threat to limit the freedom of trade with China; but this in no way affected the determination of the cabinet, supported by the clamour of public opinion, to act where possible in accord with the United States.

VI

One of the most bitter disputes over neturality in which Britain was engaged during the war was with Spain, and it arose out of both Spanish and British concern over Gibraltar. The Treaty of Utrecht had decided British sovereignty over Gibraltar but it also had bequeathed to succeeding generations the problem of defining the limits of British sovereignty over the waters of the bay. By 1898 developments in artillery since Utrecht had produced guns of far greater range than when Gibraltar was ceded, so that siege guns erected on Spanish soil across the bay could potentially neutralize the fortress. However, the chief difficulty was that as the bay was so narrow the three mile limit of British sovereignty from Gibraltar and the three mile limit of Spanish sovereignty from the Spanish shore overlapped.[82] This meant that Britain and Spain would be faced with a very complicated problem if either became engaged in a war in which the other were neutral.[83]

The problem as it arose out of the Spanish-American War was presented to Britain in two ways, firstly by a request from the governor of Gibraltar for instructions to govern his actions in case of any breach of neutrality, and secondly by the action of the Spanish in erecting fortifications opposite Gibraltar, ostensibly to guard against any American attack in the bay. The manner in which both aspects of this problem were handled reveals just how united all branches of the administration became once the war related specifically to an area vital to the security of the United Kingdom.

"In view of the contingency during the present state of war between the United States and Spain of possible attempts to capture, or other belligerent action within the waters of the bay, or attempts to violate neutrality,"[84] the governor of Gibraltar, Major-General Sir Robert Biddulph, sought from the Colonial Office a statement of principle to guide his action in any emergency. The request was forwarded to the Foreign Office, the War Office, and the Admiralty. The Admiralty was the first to reply, and without consulting the Foreign Office[85] Chamberlain directed Biddulph in terms of the Admiralty's advice. "Her Majesty's forces should enforce the provisions of the neutrality proclamation within the line [known as the *medium filum*] proposed by them in the negotiations of 1879-1883, but with regard to any action of belligerents or others constituting a danger or menace to the fortress or shipping in the port the full three mile limit should be enforced."[86] The Colonial Office legal officers considered this "an excellent solution of a very difficult point."[87] When this was made known to the Foreign Office on 29 July, Villiers immediately fastened upon what he considered the inconsistency involved in using the three mile limit for one situation and the line of the *medium filum* for another. When referred to, Salisbury ordered the matter to the Foreign Office legal officers (Webster and Finlay). Their initial reaction was to agree upon adherence to the line of the *medium filum*, but they could not agree that British action should extend beyond this line in any circumstances.[88]

Having obtained all the relevant papers, the legal officers

Webster and Finlay brought in their considered opinion on 11 August. They began by agreeing that the Admiralty advice was inconsistent. They continued by admitting that "it may well be right on the part of the Governor of Gibraltar to prevent any action even outside the territorial water, which endangers the port or shipping, but this must rest on the right of a neutral to prevent warlike operations involving direct injury to self." They concluded by adding:

The questions relating to the safety of the fortress of Gilbraltar are so important and delicate that we think no attempt should at present be made to define exactly the limits within which the Governor may act. We think it quite right that the Governor should be instructed to enforce the proclamation of neutrality only within the line marked in the bay and up to the three mile limit elsewhere, but no admission should be made which might hamper the right of the Governor to take any action in any part of the bay which may be essential for preventing injury to the fort or shipping.[89]

This decision was sent off to Biddulph and with all the relevant correspondence to Drummond Wolff in Madrid. However, in the long run, the influence of the Admiralty and the War Office won out over the niceties of international law. Both departments concurred in Chamberlain's proposal to send the statement of the limits of jurisdiction to Gibraltar and Madrid "subject to the strenuous maintenance of paragraph c of Station Orders for Her Majesty's ships."[90] As Chamberlain pointed out to the Foreign Office, this paragraph laid it down "as beyond all doubt and question that between the New Mole and Europa Point British jurisdiction extends as far as the guns of the fortress will range and that every act of violence within these limits is a violation of the sovereign rights of Great Britain."[91]

This decision involved an extension of Britain's territorial jurisdiction beyond the line of the *medium filum* and beyond the three mile limit. It involved also disregard of the opinion

SKETCH MAP

OF

THE BAY OF ALGECIRAS SHOWING
GIBRALTAR AND ADJOINING SPANISH TERRITORY

Copied from an Admiralty sketch, FO72/2096

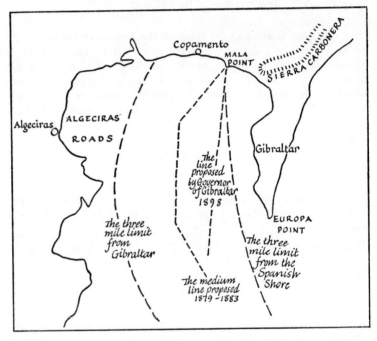

of the law officers. Nevertheless Lord Lansdowne at the War Office, Goschen at the Admiralty, and Chamberlain all agreed that the instruction should be sent to Biddulph.[92] A corollary was, of course, that the law officers should once more "take the matter into consideration," giving special attention to the latitude suggested in the right of neutrals to prevent warlike operations dangerous to themselves.

This triumph of the necessities of defence over international law must be evaluated against the crisis in Anglo-Spanish relations arising out of the Spanish attempt to defend her coasts against possible aggression. From Madrid, in May, Drummond Wolff had sent frequent reports[93] of a movement of Spanish infantry, sappers, and cavalry to the vicinity of Gibraltar and Algeciras. These, he was informed, were being assembled mainly for movement overseas to reinforce the Philippines and to protect Spanish possessions on the coast of Africa, while some were to be used to construct fortifications and battery emplacements on the Sierra Carbonera.[94] In June the works continued, but the troops had not been despatched overseas, and on this Wolff, as usual tending to favour the Spanish interest, commented in a manner indicating that he foresaw and endeavoured to forestall criticism of Spain. He indicated that the position of the Spanish battalions near Gibraltar did not support the view that they were to be transferred to the Philippines; in his opinion the disposition of the troops was more probably "a defensive measure in anticipation of an Anglo-American alliance and an outbreak from Gibraltar." There was a popular demand in Spain for the erection of fortifications in the Sierra Carbonera and other points round the Bay of Gibraltar. He summed up by arguing that "the very smallness of this force is a guarantee that nothing offensive is intended."[95]

Throughout July further reports came from Madrid of the progress of the fortifications, usually accompanied by Wolff's assessment of the reason, for example that Spain expected an American squadron to attempt to coal in the Bay of Algeciras and was therefore erecting fortifications to prevent this.[96] These periodic reports from Drummond Wolff brought no response from Salisbury or any member of the cabinet. However, at the end of the month matters took a new turn. The governor of Gibraltar had forwarded a lengthy memorandum, based on his intelligence reports, concerning the threatening nature of the fortifications opposite the fortress. This report spurred both the Admiralty and the War Office into action. On 17 July Mr. Goschen forwarded the memorandum to Salisbury, commenting that "the danger as you know has always been kept in mind and we thought that any attempt to fortify these heights would have to be protested against *effectively* at once. Will you think the matter over?" He reminded Salisbury also how closely Spain and France were acting together.[97] Lansdowne at the War Office was so far impressed as to suggest that Salisbury should consider "whether the time has not come to ask the Spanish Government to explain its actions."[98] He pointed out that "though the works were ostensibly directed against an assailant from the sea, yet they actually occupied the most favourable position for directing fire on to the south end of Gibraltar." He corroborated Drummond Wolff's reports of the Spanish fear of an Anglo-American alliance followed by combined action to extend British sovereignty around Gibraltar. Finally, intelligence reported that plans had been made by the Spanish government to move 25,000 troops into the area.

At this point issue was joined with the Spanish government. The dispute became bitter and angry exchanges of protests and counter-protests continued until long after the war. The complete history of the case need not be followed; the chief interest relevant to this argument is the clear evidence provided of cabinet and embassy attitudes to the problem of securing British interests during the United States war with Spain. Nevertheless it is necessary first to examine Spanish policy in order to appreciate fully the British reaction.

Put succinctly, the Spanish attitude was that the fortifications were a necessary defence against possible attack, that they were no more directed against Gibraltar than Gibraltar was intended for an attack against Spain, and that England should be as prepared to accept Spanish assurances about this as Spain was prepared to accept those of the British.[99] Finally, Spain was prepared to give the fullest and most explicit undertakings that the fortifications would not be used against Gibraltar. Now by Article 10 of the Treaty of Utrecht, England had been ceded Gibraltar "to be held without exception or impediment for ever," and successive Spanish governments had acquiesced in British occupation and had not until the Spanish-American

War erected "impediments" in the form of fortifications which could neutralize the fortress.

Spain's reluctance to agree to Britain's demands for the removal of all guns and fortifications which in her view threatened Gibraltar stemmed firstly from a real fear of United States action against the Spanish coast,[100] and of a possible combined action against her by which Britain would extend her control over the Spanish mainland in the rear of the rock.[101] This fear was the result of the British cabinet's refusal to participate in any strong move to dissuade the United States from her chosen course,[102] and of Queen Victoria's sympathetic but unhelpful replies to the Queen Regent's plea for aid.[103] It fed upon the rumours in the French, American,[104] and Spanish press,[105] on the enthusiasm of much of the British press for an Anglo-American understanding,[106] and seemed in Chamberlain's speeches[107] and his visit to America[108] to find proofs of these fears and suspicions. Any suggestion that Chamberlain was in the United States actively seeking an alliance was expressly denied by the Foreign Office,[109] but these denials did little to allay Spanish fears. Further proof of British hostility to Spain was thought to be apparent in Britain's expulsion of Caranza, her refusal to expel Carroll, and the assistance offered Philippine rebels in the Far East.[110] Wolff reported on 17 August that there was very strong feeling against England "to whom is ascribed all Spain's misfortunes."[111]

A second reason for the Spanish government's refusal to meet Britain's demands can be found in the state of Spain's domestic politics. The Queen Regent and her government were upholding a very unstable throne, and they, with France and England, feared a Carlist revolution if they followed a foreign policy which could be exploited to alienate public opinion from the existing regime.[112] There was, according to Drummond Wolff, a popular demand for the fortification of the areas opposite Gibraltar, and there was very strong anti-British feeling among the Spanish army authorities who were a most powerful force in Spanish domestic politics. This had been made clear to Wolff on various occasions and was put explicitly by the

Spanish Minister for Foreign Affairs, who feared that "demolition of the armaments might lead to the most untoward events in Spain." Wolff added that in the circumstances the meeting of the Cortes was fraught with danger.[113] Because of the weakness of the government and the strength of the Carlists, matters of Spanish prestige became of great moment, even delaying Spain's decision to sue for peace. As the Spanish Foreign Minister put it to Wolff,[114] for Spain to submit to England would not only place Spain in the position of being an inferior power, it would endanger the very supremacy of the Spanish government itself.

A third reason for Spain's attitude is to be found in the support lent to her opposition by other European powers. Austria, of course, endeavoured to support Spain, her ambassador pointing out to Wolff that France would be likely to side with Spain in any difference with England, and that Spain's capitulation to England would result in the forced abdication of the Queen Regent and a Carlist revolution.[115] Wolff believed that French support for Spain was the secret of Spanish intransigence. He argued that Spain was dominated by France and that British influence only remained at all in Spain because of Gibraltar. In his own words:

In the minds of all the diplomats at Madrid there now exists the belief that Spain has become practically the vassal of France. It is France that from her position commands the dynasties or other form of government adopted by Spain. France has bought nearly the whole press. France possesses the railways and disposes of the money market and shares with Spain the whole of the Western shores of Mediterranean Europe. In case of war France could overrun in a very short space the country [sic] from one end to the other including the lands to the north of Gibraltar.

In these circumstances Wolff believed that "over-pressure would probably cause an appeal to France and consequently to Russia."[116]

Wolff's sympathy for Spain and his reluctance to use the strong language urged upon him by cabinet probably led him continually to over-emphasize French influence, for Hanotaux had resigned in June and Delcassé, who was much more friendly to England, was Foreign Minister. However, it was not until after Fashoda that the *bonne entente* that Delcassé sought was to make any progress. In August it is quite likely that Wolff was to some extent correct in assuming that France was encouraging Spain,[117] and that Spain might appeal to France and Russia against overpressure. Sir John Ardagh, the Director-General of Military Intelligence, certainly believed that the threat to Gibraltar was now greater than ever because of the increase in French influence over Spain. He believed that France would support Spain because "every gun placed within range of Gibraltar is from her point of view so much gained."[118] In September Wolff was at first confirmed in his view by the opinions of the Italian and Austrian ambassadors (both probably suspect sources of information because of their pro-Spanish sympathies), by other "good but less reliable sources," by the fact that the French press first started the rumours that Britain was seeking more territory from Spain, by the fact that the French ambassador countenanced the press reports, and by the very unfriendly attitude of the French embassy.[119] Later, however, according to his friend the Russian ambassador, the Italian ambassador modified his view.[120]

Wolff's error lay in over-estimating the efficacy of the appeal to France which he feared would be made. As Balfour pointed out, French economic investment in Spain in bonds and railways was a powerful reason for her to desire peace between England and Spain.[121] In September, Sir Edward Monson, Britain's ambassador at Paris, in whom cabinet placed more trust than in Wolff, believed that France was endeavouring to increase her influence in Spain but was not inciting Spain to raise difficulties with England.[122] He did not believe that French policy would lead France to risk a collision with any foreign power and added that at the time M. Delcassé was very friendly toward England. This estimate of the limits of French policy was amply borne out by the diplomatic actions of France in the Fashoda incident.[123]

One other circumstance led Spain to refuse to comply with the British demands even after her defeat was manifest. The occasion appeared to the Queen Regent and the Duke of Almadovar (the Minister for Foreign Affairs) to be an excellent opportunity to bargain with England.

I have received [wrote Wolff on 23 August] a very slight indication that if Her Majesty's Government will give their good offices to Spain with the United States in settling the Philippine question, and some moral support in that of the Cuban debt, Spain would give a private undertaking in writing as to the limitation of the works round Gibraltar in a manner to be agreed.[124]

The Foreign Office were not prepared to go as far as the Spanish desired, but the matter was discussed, and Sanderson sent off to Wolff the substance of a plan sketched by Balfour with a request to send Lord Salisbury his opinion of what the Spanish government's reaction would be.

As a way out of the difficulty Balfour suggested that England should by treaty or otherwise guarantee Spanish sovereignty over the regions immediately surrounding Gibraltar and should guarantee to oppose the invasion of that region by any foreign power. Spain would be required in return to pledge herself not to maintain or erect within the region, military works or fortifications of any kind. Balfour thus sought to reassure Spain against any fear of American use of Gibraltar as a base. Salisbury, with greater insight into the Spanish character than his younger protége, minuted "my fear is that the Spanish Government will look upon the offer of protection as more insulting than the demand for liberty to inspect." Salisbury was confirmed in his view by Wolff's reply which was to the effect that the plan, no matter how judicious, "could not at this moment be brought forward alone as in their sensitive mood the Spanish would look on it as an offer of a protectorate and consequently a humiliation without any great advantage."[125]

The Queen Regent's conception of what she would consider an acceptable bargain was contained in an explicit proposal in

September when she was seriously considering, as a solution to the difficulty, a convention between Spain and England by which England would guarantee Spanish ownership of the Canaries, the Balearic Islands, and Ceuta, in return for which Spain would agree not to join with the enemies of England.[126] During the absence from the cabinet of the Marquis de la Vega de Armigo, this proposal had been originally put forward by Senor Moret who was opposed to the increasing influence of France in Spain.[127] The Queen Regent and two of her advisers, Segasta and Almadovar, were all prepared to accept Moret's proposal, but endeavoured to require, as a pre-condition, Britain's support of Spain's attempts to escape the Cuban debt and either to retain portion of the Philippines or obtain greater compensation for their loss.[128] Although Salisbury and the cabinet approved the plan for the convention, in so far as it applied to Ceuta, the Canaries, and the Balearic Islands, and although the Queen Regent and Almadovar were not prepared to make the Cuban and Philippine conditions an insuperable stumbling block, the matter was not concluded successfully because of the return of the Marquis de la Vega de Armigo. He was bitterly opposed to British possession of Gibraltar, he was convinced that Britain had been encouraging the United States to acquire the Philippines, and he would only agree to the convention provided that Britain would obtain some provision favourable to Spanish aims and interests in the Philippines.[129] He was able to influence Almadovar and the Regent's influence was insufficient to retrieve the situation.

The attitude of the United Kingdom to the Gibraltar dispute was determined by three considerations. In the first place Gibraltar was the hub of Mediterranean and Atlantic defence and any threat to its security was a threat to the basic structure of empire. Secondly, the incipient threat of the Spanish fortifications was made extraordinarily urgent by the twin bogeys of French influence in Spain and the deterioration of British-French relations from late August until the settlement of the

Fashoda affair on 4 November. Finally, England was determined neither to permit any incident to impair Anglo-American understanding nor to interfere in any way between Spain and the United States. The degree of intensity of British pressure upon Spain reflected the urgency of the international situation and the variety of personalities in the cabinet, the War Office, the Admiralty, and court circles.

Both Balfour (acting as Foreign Minister during Salisbury's absence) and Sir John Ardagh (Director-General of Military Intelligence) were concerned to emphasize Britain's early restraint and patience. Ardagh made no comment until 18 August when he justified his reticence by stating that "he conceived that the right of self-perservation was a sufficient justification" for the Spanish action.[130] Balfour pointed out to Drummond Wolff the consideration cabinet had shown in delaying any remonstrance despite "frequent and early notification" of the Spanish works.

Until our military and naval advisers here and in the colony urgently impressed upon us that some of these works appeared to be directly solely or mainly against the British fortress and harbour and that if completed they would threaten both very seriously, we were reluctant to make representations. Even then we delayed our instructions in order that they might not arrive at what appeared to be a critical moment for Spain.[131]

If British assumptions are accepted, Balfour's claim that Spain had received generous consideration was sound, for the war was virtually over by the end of July and the first British protest, suavely worded by Salisbury, was not delivered until 3 August. However, once the issue was joined with Spain, the British Foreign Office, backed by a united cabinet and particularly by the urgent advice of the War Office and the Admiralty, took a firm and completely uncompromising stand which left no room whatever for doubt as to the seriousness of British intentions. The various expressions of the position adopted are an interesting reflection of the personalities and groups involved.

It was Salisbury who worded the first remonstrance, and his statement is a model of his studied consideration and reserved formality which yet permitted the steel to be perceived through the velvet. He instructed Wolff to draw the attention of the Spanish government to the works threatening Gibraltar and to say that Her Majesty's government presumed they were for defence against a possible action by the United States in this area.

It may relieve the Spanish Government from solicitude on this point if Your Excellency informs them that Her Majesty's Government are quite ready to give them an assurance that such an operation against Spain would not be permitted to be carried on or even attempted from within the territorial waters of Great Britain in the Bay. . . . Her Majesty's Government entertain no doubt that the Spanish Government on receiving this assurance will not consider it necessary to continue the construction of the works I have specially mentioned.[132]

Giving rein to their pride and to their resentment against Britain's alleged support of the United States, the Spanish government replied briefly that the matter was within their sovereignty and pointed out that they had made no protest to England concerning the fact that Gibraltar's guns could be turned against Algeciras. This rebuff brought rejoinders so blunt that Wolff was quite alarmed and delayed action upon his instructions.[133] On 9 August the Foreign Office forwarded to Madrid an Admiralty recommendation protesting against the fortifications on the Sierra Carbonera and suggesting that the British ambassador should say "that permanent batteries in such a position cannot be tolerated, and that they must be removed at the conclusion of the war with the United States."[134] Balfour followed this up on 12 August with an instruction drafted in his own hand that Wolff should make explicitly clear to the Spanish government that Her Majesty's government "would shrink from no consequences to avoid the batteries rendering Gibraltar useless."[135]

Having thus made clear in such outspoken language Britain's determination to protect her interests, cabinet was once more prepared to consider the difficulties in which Spain found herself in attempting to salvage from the peace negotiations what little she could of empire and prestige. The matter was considered by the Admiralty and the War Office, who decided that it would be inopportune to press the matter during the peace negotiations between Spain and America, that the Spanish explanation should be noted, that it should be assumed that peace would mean reversion to the status quo ante bellum and that if the emplacements remained after the peace settlement, then remonstrances should be resumed. To this the Colonial Office and Foreign Office agreed and on 20 August Balfour informed Wolff to that effect.[136]

These early decisions set the atmosphere of the prolonged negotiations which followed, that is to say an immovable determination to achieve British aims, but in negotiations to display the restraint of a self-confident power, certain of its strength, dealing with a proud, once great but now weak, monarchy. Balfour and, after his return to the Foreign Office, Salisbury pointed to their early patience and reticence. They referred Spain to the ancient treaty rights of Britain at Gibraltar. They insisted that they were willing to wait until the victory had been won or lost. They emphasized the importance of Gibraltar to Britain and the empire, and their readiness to give undertakings that Gibraltar would not be used against Spain, nor would any operations of Spain's enemies be permitted from the vicinity of Gibraltar. Then, when Spain still pressed on with the construction of the fortifications, stern language was again used. Drummond Wolff, as usual seeking to minimize the conflict, had asked Balfour for further advice. He received a rather testy reply: "You ask my views. They were expressed in my tele. No. 102 private of yesterday.[137] . . . In as much as peace with the U.S.A. is now assured, these armaments can be directed against no one but ourselves." He went on to point out that Spain would be most unwise to force Great Britain in self-defence to go beyond friendly representations. Wolff was to delay no longer and to make cabinet's view clear to the Spanish Minister for Foreign Affairs.[138] This was followed next day by a warning even more blunt. "Please note," wrote Balfour to Wolff, "that Lord Howden in 1851 informed the Spanish Government that the construction of forts menancing Gibraltar would be regarded as an act of incipient hostility and would be dealt with as such."[139] This abrupt direction was no doubt a reflection of the tension in British-French relations in the Sudan.

Cabinet, it can be seen, was determined to prevent any threat to Gibraltar from developing out of Spanish defence measures in the war. Cabinet was equally determined that Spanish policy should not in any way be permitted to disrupt the harmony existing between Britain and America in the Far East. This is most evident in the succession of blunt rebuffs made to all Spain's attempts to use the Gibraltar affair as a lever with which to force the United Kingdom to support Spain against the American claims in the Philippines.[140] When Wolff first reported the "slight indication" that Spain would appreciate British good offices in her effort to escape the Cuban debt and to keep the Philippines, Balfour drafted in his own hand a reply which set the tone of all future cabinet directions.

If there is any foundation for your suspicion it puts Spanish action in connection with Gibraltar in a serious light: for it shows they are contemplating works which threaten the fortress, but are ready to be bought off if we help them against America. I cannot consent to mix up the question of Gibraltar with any other: and though most anxious to do nothing which can at this moment add to the difficulties and perplexities of Spain, it would evidently be impossible for us quietly to allow the strategic value of the harbour to be destroyed under our very eyes.[141]

This decision was made clear to Spain, whose government

nevertheless continued its attempt to bargain. In October the request for Britain's good offices was renewed but Wolff replied that the matter of the disposal of the Philippines was for the peace commissioners to decide.[142] In November Wolff was of the opinion that the United States demand for the cession of the whole of the Philippines without sufficient compensation was the chief difficulty in the way of a settlement with Britain.[143] When discussing Senor Moret's suggestion for the convention mentioned above, Wolff pointed out to the Regent that even in this context the question of the Philippines would not be considered. On 7 November, the Queen Regent went so far as to promise that if England would use her good offices with the United States to enable Spain to keep the islands, Spain would make over "a substantial portion of the archipelago to Britain." The Spanish minister conveying the offer also pointed out that no similar offer had been made to any other power.[144] Despite Wolff's refusal to entertain the suggestion, the Spanish Foreign Minister persisted, pointing out that if England would only take the lead something might be saved for Spain, as other European powers would follow England's lead.

These futile and rather pathetic arguments were recounted at length in Wolff's telegrams and despatches, until even Salisbury lost some of his patient reticence. He telegraphed bluntly to Wolff: "The questions of Gibraltar and the Philippines should be kept distinct. We have no desire to possess any one of the Philippines and we have no influence that could induce the United States to abandon whatever policy they have resolved upon, especially after the elections recently decided in America."[145] Although the Queen Regent had in September ordered the construction of fresh works to cease, this was not enough. As Salisbury put it: "What we want is no guns to be mounted. Guarantees from Spain are perfectly worthless first because she could not make them good: second because a war with her would forthwith annul them."[146]

The dispute continued long after the settlement between

Spain and America, until finally Britain was successful in bend-
ing Spain to her will. However, as the remainder of the dispute
sheds no new light upon British policy during the war or upon
British-American relations in the Philippines and the Far
East, the matter ceases to be relevant. Enough has been said to
demonstrate once more that the British cabinet was not prepared to allow any issue arising out of the Spanish-American
War to become a threat to Britain's basic security interests,
and that the preservation of this security should not be permitted to interfere with the development of amicable relations
between Britain and the United States.

VII

Among the neutrality problems which arose in the Far East
during the Spanish-American War, the one which more than
any other has been held to supply the clearest evidence of
British friendship for the United States was the behaviour of
the British squadron under Captain Chichester during the
battle in Manila Bay between the American and Spanish fleets.
Put succinctly, the traditional account still current in some
textbooks[147] is to the effect that in the friction between the
German and American commanders Chichester consistently
supported Dewey as against Von Diederichs, and that during
the American bombardment of Manila, Chichester prevented
any German interference with the American fleet by manoeuvring into such a position that it would have been impossible
for the German ships to fire upon the Americans without
involving the British. In the past some authors ascribed tremendous significance to this event. It was believed to have
played an important part in overcoming those anti-British
tendencies so rampant in America after the tension which developed during Grover Cleveland's presidency.[148] In more
grandiloquent terms, it was argued that "the position maintained by Captain Chichester convinced Admiral Von Diede-

richs that Great Britain would resist German aggression to the limit. In other words, Germany was not yet prepared to meet the British in a great conflict. The union of the American and British nations held the balance of world power as Joseph Chamberlain had planned."[149]

In the light of these estimates of the effects of British action, it is somewhat ironic to find that there is no basis in fact for the traditional account upon which such estimates are based.[150] The evidence for this is quite conclusive, for neither the German nor the British governments anticipated or intended intervention in the interests of Spain or the United States, and the German and British naval commanders faithfully obeyed the spirit and the letter of their instructions.

Germany's naval force was kept in the vicinity of the Philippines in order to represent her interests in case America decided not to annex the archipelago.[151] The only instruction given Von Diederichs by his government was "to proceed to Manila in order to form personally an opinion on the Spanish situation, mood of natives and foreign influence upon the political changes."[152] The logs of the German ships reveal that they were anchored and were not cleared for action during the bombardment of Manila. The only comment upon the movement of the British ships made by Von Diederichs was a complaint that they so obscured observation that one of his ships was forced to alter position. These facts hardly suggest the existence of any hostile plan on the part of the German admiral.

Like the German policy, Britain's[153] was to have a fleet on hand to protect British nationals, to watch over the extensive economic interests of British subjects in the Philippines, to report to the Admiralty and Foreign Office upon the ambitions and activities of foreign powers, and to observe the efficiency or otherwise of the United States fleet. Again, like the German the British ships were not cleared for action, and they anchored once they reached their position of observation. Chichester did not even take his complete command with him, but left two gunboats at their anchorage in Cavité. Finally, in all the detailed reports sent to the Admiralty by Chichester, and in the many reports forwarded by the Admiralty to the British Foreign Office, there is no mention whatsoever of any anticipated or intended intervention, nor of any situation which might in Chichester's estimation have made such intervention desirable.[154] It is inconceivable that an officer as efficient as Chichester would have omitted to report any situation involving the possibility of an armed clash between Britain and Germany.

From the American point of view neither Dewey's official reports[155] nor the account published in his autobiography attach any significance to Chichester's manoeuvres.[156] However, in the unpublished manuscript prepared by Captain Nathan Sargeant as a draft for Dewey's autobiography, the account is slightly different.

Captain Chichester got under way also, and with the "Immortalité" and the "Iphigenia" steamed over toward the city and *significantly* took up a position which placed his vessels between ours and those of the foreign fleet. *This manoeuvre was quietly executed, but it meant much, and no doubt was as thoroughly understood by the foreign men of war as it was appreciated by our own.*

The words in italics are those which appear in Sargeant's manuscript (held in the Library of Congress, Washington), but do not appear in the published account.[157] It is to be noted, however, that this account was not written by Dewey himself. It was not written until after the matter had become the subject of popular dispute, and it was not included in the published autobiography. Furthermore at the time not one of the twenty-four press correspondents with the fleet attached any significance to the movements of the British and German fleets.[158] It is therefore reasonable completely to discount this manuscript evidence.

It is apparent then from Professor Bailey's work and from Foreign Office records that the one incident most famous as providing positive evidence of Britain's willingness on behalf of the United States to jeopardize her neutrality during the Spanish-American War has been completely misinterpreted. The British commander acted throughout strictly within his function as a neutral observer. It remains to indicate briefly how the legend of intervention grew. This will serve two purposes. It will expose the legend in its true light, and it will reveal that at Hong Kong and Manila, as well as in London, British friendship for America as against Spain was most marked, even though the conventions binding a neutral naval force were most strictly observed.

In essence, the exaggerated accounts of the British manoeuvre in Manila Bay grew out of the mass of reports and rumours published in German, British, and American newspapers.[159] The rumours particularly emphasized on the one hand British acts of consideration for American nationals and interests, and on the other the frequent and sometimes violent disagreements between Dewey and Von Diederichs. These rumours were the more readily believed because of American suspicion of German aims and official American reports of friction between the two admirals.

Although the official German press had changed its tone from hostility to cordiality, the popular papers remained hostile to the American action against Spain and disdainful of American prowess. This type of German criticism was repeated in the American journals and seemed to lend colour to the frequent reports from the English press of Germany's intention to acquire territory in the Philippines and Carolines. So frequent were these repetitions in the *New York Times,* the *New York Herald,* and the *New York Tribune,* that Mr. Henry White (United States ambassador to Germany) saw fit to warn the Secretary of State against them. Holleben (the German ambassador at Washington), also complained of the matter,[160] highlighting the heading in the *Washington Post* "Kaiser Nurses a Plot," and the suggestion that the State Department should seek an explanation from Germany.[161] The atmosphere of suspicion created by these press reports was made more intense by the knowledge that the German fleet was (until 31 July, when American reinforcements arrived) much more powerful in both tonnage and armament than the American. It was quite needlessly large for its purpose.

At the very time when rumour and suspicion were spreading rapidly in the United States, very serious disagreements developed between Dewey and Von Diederichs. Dewey protested vehemently to Von Diederichs against the German's failure to adhere to the rules of blockade. Von Diederichs disclaimed any breach of international law and made a countercharge that one of his vessels, the "Irene," had been illegally halted and boarded by a United States ship. This provoked an explosion from Dewey and a threat to fire upon any ship which refused to stop for identification.[162] Von Diederichs was prepared to establish the identity of his ships by communication, but was not prepared to permit the *droit de visite,* which involved "visit and search." He was upheld in this by Chichester and other neutral captains, but Dewey had already disclaimed any intention of enforcing the *droit de visite.* This was just as well, for Von Diederichs had issued specific orders to his captains to repel by force any attempt to board their vessels, except at night.

The greatest excitement in the United States press was caused by a telegram from Dewey given to the press by the Navy Department. "Aguinaldo informed me his troops had taken all of Subic Bay except Isla Grande, which they were prevented from taking by the German man-of-war 'Irene.' On 7th July sent the 'Raleigh' and the 'Concord' there; they took the island and about 1,300 men with arms and ammunition. No resistance. The 'Irene' retired from the bay on their arrival."[163] The intentions and actions of the "Irene" are almost irrelevant for the Navy Department released Dewey's telegram to the press. This was interpreted as being official evidence of German interference with United States activities in the islands.

Against this background of suspicion and hostility, friendly gestures by British officials stood out in high relief. One or two of these gestures can be quickly catalogued as examples. Dewey was given every facility possible at Hong Kong, both before and after the outbreak of war,[164] and cabled the Secretary of the Navy, Long, that the British in both Manila and Hong Kong were most friendly.[165] This active friendship was reflected in the press; as Holleben complained to Hohenlohe,[166] the Far Eastern English press was most partial to the Americans and their cause. The *New York Times*'s estimate of the press in England was not quite correct, but is illustrative of the current American belief in British friendship. In the *Times*'s opinion, "Of all the English newspapers of London, only two, and they are minor ones, in any way suggest any pro-Spanish feeling . . . going straight through, the English press stand unanimous in favour of the United States."[167] Accompanying this pro-American sentiment were constant warnings repeated in the United States press of Germany's territorial aims in the Far East. The London *Times* was prepared to contemplate possession of the Philippines by the United States "with equanimity and indeed with satisfaction. We can only say that while we would welcome the Americans in the Philippines as kinfolks and allies united with us in the Far East by the most powerful bonds of common interest, we should regard very differently the acquisition of the archipelago by any other power."[168]

In the light of the United States suspicion of Germany and the friction between Dewey and Von Diederichs it is easy to understand how such statements as this assumed unwarranted significance in the public mind, particularly when the American press exaggerated the situation.[169] In this way the breeding ground for the growth of the intervention legend was prepared.

For some years after the war, the British, American, and German admirals had nothing to say about the Manila episode, but towards the end of 1898 and throughout 1899 the history of the battle was written and re-written in sensational journalese by observers, press correspondents, and others.[170] The clash between Dewey and Von Diederichs was made public by Captain Coghlin of the U.S.S. "Raleigh," and was given nation-wide publicity. Coghlin's story lent vivid colour to the picture of German hostility and British friendship painted by these post-war writers. "Drawing upon these accounts and presumably also upon his imagination, Henry Cabot Lodge published in 1899 the first full-blown version of the legend"[171] that Professor Bailey could find.

The matter then became a part of the propaganda contest for American goodwill which took place between England and Germany, and played its part in the 1902 quarrel over the respective roles of these two powers in the proposed mediation between Spain and the United States in 1898. In 1913 Dewey published his autobiography, and this brought forth a heavily documented rebuttal by Von Diederichs. However, the myth persisted despite the documentary evidence available to disprove it.

The episode in Manila Bay has been shown to lack completely the drama previously associated with it and it must not be taken, as it has been in the past, as evidence that the British Foreign Office and Admiralty were prepared to go so far as to risk war with Germany in the interests of Anglo-American goodwill. However, the incident did become an occasion for a clear demonstration of the friendly disposition of the British toward the United States, and of the popular belief in Britain in the identity of American and British interests in the Far East.

VIII

From this somewhat detailed examination of matters concerning neutrality raised with the Foreign Office by the Colonial Office, by Foreign Office officials, by colonial administrators, by the War Office and Admiralty, and by the Spanish and American governments, a clear pattern of English policy and of English attitudes to the United States during the war can be constructed.

Initially the chief concern was for the security of the sea lanes and the continued freedom of commerce. Some effort was made to extend the British version of the neutral shipping regulations, and representations were made to Spain and the United States concerning their attitudes to the maritime provisions of the Declaration of Paris, 1856. Once this matter was decided, neutrality became a matter of the nice adjustment of international law to the requirements of British policy and security. Chamberlain and the Colonial Office were prepared to strain and even to disregard international law in an effort not to offend the United States. Salisbury was inclined to be legalistic and formal, but where British security was involved, as in Gibraltar or Honk Kong and the Far East, he was prepared if possible to accommodate British action to American needs, and if necessary to ignore international law in order to ensure Britain's countinued security.

In colonial territories in the Pacific the tendency was for the administration of neutrality regulations to reflect colonial enthusiasm for a United States victory and colonial concern that interests other than those of the United States and the United Kingdom should not be furthered by the war. In Egypt, where if necessary the legal fiction of the power of the Khedive and the authority of the Turk could have been invoked to prevent it, the neutrality regulations were enforced in a situation where such action could operate only against Spain. The action of the Admiralty particularly at Manila Bay reflected clearly the intention of the Foreign Office not to become involved, while yet watching carefully for any possible infringement of British rights by a third power. In the western hemisphere[172] British naval power was insufficient to be decisive and neutrality was as much self-preservation as a technical matter of international law. In these circumstances the colonial officials observed strict neutrality, but British consuls in Spanish territory, here as elsewhere, earned justly enthusiastic eulogies from the United States press and government for their extraordinary service to United States nationals and prisoners of war.

In a word, British action, whether by the Foreign Office, the Colonial Office, or by local colonial officials, tended to be "neutral" in favour of the United States. This reflected the variety of attitudes expressed during the formulation of the official British policy toward the Spanish-American dispute and was the expression of the realistic intention of the cabinet to make Anglo-American friendship a basis of Britain's foreign policy.

Notes

1. *Foreign Relations of the United States, 1898*, pp. 750-60.

2. W. Mills, *The Martial Spirit: A Study of Our War with Spain* (Boston & New York: Houghton Mifflin Co., 1931), deals with the rivalry between Hearst's *New York Journal* and Pulitzer's *New York World* and its effect upon United States public opinion at this time.

3. FO72/2091, F.O. to Customs, 17 March 1898.

4. This was defined in terms of the Foreign Enlistment Act, the precedents of the Franco-German War of 1870, and the Neutrality Laws Commission of 1867.

5. FO72/2091, F.O. to Customs, 2 April 1898.

6. *Ibid.,* C.O. [Colonial Office] to F.O., 5 April 1898.

7. *Times* (London), 6 April 1898. *Hansard,* 1898, LVI, 5 April 218.

8. E.g. a memorial to the F.O. from British merchants urging the government to prevent any unnecessary interference with trade. Among the signatories were the Chartered Bank of India and the Hong Kong and Shanghai Banking Corporation. FO72/2084.

9. E.g. letter to the *Times* (London), 16 April 1898, by Sir George Baden-Powell urging the government to decide these questions in the interests of British shipping. See also *Hansard,* 1898, LVI, 4 April, 47, 5 April, 217, 21 April, 663, questions by Lord Charles Beresford.

10. Minute of 14 April, Villiers to Salisbury, FO72/2094.

11. *London Gazette,* 26 April 1898.

12. FO72/2091, Pauncefote to F.O., Telegram No. 55, 23 April 1898. British claims for wrongful seizure were dealt with upon the basis of this decision by the United States. These claims, lodged in London and Wash-

ington, did not produce any conflict whatever between the United States and Great Britain. The British government asked for no special privileges and without protest accepted the decisions of the commission appointed to deal with the claims. Pauncefote's knowledge of international law and his experience in the Behring seals dispute enabled him to handle the situation with surety and tact. The commission awarded a total of $425,000 compensation for wrongful seizure. See also Mowat, *op. cit.*, p. 209, n. 1.

13. Bemis, *op. cit.*, p. 396.

14. C. Savage, *The Policy of the United States Towards Maritime Commerce in War* (Washington: United States Government Printing Office, 1934), 63-73, quoted Bemis, *op. cit.*, p. 336.

15. FO72/2091, Pauncefote to F.O., Telegram No. 55, 23 April 1898.

16. *Ibid.*, Barclay to F.O., Telegram No. 26, 23 April 1898.

17. *Ibid.*, Milbanke to F.O., Telegram No. 18, 19 April 1898.

18. G. Smith, *The Treaty of Washington, 1871* (Cornell: Cornell University Press, 1941).

19. FO72/2092, F.O. to Lascelles, 25 April 1898.

20. *Ibid.*, Lascelles to F.O., Draft of Despatch No. 8 (undated, approx. 27 April).

21. *Hansard*, 1898, LVI, 21 April, 662.

22. Salisbury at this time was convalescing at Beaulieu and Balfour deputized at the Foreign Office until Salisbury gradually took over during the latter half of March.

23. FO72/2091, Sanderson to Davidson, Private, 21 April 1898. For Salisbury's consideration of the United States fleet in the Far East see pp. 65-68.

24. *Ibid.*, Minute, C.O. to F.O., 23 April 1898. See also Mowat, *op .cit.*, p. 210.

25. FO72/2096, Series of Despatches and Minutes, 24-25 July, re United States vessels in Canadian waters.

26. *Hansard*, 1898, e.g. (i) LIX, 47: "In view of the protracted residence in Toronto of the late Spanish minister to Washington and the activity of other Spanish agents . . . in the dominions . . . what powers if any are possessed by Colonial Governments to prevent the hospitality of their soil being exploited in the interests of a particular belligerent . . . ?" 13 June, Mr. J. F. Hogan to the Attorney-General. See also (ii) LXIII, 437, (iii) LVI, 1210.

27. Mowat, *op. cit.*, pp. 210-11.

28. *Hansard*, 1898, LXIII, 29 July, 437.

29. FO72/2096, Governor of Gibraltar to C.O., 1 July 1898.

30. *Ibid.*, C.O. to Biddulph, 6 July 1898.

31. *Ibid.*, Governor of Gibraltar to C.O., 14 July 1898.

32. *Ibid.*, C.O. to F.O., Downing Street, 22 July 1898.

33. Spain had already protested against the expulsion of Caranza, 16 June 1898, and complained of the activities of Carroll and others. FO72/2095, Wolff to F.O., Telegram No. 172, 16 June 1898.

34. Appended as a minute to Chamberlain's submission to the F.O.

35. General Aguinaldo had been a leader of Philippine insurgents against Spanish rule and had been exiled from the Philippines.

36. *Singapore Free Press*, 2 May 1898. Included in FO72/2097.

37. FO72/2096, Spanish consul's charges and Attorney-General's comments, 27 May 1898.

38. *Ibid.*, Straits Settlements, No. 107 to Louis Marinos, consul for Spain.

39. *Singapore Free Press*, 2 May 1898 and 4 May 1898.

40. FO72/2096, Spanish consul's charges and Attorney-General's comment, 27 May 1898.

41. *Ibid.*, Administrator of Hong Kong to C.O., Despatch No. 151, 20 May 1898.

42. *Ibid.*

43. *Ibid.*, Minute attached to Despatch No. 151, 20 May 1898.

44. FO72/2097, Pauncefote to F.O., Treaty No. 5, 5 September 1898.

45. See above, chap. i. It must also be emphasized that colonial officials would have been well informed concerning Chamberlain's desire for friendship with the United States. His public speeches and press statements alone would have ensured this.

46. See pp. 58-85 and pp. 109-113.

47. FO72/2094, Note by Legal Officer re Export of Arms, 19 June 1898.

48. See also chap. i, pp. 6-7 and chap. iii, pp. 109-113.

49. A. P. Newton, *A Hundred Years of the British Empire* (London: Methuen & Co. Ltd., 1940), p. 249.

50. FO72/2096, Cromer to F.O., 29 June 1898.

51. *Ibid.*, 23 June 1898.

52. *Ibid.*, copy F.O. to Drummond Wolff, 4 July 1898.

53. *Ibid.*, Cromer to F.O., 27 June 1898.

54. *Ibid.*, Wolff to Salisbury, Telegram No. 198, 5 July 1898.

55. *Hansard*, 1898, LX, 1 July, 800.

56. Cf. Salisbury's attitude to Spain. See p. 105.

57. FO72/2096, Cromer to F.O., 23 June 1898.

58. *Ibid.*, Minute by Villiers.

59. Rule three in the neutrality regulations circularized to all colonial officials on 20 April.

60. FO72/2096, Cromer to F.O., 24 June 1898.

61. *Ibid.*

62. *Ibid.*

63. *Ibid.*, 26 June 1898.

64. *Ibid.*, Further from Cromer, 26 June 1898.

65. *Ibid.*, Minute by Davidson, 26 June 1898.

66. *Ibid.*, Cromer to F.O., 27 June.

67. *Ibid.*, unsigned Minute of 28 June.

68. *Ibid.*, Cromer to F.O., 29 June and 1 July.

69. *Times* (London), 13 July 1898. *Hansard*, 1898, LXI, 12 July, 667. *Parliamentary Papers Egypt*, No. 19, 1885, p. 292.

70. See p. xix.

71. G. Dewey, *Autobiography of George Dewey* (New York: C. Scribner & Sons, 1913), pp. 170-72.

72. *China Mail*, 17 May 1898.

73. H. B. Morse and H. F. McNair, *Far Eastern International Relations* (Boston and New York: Houghton, 1931), p. 427.

74. The United States ship sent to convey Aguinaldo and his company to the Philippines.

75. I.e. Mirs Bay.

76. FO72/2096, Despatch No. 151, Major-General Black to C.O., forwarded by F.O., 20 May 1898.

77. This became the boundary of the British area of Kowloon opposite the island of Hong Kong.

78. Sir Claude MacDonald to F.O., No. 185. Referred to in FO17/1341, Minute on back of Sir Claude MacDonald's Telegram No. 198 of 9 June 1898.

79. *Ibid.*, Minute on the back of Sir Claude MacDonald's Telegram No. 198 of 9 June 1898.

80. *Ibid.*, No. 202, F.O. to MacDonald, 9 June.

81. T. A. Bailey, "Dewey and the Germans in Manila Bay," *American Historical Review*, XLV, No. 1 (October 1939), 59-60.

82. See map, p. 72.

83. This question had been the subject of a prolonged dispute 1879-83, when a suggestion was put forward that a line (known as the *medium filum*) should be drawn on the map to divide the waters of the bay equably between British and Spanish sovereignty.

84. FO72/2097, quoted in Law Officers' report of 11 August 1898.

85. *Ibid.*, Minute Villiers to Salisbury and Balfour, 22 August 1898.

86. FO72/2095, Telegram Chamberlain to Governor of Gibraltar, 24 May 1898.

87. *Ibid.*

88. FO72/2096, Minute on Villiers to Salisbury, 29 July 1898.

89. FO72/2097, Law Officers' report "Limits of Territorial Jurisdiction," Royal Courts of Justice, 11 August 1898.

90. *Ibid.*, War Office, 3 September 1898, Minute to F.O., 21 September 1898.

91. *Ibid.*, C.O. to F.O., 21 September.

92. This was done 15 November 1898. *Ibid.*, Chamberlain to Governor of Gibraltar.

93. E.g. FO72/2098, Wolff to F.O., 22 and 23 May 1898.

94. See map, p. 72.

95. FO72/2098, Wolff to F.O., 12 June 1898.

96. *Ibid.*, Despatch No. 213, 2 July 1898.

97. Salisbury Papers, unbound, Goschen to Salisbury, July 1898—October 1900.

98. FO72/2098, Lansdowne to Salisbury, 27 July 1898.

99. *Ibid.*, Wolff to F.O., No. 319, 27 August 1898.

100. From mid-June to July, Dewey's position in the Philippines was quite precarious because of the presence of large foreign "observer" contingents, the fear of Spanish reinforcements (Admiral Camara's fleet), and the delay in the arrival of United States reinforcements. On 27 June Dewey advised the United States Secretary of the Navy that a diversionary expedition against the coast of Spain would force Camara to return. On 29 June Secretary Long let Dewey know that a squadron under Commodore

J. C. Watson was being prepared for this purpose and added that the Spaniards knew it. *House Documents, Vol. XII, 55th Congress, 3rd Session, 1898-99.* Reports of the Navy Department 1898, No. 3, Navigation Bureau Appendix [hereinafter *House Documents*] (Washington: Government Printing Office, 1898).

101. FO72/2098, War Office to F.O., 27 July, Wolff to F.O., 12 June and 28 August. So widespread was this belief that Wolff was questioned "in a friendly fashion" by the Russian ambassador.

102. See above, chap. ii. FO72/2065, Wolff to F.O., Despatch No. 322, 15 September 1898, reports the *Diaro de Barcelona* as typical of all the Spanish press, saying that "if all the despatches preceding the war were published, it would be revealed that England is responsible that America was encouraged to declare war on our country."

103. G. E. Buckle (ed.), *The Letters of Queen Victoria.* Series III 1886-1901 (London: Murray & Co., 1930-32), III, 236.

104. *New York Times,* 4 May 1898. The suggestion was made that the Philippines might be turned over to Great Britain. *New York Times,* 15 May and 16 May 1898.

105. See Monson's reports of the French press, chap. i, n. 63, and Wolff's report of the Spanish press in G. P. Gooch and H. W. Temperley (eds.), *British Documents on the Origins of the World War, 1898-1914* (London: H.M.S.O., 1926-38), II, No. 300 and No. 301, 253. Articles and reports from the British press were widely circulated in the Spanish press and were the subject of complaints to Queen Victoria by the Queen Regent. (For Salisbury's reply see Buckle, *op. cit.,* III, 279.)

106. See p. 156.

107. See above, chap. i, n. 3.

108. Reported at length in *New York Times,* 8 September 1898. FO72/2083, 25 September 1898, Sanderson assured the Spanish ambassador, who questioned the F.O. on the subject, that Chamberlain's visit had "no political object whatsoever."

109. FO72/2098, F.O. to Wolff, Telegram No. 106, 20 August 1898.

110. *Ibid.,* Wolff's report of conversations with the Queen Regent. Wolff to F.O., 2 November 1898.

111. *Ibid.,* Wolff to F.O., Telegram No. 329, 2 September 1898.

112. L. Bertrand and C. Petrie, *The History of Spain* (London: Appleton Century & Co., 1945), pp. 343-48.

113. FO72/2098, Wolff to F.O., Despatch No. 320, 27 August.

114. *Ibid.*

115. FO72/2098, Wolff to F.O., Telegram No. 329, 2 September 1898 and Telegram No. 322, 29 August 1898.

116. *Ibid.,* Despatch No. 294, 17 August.

117. The Italian ambassador informed Wolff to this effect 29 August. *Ibid.,* Telegram No. 321, 29 August.

118. *Ibid.,* Observations by Sir John Ardagh, Director-General of Military Intelligence, 18 August 1898.

119. *Ibid.,* Telegram No. 329, Wolff to F.O., 2 September.

120. *Ibid.*

121. *Ibid.*, Balfour to Wolff, No. 117, 31 August.

122. *Ibid.*, Monson to F.O., Telegram No. 126, 2 September, repeated to Madrid. Fashoda did not develop until 19 September.

123. See W.L. Langer, *The Diplomacy of Imperialism* (2nd ed.; New York: A. A. Knopf, 1951), p. 564.

124. FO72/2098, Wolff to F.O., 23 August, Private and Secret, For Mr. Balfour only.

125. Salisbury Papers, Vol. CXXXI, No. 97, F.O. to Wolff, 6 September 1878 and Vol. CXXXIII, No. 32, Wolff to F.O., 8 September 1898.

126. FO72/2098, Wolff to F. O., Telegram No. 344, 12 September 1898.

127. *Ibid.*, Despatch No.446, 17 December. Note re Armigo and Moret, and Telegram No. 344, Wolff to F.O., 12 September 1898.

128. *Ibid.*, Despatch No. 382, 2 November 1898.

129. *Ibid.*, Despatch No. 446, 17 December.

130. *Ibid.*, Observations by Sir John Ardagh, Director-General of Military Intelligence, 18 August 1898.

131. *Ibid.*, Private, Balfour to Wolff, 13 August 1898.

132. *Ibid.*, Salisbury's draft of 3 August 1898. This was submitted to the Colonial Office and Chamberlain's suggestion to omit any delimitation of territorial waters because of the current dispute (referred to on p. 71) was accepted.

133. Cf. Garvin, *op. cit.*, p. 297. As early as 12 November 1897 Chamberlain had been approached "rather in the Spanish interest by his old friend . . . Sir Henry Drummond Wolff," whose sympathies were well known to be with the Queen Regent, and the whole tone of his diplomatic despatches reflected this.

134. FO72/2098, Admiralty to F.O., 9 August, repeated to Madrid.

135. *Ibid.*, Balfour Telegram to Wolff, 12 August 1898.

136. *Ibid.*, Balfour to Wolff, 20 August 1898.

137. Quoted p. 83.

138. FO72/2098, Balfour to Wolff, Telegram No. 109, 24 August 1898.

139. *Ibid.*, F.O. to Wolff, Telegram No. 110, 25 August.

140. See above, p. 79.

141. FO72/2098, Balfour to Wolff (Private), 23 August.

142. *Ibid.*, Wolff to F.O., Telegram No. 355, 6 October 1898.

143. *Ibid.*, Telegram No. 404, 6 November 1898.

144. *Ibid.*, Telegram No. 406, 7 November 1898.

145. *Ibid.*, Salisbury to Wolff, Telegram No. 137, 9 November 1898.

146. *Ibid.*, Telegram No. 138, 11 November 1898.

147. Ensor, *op. cit.*, pp. 256-57. R. B. Mowat, *The American Entente* (London: Oxford University Press, 1939), p. 137.

148. Ensor, *op. cit.*, p. 257.

149. Reuter, *op. cit.*, pp. 148-49. A more cautious estimate was made by Gelber, *op. cit.*, pp. 28-29: "The delicacy of the whole Manila episode should not be exaggerated. It would have been rash for Germany to misprize the latent naval strength which inhered in a *rapprochement* between the English-speaking powers. Her blunders and intrigues were

shorn of their peril through the insurance afforded American arms, on land and afloat, by British mastery of the seas."

150. The facts concerning the intentions and activities of the Germans in Manila Bay have been conclusively established by Professor T. A. Bailey, *op. cit.* The episode is included here because it forms an integral part in the pattern of British-American relations. Bailey used the documents published in *Die Grosse Politik*, German Admiralty and Foreign Office records, and the logs of the German ships involved, as well as Vice-Admiral Otto Von Diederichs' publications on the subject. He also used American naval records and the published and private papers of Admiral Dewey. The Secretary of the British Admiralty made available to him transcripts of the relevant British naval documents. Captain Chichester's report was published in Gooch and Temperley, *op. cit.*, I, 105-7. Since Professor Bailey's definitive article was published, the reports made to the British Admiralty by Chichester which were in the opinion of the Admiralty sufficiently important to be forwarded to the Foreign Office have been made available by the Public Record Office; they are to be found in the volume FO72/2096.

151. Shippee, *op. cit.* This article is based upon a thorough examination of the documents in *Die Grosse Politik*.

152. Quoted Bailey, *op. cit.*, p. 61.

153. For a full consideration of British policy in the Philippines, see below, chap. iii.

154. FO72/2096. Chichester's detailed reports were concerned with those aspects of British policy mentioned in the above paraghaph.

155. *House Documents*, pp. 65-130.

156. Dewey, *op. cit.*, p. 277.

157. Quoted by Bailey, *op. cit.*, p. 80, n. 87.

158. *Ibid.*, p. 77 and n. 70.

159. The evidence which follows is most admirably presented by Bailey, *op. cit.*

160. *Die Grosse Politik*, Band XV, Nr. 4148.

161. The only official action by the State Department was an instruction to White to ascertain "without making embarrassing enquiries, official or otherwise" whether the German fleet was to remain at Manila or to be recalled or to be reduced in size. This was ten days after the "Irene" incident mentioned below. Bailey, *op. cit.*, p. 72.

162. See *ibid.*, p. 67. *Die Grosse Politik*, Band XV, Nr. 4160, n. 2.

163. *House Documents*, pp. 110-11. Dewey to Secretary of Navy, 13 July 1898. For Bailey's evaluation of the incident, see *op. cit.*, p. 66.

164. Dewey, *op. cit.*, pp. 240-41. Cf. the Mirs Bay episode. See above, p. 65.

165. *House Documents*, p. 119, No. 412D, p. 120, No. 437D.

166. *Die Grosse Politik*, Band XV, Nr. 4148.

167. *New York Times*, 1 May 1898. The *New York Times* omitted the *Saturday Review* from its list of pro-Spanish papers.

168. *New York Times*, 25 May 1898, quoting *Times* (London), 24 May 1898.

169. The *New York Herald*, 2 August, commented that the United States

should keep the Philippines if only as a mark of friendliness to England who "stood by us" and showed herself ready to give material aid if it had been needed. This was reprinted in the *Times* (London), 3 August. Wolff feared harm would be done by this report. Salisbury merely replied that the F.O. had no influence with the *Times*.

170. For the following details see Bailey, *op. cit.*, pp. 79-81 and H. C. Lodge, *The War with Spain* (New York: Harper & Bros., 1899), pp. 215-16.

171. Bailey, *op. cit.*, p. 80.

172. The war in the Caribbean has been so thoroughly treated by United States experts that the British documents in the Foreign Office have nothing new to say. For this reason that area has not been included in this study.

Britain and the Peace

III

BOTH BEFORE AND DURING the conflict, the European powers had, for a variety of reasons, refrained from any interference. If they were in any way to use the situation to aid their struggle for power, in Europe or Asia, a last opportunity would be offered during the attempts to define the basis of a peace settlement between Spain and America. British policy during this period has been the subject of a wide variety of interpretations. The Spanish view was that the United Kingdom used the situation to extend her influence over China[1] and to seek territorial concessions for herself in the Pacific at the expense of Spain, and that she acted in a way designed to further the American cause rather than the Spanish. The German press accused England of urging Spain to make an early settlement because of a fear that delay would lead to an increase in America's territorial holdings in the Pacific and this, said Germany, would be inimical to British interests there. On the other hand, American writers have interpreted British policy as an attempt to use American expansion as a counterweight to European competition in Asia. English historians also have accepted the view that Britain encouraged and supported the imperialist ambitions of the United States during the war. In view of these conflicting claims it is necessary to trace carefully British diplomatic action as distinct from public opinion, and to make an appreciation of the aims and motives of those who formulated and carried out cabinet's policy during the peace negotiations.

I

From May to July 1898, the Spanish government sought, through the British ambassador at Madrid, to obtain England's assistance in devising a plan for mediation by the great powers. To any Spanish appeals for international action to initiate negotiations to end the war, Salisbury was even less responsive than Balfour and Chamberlain had been to appeals to prevent the outbreak of the war. It was this attitude that confirmed Spain in the view mentioned above. The Spanish court and cabinet found it difficult to believe that England was not wholeheartedly supporting the United States. This belief was engendered by the disputes dealt with in chapter two, and by the tone of the English and American press. Then on 13 May came Chamberlain's startling speech advocating the desirability of an Anglo-American alliance, or at least the closest possible entente between the two Anglo-Saxon powers.

"The report of Mr. Chamberlain's speech," wrote Wolff, "has created a great turmoil as the papers believe Anglo-American Alliance to be directed against Spain. They are pointing out how Spain can assist the adversaries of England at Gibraltar and elsewhere." The Duke of Almadovar (Minister for Foreign Affairs), although more friendly to England than other members of the Spanish cabinet, informed Wolff that he did not consider Chamberlain's speech to be "entirely neutral," advocating as it did an alliance with a country with whom Spain was at war.² This belief in England's partiality toward the United States was the basis of understandable hostility; but it did not prevent the Spanish court and the cabinet from realizing that England was the one power which could if it so desired support Spain against exorbitant territorial and financial demands from the victorious republic. Salisbury was well aware of this, both from his assessment of the international situation and from Wolff's frequent reports. "As I have before stated," wrote Wolff on 10 June, "everyone here both Spanish and foreign is continuously dwelling upon the great advantage that would accrue to Spain were England to take up her cause with the United States." The recent friendship between the United States and England would, he believed, predispose "the Government of the United States to listen to representations from Her Majesty's Government with greater deference than to any other power."³ He reported further that most Spanish politicians were afraid to take any steps directly with the United States or even to ask directly for mediation. They expected the European powers to intervene to prevent the spread of war. The Austrian ambassador at Madrid confirmed Wolff's assessment, assuring him that Spain would not sue for peace except under pressure from the powers, and that "if anything were to be done in this manner it must be at the instance of England as being the only power to which the United States would pay any attention."⁴ Wolff believed that Spain would accept any well considered plan, but knew Salisbury's opinion well enough to assure foreign ambassadors and "unofficial" Spanish enquirers that he could not possibly approach the Duke of Almadovar without instructions and these he "could not conceive would be given."⁵

Except for a short period in June when Spain apparently hoped for German assistance,⁶ Wolff received frequent unofficial enquiries from Spanish senators as to Britain's opinion as to what would constitute a possible basis for peace, but Salisbury would not even pass such enquiries on to Pauncefote at Washington. In answer to a question in parliament, Balfour could say that "Her Majesty's Government will gladly take any favourable opportunity of promoting a cessation of hostilities and negotiations for a definitive peace. But any action on their part . . . can only be undertaken if there should be reasonable prospects of its being well received by both parties and of its leading to an agreement between them. There is unfortunately not sufficient ground as yet for believing that these conditions exist."[7] Friendly in tone as this appeared, it was generally recognized, as by the Austrian ambassador at Madrid, that any state would have said the same.[8] The realistic attitude adopted by cabinet towards appeals from Spain can be clearly discerned from the tone as much as from the content of the correspondence between Salisbury and Ambassador Wolff. The Prime Minister was quite determined not to intervene without an assurance that any such action would be welcomed by America, and in the end he became quite impatient with Wolff's attempts to plead the Spanish cause.

During May the Spanish Minister for Foreign Affairs spoke to Wolff of his desire for peace and asked "whether when the time came, Her Majesty's Government would accede to a request and join with others in a mediation."[9] In reply Salisbury forwarded to Wolff copies of his previous instructions to Pauncefote together with Pauncefote's comments upon the problem. His purpose in doing this was to demonstrate the action he had taken "to obtain immediate information of any opening for the promotion of peace." "If you should think now or at any future stage in this unhappy war," wrote Salisbury to Pauncefote, "that offers of mediation from the European Powers would be welcomed or received favourably by the United States, please inform me."[10] Pauncefote sounded the United States government and reported:

From my private and confidential conversations with the Secretary of State I am confident that he will not fail to inform me should circumstances render an offer of mediation by the European powers acceptable to his Government. In the present state of public feeling here, I think it doubtful whether the abandonment of Cuba and the payment of a war indemnity would satisfy Congress, even if Spain should consent to such a sacrifice. But the President is anxious for the termination of the war and it is not improbable that in the event of a further naval disaster to Spain an effort by the Powers to bring about such a solution might be successful.[11]

Despite this clear statement of cabinet's policy and perhaps encouraged by the sympathetic tone of Salisbury's early instructions Wolff continued to press Spain's interest. He was insistent in suggesting that as Spain would not sue for peace save under pressure, England's intervention would be the only effective means of preserving anything of prestige or stability for Spain. Salisbury's rather testy reply effectively quashed any further such efforts: "You ask me to send you instructions," he wrote.

I have nothing to add to what I have already said. Your informant says that Spain cannot make any communication directly or indirectly to the United States as this would be to own herself in the wrong. I understand the United States say they cannot make any offer to Spain, or Spain would infer that the United States are feeling the strain of war and she would therefore be encouraged to persevere. Until one or the other modifies their view, no negotiations can take place. It is obvious that the other powers will not take any active part in a quarrel in which they are not concerned.[12]

In Paris M. Hanotaux earlier had reached a similar conclusion. He had informed Monson, the British ambassador, "that Spain would not be able to make peace until some signal disaster had impressed upon the public mind the necessity of such a course."[13]

This attitude of Britain toward Spain was of course the expression of policies already decided upon; that is, to remain neutral, not to take any action which had not been previously concerted with the United States, and certainly not to lead any European action in the interests of Spain as against the United

States. With American arms victorious in Cuba and in the Philippines, it was for the vanquished to admit defeat, to face the realities of the power situation, and to enquire of the victor the terms upon which peace would be acceptable. Spain, knowing the British cabinet's previous decisions, could expect no more than the negative response her appeals to England produced. Furthermore, as Pauncefote's report made clear, there was little if any hope for a peace settlement which did not involve great territorial and financial loss to Spain. Even if Spain were to suffer further disasters before this fact was accepted, she was left in no doubt that England would intervene, if at all, only upon an occasion chosen and for reasons decided by the United States. Hence Spain was confirmed in the belief that Britain's conduct during the war was proof positive of a policy designed to assist the United States rather than Spain.

II

After Salisbury's direction to Pauncefote to inform him of any opportunity for mediation, it might well be assumed that the Prime Minister was prepared to take advantage of any such opportunity, provided of course that it was approved by the United States. Surprisingly enough, however, when Pauncefote in fact did recommend action, Salisbury would not countenance any English initiative. Rumours of this contradictory policy spread through Europe and by 1902 the facts had become so distorted that the semi-official German journal, the *Kreuz Zeitung*,[14] could accuse England of having endeavoured in June or July 1898 to induce Spain to sue for peace, in order to prevent the United States from acquiring territory in the Pacific where such action would in the opinion of the German government be more annoying to England than to any other power. It is true that the British ambassador to the United States suggested that a tentative approach should be made to Spain to make peace, but Salisbury for a variety of reasons refused to act on the suggestion.

On 10 May Pauncefote received instructions from Salisbury to inform him immediately if at any time offers of mediation from the European powers would be welcomed or received favourably by the United States.[15] Referring to this telegram, Pauncefote on 4 June advised Salisbury in the following terms:

For various reasons I believe [the] present time opportune for [an] effort to arrange terms of peace. I am assured on [the] best authority that the cost of the war incurred by the United States amounts already to the enormous sum of $400 m., plus $16 m. in claims. Spain could never pay such an indemnity and the question arises whether she . . . would make peace on the basis of territorial concessions. For instance, would she consent to evacuate Cuba, and in lieu of a war indemnity cede to the United States the island of Porto Rico and a port in some part of the Philippine Islands. I have no authority, but from most confidential conversations I have sufficient reason for the belief that the United States would make peace on these terms. Would it be possible very secretly to discover the disposition of Spanish Government with regard to such a basis of arrangement. If favourable it would certainly afford an opening for mediation of Great Britian or of the European Powers.

In Pauncefote's opinion, if Britain were favourably disposed, then this was the opportunity for her to offer mediation. He was supported in his reading of the situation by the French ambassador, who reported that "his advices from New York were that a gloomy view was taken in financial circles there, and that terms of peace were openly discussed on a basis of territorial concessions."[16] Furthermore Mr. William R. Day (acting Secretary of State) cabled to the United States ambassador at London the terms the United States government would accept if offered promptly by Spain. The terms were substantially those already indicated by Pauncefote,[17] but went further. An island in the Ladrone group was required as a coaling station and the threat was added that these demands might change if the war was prolonged.[18]

Salisbury's reply was prompt and definite. He refused to act on the ground that "England could not propose [the] cession of the Philippines." He instructed Rumbold in Vienna to sound the Austrian government to see if they were "disposed to come forward, explaining that you do so because we feel bound [to convey to those most concerned the knowledge of our ambassador's view]. But we would not ourselves propose any cession of the Philippine Islands or appear as initiating the consideration of these terms."[19] According to Dennis, Salisbury went further and advised the Austrian government that Spain should take advantage of the President's liberal disposition while it was yet possible.[20] It is therefore apparent that on this occasion the British government was not prepared to urge peace upon Spain. It is also apparent that even though unwilling to propose the cession of the Philippines to the United States Salisbury was quite prepared to see Austria do so.

Salisbury's attitude to the United States needs further explanation. It had been conditioned by the disputes over Venezuela, the Behring Sea, the Canadian boundaries, and the attempts to reach agreement upon a general treaty of arbitration. The suspicion and scepticism of American officials engendered by the negotiations over these subjects deeply affected the members of the British cabinets concerned as well as the permanent officials in the Foreign and Colonial Offices. Lord Rosebery's reaction was typical. Minuting a paper referring to the proposed treaty of arbitration he wrote:

Extraordinary care must be taken in the wording of any such treaty. It must be submitted to the best experts and strained through the severest sieve of criticism. For our cousins are extremely acute, and, as we have had woeful experience, do not allow a common blood, language and literature to control their desire to get the best of us by hook or by crook.

Lord Kimberley entirely agreed with Rosebery, adding, "I cannot say I feel implicit trust in the professions of the Americans."[21] In 1896 Salisbury could write privately that "a war with America—not this year but in the not distant future—has become something more than a possibility."[22]

In addition to his experience of American diplomacy, Salisbury was by temperament, training, and tradition out of sympathy with the American way of doing things. He deplored the bumptiousness and lack of finesse that marked the United States conduct of negotiations. His reticent and aristocratic temperament and his polished address assured Pauncefote of a sympathetic audience when he wrote to his Prime Minister deploring the "bad taste" and "bad form" of American diplomatic notes, the main characteristics of which were as he expressed it on another occasion "vulgarity and verbosity."[23]

Another important element in this background to Salisbury's attitude to the United States was his lack of personal experience in the country itself. By marriage, personal friendships, and frequent and sometimes prolonged visits, Chamberlain and Balfour acquired an understanding of the United States political scene and a sympathetic appreciation of Americans and their way of life which, although sometimes rather limited, was sufficient to cancel out in a degree never apparent in their leader the hostility inherited from past conflict. An accommodation of difficulties with the United States became with Salisbury a politic measure, but it was never a personal enthusiasm as it was with the younger members of his cabinet and some of the Opposition such as Sir William Harcourt. Against this background, Salisbury's sympathy for Spain is understandable. To him the war was a most melancholy affair and he was very reluctant to see Spain humiliated. His attitude in this reflected his respect for the monarchical principle and the sympathy of Queen Victoria and court circles for the Queen Regent of Spain.

However, his personal sympathies and antipathies were never permitted to determine policy toward either the United States or Spain. This he made quite explicit to Wolff in a long personal letter in which he stated his view of "friendship" as an element in foreign policy. The letter refers to the Spanish situation and was written in July 1899 but was elaborated at such length and written with such emphasis that it is clearly a well thought out position held as a basic guide to diplomatic action. He wrote to Wolff to say that he ought not discourage him, as he had done in the past, from countermining the various powers which were trying to establish an influence in Spain, without explaining his views concerning the establishing or building up of a party in a foreign country. He agreed that he might be thought cynical, but the longer he lived the more convinced he was of their truth.

"My doctrine," he wrote, "is briefly this, that you cannot build up in any desirable form an influence or popularity among the governing classes of another society." Any such influence must be momentary and "must needs be quite flimsy and absolutely transitory." It would disappear with the statesmen and diplomats who created it and the circumstances which enabled its creation. He then proceeded to illustrate his thesis with several historical examples and concluded that no importance whatever could be attached to an elaborate structure of influence for "a change in the wind of politics will blow it down. It is waste labour."

But he went on, *"Influence disappears, territory remains."* This was placed in quotation marks and heavily underlined. He then read to Wolff the practical application of this principle to the Spanish-American peace negotiations. As it was notorious that more than one European power was anxious to coax Spain to alienate valuable European and African islands such as the Balearic, Canary, and Cape Verde groups, every effort should be made "to counteract the influence which was likely to end in a bargain of this kind."[24]

This principle is one of the keys to Salisbury's policy toward the war as a whole and in particular to his view of the possibilities of the peace. He had never shown the enthusiasm in England's search for allies that marked Chamberlain's restless activity, for he was never so convinced of the dangers of British isolation.[25] Nor was he such a keen advocate of an understanding with the United States as was Balfour.[26] But it cannot be shown that he was reluctant to see the United States acquire territory in the Far East or the western Pacific. On the contrary, although he disapproved of the official manners of the United States and of her attack upon Spain, he did not believe that this expansion in the Pacific would be against British interests. He had given his approval to the request for the United States to stand with the United Kingdom in China to stabilize the Far East, and had approved Balfour's maiden speech which advocated friendship with the United States.[27] Further, even after the United States had refused to co-operate with Great Britain and after she had defeated Spain, Salisbury could state publicly that "no one can deny that their [United States] appearance among the factors of Asiatic at all events and possibly European diplomacy is a grave and serious event which may not conduce to the interests of peace though I think that in any event it is likely to conduce to the interests of Great Britain."[28] Obviously then if American expansion into the Pacific was likely to conduce to the interests of the United Kingdom, it was not for the Foreign Office to prevent the United States from acquiring territory there. It would however continue to be necessary to prevent any further acquisition of territory by the European rivals of Great Britain.

It is in this that there is to be found the chief explanation of Salisbury's refusal to initiate any moves for peace. His reluctance sprang from a variety of motives, but certainly not from any opposition to the extension of American power into the Pacific. In the first place he was determined not to initiate any move which would lay England open to the charge of seeking territorial gains for herself, for this would only have served to increase the suspicion and antagonism of Germany, Russia and France and thus have turned the question into an international struggle for concessions. That this was Salisbury's belief is borne out by statements both during and after the peace negotiations. Hay wrote to McKinley on 2 August, saying that it would disappoint the United Kingdom if the United States abandoned the Philippines, that Germany was most anxious for a foothold, and if they did abandon them then there would be grave danger of European complications.[29] Balfour told Henry White that Britain would make no demands if the United States kept the Philippines, but expected German intervention if part were ceded to Britain or any other power,[30] and Salisbury told White in November that the United States avoided another Kiaochow by the annexation.[31]

Another reason for Salisbury's inaction was that he desired not to have any part in a move which would despoil Spain of her colonial possessions, particularly as English ambassadors and consular officials were representing American interests in Spanish territories. Finally, his decision not to act was taken because of his belief that for England to have recommended any course to Spain would have been to ensure its rejection. There is no direct statement available to prove this last point, but it is a reasonable assumption given the nature of the relations between Spain and the United Kingdom at this time. The press and official circles in Spain believed that England's friendship with the United States was a danger to Spanish security.[32] The hostility to England engendered by this belief, encouraged by France and sharpened by fear of an American naval attack on the peninsula, led to furious attacks on English policy and, of more weight with the cabinet and War Office, it led to Spain's attempt to erect fortifications opposite Gibraltar. It must be remembered also that it was just at this time that Spanish hopes of German assistance were high, and there were rumours that Spain was seeking German aid by promises of territorial concessions.[33] In a letter to Queen Victoria, the Queen Regent of Spain summed up the Spanish government's assessment of British policy prior to August in these words: ". . . à mon grand chagrin j'ai vu que les sympathies de son gouvernement se prononçaient en faveur de nos ennemis. Les Amèricains trouvaient dans les ports anglais du charbon, des ressources qu'on refusait à nos vaisseaux. Les insurgés des Philippines purent équiper et armer à Hong-Kong une expédition qui à Manille aida les Américains."[24]

In this atmosphere of suspicion and recrimination a government already convinced of Britain's hostility would be most unlikely to have accepted any British suggestion that Spain should cede territory. As Wolff in Madrid put it: "Any step we might propose would be attributed to our desire to serve the interests of the United States. This feeling is stimulated by the Austrian ambassador and the Archduchess, the Queen Regent's mother."[35] With this the British ambassador in Vienna agreed. Before acting upon his instructions, he pointed out to Salisbury that the conditions suggested would be regarded in Austria as those warranted only by the complete defeat of Spain. He also was certain that the Austrian government would tell him that acceptance of such conditions would "involve the gravest consequences to the Dynasty." He concluded, "nor can I conceal from Your Lordship my apprehension that the mention of a port in the Philippine Islands coming from us even indirectly may lay us open to unpleasant misconstruction,"[36] that is, that Britain was seeking territorial gain to herself from the dispute. Despite misgivings, Salisbury repeated his instruction, recommending Rumbold to "take care that there is no mistake in Count Goluchowski's mind and that he clearly understands that I simply repeat a suggestion which has been transmitted to me without expressing in the faintest degree the opinion of Her Majesty's Government in respect to it."[37]

After Salisbury's message had been conveyed to him, Goluchowski replied that the suggested conditions amounted to the loss of all Spain's colonies and could only be accepted as a last resort and after Spain had been completely defeated. However, Austria was not prepared to act in the Spanish interest. Although "well affected" toward Spain she had "no immediate interest in the war to justify her in taking the initiative for the proposals of mediation which ought rather to come from the great maritime powers like France and Great Britain."

Austria would join such a mediation but would not take any initiative. Spain should address herself to the powers on the subject. Rumbold's report concluded, "the only remark made by Count Goluchowski regarding the cession of a port in the Philippines was that it would be equivalent to a cession of these Islands."[38]

It would appear then that the German charge cannot be substantiated. In June 1898 the British Foreign Office favoured a peace settlement (it had never favoured the American use of force), but refused to take the initiative in any action to induce Spain to make peace. This reluctance was not in any way because of a fear that the United States would gain territories in the Far East. As will be shown later Britain quite favoured an expansion of United States territories and hence of her naval power and her diplomatic weight in the Pacific. Salisbury refused to act because he believed any such action would not be conducive to peace, but would on the contrary lay England open to the charge of seeking territorial gains for herself. For this to happen would be to precipitate a scramble for concessions and to increase dangerously the international tension in the Far East.

III

From the preceding comments it is clear that up to July 1898 Salisbury was determined not to permit England to become involved in any attempt to initiate or to influence a negotiated peace. After the defeat of their arms in Cuba, the destruction of their sea power in the Orient, and finally the fall of Manila, the Spanish government at last faced reality and sued for peace. Theatrical to the end, the government "arranged"[39] a meeting of all ambassadors to Madrid in order to give the appearance of submitting only upon the advice of the combined European powers. This act opened the last round in the struggle. During the following months, the ambitions and interests of rival imperial powers were to be revealed. The crucial issue was the fate of Spain's colonial empire and the effect its disposition would have in the Far East upon the balance of power and upon commercial opportunity. This was the chief problem for the British cabinet to consider during the manoeuvres preceding the armistice and the peace. What was to be British policy toward the disposal of Spain's Pacific dependencies?

The usual interpretations of Britain's attitude to this question are variations on the theme that Britain regarded the Spanish-American War as an opportunity to "use" the United States in the Far East in the interest of British territorial and diplomatic aims as opposed to German and Russian objectives there. The most forthright of such works is that by R. H. Heindel. Writing in 1940 of England's attitude to the Spanish-American War, he claimed that "her desire to use us [the United States] affected vitally many steps in British diplomacy and in spite of the American Senate and isolationism, she tried to make American expansion a counterweight to European competition and a reinsurance of the *status quo* satisfactory to Great Britain."[40] A more moderate thesis had been developed two years earlier by L. M. Gelber.[41] His argument very briefly was that "towards the close of the nineteenth century, as in the days of Monroe and Canning, the New World was called into existence to redress the balance of the old."[42] In this process the crucial event was the entry of the United States into world politics. This obviously would upset the balance of power. "To capitalise that alteration in favour of Great Britain, to capture the goodwill of the United States for its own sake and before it was obtained by others, became now an object of British diplomacy."[43] Britain's great opportunity was provided in 1898. In that year "in international affairs Anglo-American friendship first became a decisive factor during the Spanish War when the British Government, faithfully reflecting public opinion, manifested goodwill towards the United States and supported her growth as a colonial power."[44]

Contemporary opinion would seem to provide corroborative

evidence for this type of interpretation. The Spanish government, as has been shown, firmly believed the United Kingdom
to be encouraging the United States in imperialist adventures.
The Kaiser in a hot-tempered outburst professed to see England
in 1898 stirring up the powers with the intention of allying
herself with the stronger of the combatants, whom she would in
turn incite against the continental powers.[45] The theme of
English and American press articles during and after the war
constantly emphasized the identity of interests and the growing
friendship between the United States and the United Kingdom.
Of this, the best example is the traditional but mistaken belief
in the protective manoeuvre by the British fleet in Manila Bay.
Even the more hostile American press accepted the fact of
British friendship, but attributed it to political realism rather
than to idealism or any affinity of spirit or of blood. Comment
by the *Boston Herald* was typical: "She [Britain] is seeking our
favour now because she is out of favour with her sister powers
in Europe and would like us for an ally in her conflict with
them. As the field of such a conflict is likely to be the East, she
would like us to go there and hence her reason for advising us
to take the Philippines."[46]

Added weight to this view is provided by the statements of
public men and the private correspondence between English
officials and members of the United States executive. Harcourt
and the Liberals as well as Balfour and Chamberlain favoured
the expansion of the United States as a Pacific power. Cecil
Spring Rice, writing as a private person from his position as
second secretary in the British embassy in Berlin, bombarded
Hay with letters urging the American annexation of Hawaii
during the war and before any peace settlement was achieved
with Spain.[47] This in his opinion was the only way of ensuring
American ownership and of forestalling German claims for
compensation. When the news of annexation reached him he
wrote jubilantly to his friend Cabot Lodge: "I can't tell you
with what pleasure I see that Hawaii is at length to be annexed
. . . I think there can be no doubt that there is an intention

(and a natural one) to depose English civilization (I mean yours as much and more than mine) from the Pacific. I don't believe that England, the island, is strong enough to defend English civilization alone. . . ."[48] Again Henry Adams could write that the one topic of conversation among members of the British cabinet at Hay's dinners was the balance of power and the advent of the United States as a colonial power in the Far East.[49] It was in this atmosphere that Spring Rice advised Hay that Chamberlain and Balfour preferred the United States to keep the Philippines.

The suggestion of British initiative implied in this spoken and written evidence of private and public opinion seems at first glance to be corroborated by offical British policy both prior to the Spanish-American War and later when the disposal of Spain's Pacific colonies became the chief interest of the powers. The tentative approach to co-operation in the Far East between England and the United States from the 1850's is well known, the highlights being the diplomatic prelude to the Treaty of Tientsin and the policies and methods of Secretary of State William H. Seward and his minister in China, Anson Burlingame. From 1895 Lord Kimberley kept the State Department informed of his assessment of Russo-Japanese relations and of Russian aims in China, and sought an indication of the attitude of the United States.[50] Referring to the Far Eastern situation, Chamberlain wrote to Balfour (3 February 1898), stating: "If matters remain as they are our prestige will be gone and our trade will follow. I would not give a year's life to the Government under such conditions. . . . I would propose an approach to the United States saying, 'Will you stand with us in our China policy?' "[51] Finally on 7 March 1898, before the outbreak of the Spanish-American War, Balfour instructed Pauncefote in the following terms:

Her Majesty's Government are anxious to know whether they could count on the co-operation of the United States in opposing any action of foreign powers which would tend to restrain the opening of China to the commerce of all nations. There are two methods in which this might be effected. Either by the lease of portions of the Chinese coast under conditions which would ensure preferential treatment of that power, or of the actual acquisition by a foreign power of portions of the Chinese littoral. Can you ascertain confidentially whether the United States would be prepared to join with us in opposing such measures if the contingency should present itself?[52]

By 15 March no reply had been received and the reason for the British enquiry was revealed by a telegram sent that day to Pauncefote: "Delay of reply from United States Government is embarrassing as Russians are strongly pressing Chinese Government for lease of Port Arthur and Talienwan."[53] The United States refused Balfour's request, the President cautiously saying that he was "in sympathy with the policy which shall maintain open trade in China" but "all his advices indicate no occupation up to this time which proposes to interfere with the trade."[54] Russia and Germany assured him that no closure of trade was intended, so he felt that there was no reason for departure from the traditional policy of withholding from entangling alliances. This was supplemented verbally by Secretary Day, who told Pauncefote that the reasons for the reply were the preoccupation with the Cuban question, the traditional opposition to entangling alliances which was regarded as part of the law of the land, and the insurmountable difficulty of congressional influence on foreign policy.[55] The feeling of the Foreign Office appeared in a minute on the back of this despatch: "There is not much solid comfort in this."

It is obvious then that up to March 1898 the United Kingdom consistently sought United States co-operation in the Far East. The object was to acquire United States support in maintaining China's territorial integrity and thus Britain's territorial and trading position. Would Britain now attempt to use the Spanish-American War as an opportunity to renew the attempt to involve the United States in diplomatic and territorial commitments in the Far Eastern scene? In order to appreciate fully the motives governing British policy in this period it is essential to examine the interests and pressures governing cabinet thinking on the Philippines problems as such and then to set these considerations in the more general context of the international situation in which decisions had to be made. The perspective thus gained will accurately reveal Britain's policy, and will determine the extent to which the traditional interpretation of British policy can be sustained.

Britain's first interest in the Far East was commercial. In 1896 when the United States through Henry White first sought an indication of cabinet's attitude to the dispute over Cuba, it was not yet apparent that the trouble would involve a redisposition of Spain's colonial possessions. Salisbury could therefore emphasize that Britain's interests were purely commercial, and that the dispute was, as he said, "no affair of ours."[56] However, as the danger of war increased, trading and financial houses began to make it their affair. British investments in the area were heavy. A memorial from British merchants engaged in trade with the Philippines pointed out that there was £600,000 worth of British goods at Manila awaiting export, that 8¼ per cent of the principal exports, sugar, hemp, and coffee, and 70 per cent of the imports to and from the Philippines were British property.[57]

The pressure exerted upon the government prior to the outbreak of war to secure English commercial interests and the measures taken to this end have been dealt with in chapter two.[58] Once it was realized that war was inevitable, many representations designed to ensure the continued protection of British investments were made by interested parties to the Foreign and Colonial Offices. The fact that these representations were almost entirely concerned with the Pacific area seems to show a far greater concern with the fate of the Philippines than with that of Cuba. The reason is that because of its geographical proximity to the United States it was universally believed that the United States was certain to control the future of Cuba. On the other hand, the traditional anti-imperialism of the United States and the attitude of many in the Republican party made it very doubtful whether the United States would invest in imperialist adventures in the Far Western Pacific. This doubt was intensified by press talk of the United States either selling or giving away the Pacific dependencies,[59] and by speculation as to German ambitions in the area. The result was that English financial and trading houses became as much concerned with the possible changes in jurisdiction over the Philippines as with the security of existing investments. This concern sprang from the realization that any change in jurisdiction would probably mean a change in trading policy, a change which could only be adverse to British interests. The contemporary struggle in China to maintain equal opportunity for trade, as against the discriminatory policies favoured by Germany, France, and Russia, would be extended to the Philippines unless they remained Spanish or were annexed by the United States.

With these considerations in mind, every effort was made to make the Foreign Office and the Colonial Office aware of the hopes and fears of "the city." The general trend and tone of advice given to the Foreign Office and the Colonial Office was that summed up in a telegram from the British consul in Manila on behalf of British merchants.

Vitally important secure American or British administration entire archipelago with uniform tariffs under one central government, deprecate any partition islands under separate Governments as destructive British interests centred in Manila. Spanish rule Luzon impossible, and other islands revolting. [sic] Chichester, senior naval officer, can vouch for these being merchants general views.[60]

In May Mr. Martin, the chairman of the British North Borneo Company, was brought to the Foreign Office by Mr. C. P. Lucas of the Colonial Office to put the views of his company before Mr. Sanderson. Mr. Martin's chief object was to warn the Foreign Office that Germany "had designs upon the Sulu Islands should the Spanish rule in the Philippines go to the wall." He pointed out that the inhabitants of the islands had been cultivated by the company with whom they were on excellent terms. Distrusting the abilities of the British consul in the area to watch over British interests, Mr. Martin suggested that the Foreign Office should seek the services of a more alert representative. His chief point was that "it would not do—so far as British interests in the Far East were concerned—to have the Germans established in these islands."[61] The Foreign Office consulted with the Colonial Office, which directed the officer administering the Straits Settlements and acting as consul-general for North Borneo to "watch and report any indication of foreign claims."[62]

On 11 June, the consul-general for North Borneo reported that the Sultan of the Sulu Islands had tentatively suggested the creation of a British protectorate over the archipelago. The instruction returned to him after consultation between the Foreign Office and the Colonial Office was to assure the Sultan of Britain's friendship but to point out that the suggestion was premature and that cabinet had not given him any authority to act.[63] Again in July the North Borneo Company reported requests for the creation of a British protectorate, and in the same month the Japanese ambassador enquired if the Foreign Office had any news of the Sulus being ceded by Spain to Germany.[64]

To the support of the North Borneo Company came many other similar organizations. The Pacific Islands Company with large interests in the Caroline Islands used the British Empire League to press colonial opinion upon the cabinet. In June the League sent a memorial to the Colonial Office submitting that there was "a strong feeling in Australasia that in the event of the Islands [the Philippines] or any of them passing out of the ownership of Spain, they should not either be left in a condition of anarchy or pass under any jurisdiction which would be prejudicial to British and Colonial commercial interests."[65] Earlier than this, in April, a letter was received at the Colonial Office from the Agent-General of the Colony of Victoria,

Australia, stating that he had been instructed by his government to call attention to "the necessity of the Philippine Islands
being in possession of a friendly power, owing to the importance
of its strategical position, and also in the interests of trade, as
they command the route from Australasia to China, Japan and
the Far East."[66] The Chartered Bank of India, Australia, and
China, the Hong Kong and Shanghai Banking Corporation,
and seven other allied firms requested the friendly offices of
the British government with the United States to prevent any
unnecessary interference with the trade of the Philippines; as
this trade was "principally in the hands of British firms consequently any injury done to the trade of the Philippines would
be more felt by British subjects than Spanish."[67]

It is evident that a concern for commercial and financial
interests very quickly became a concern for the future disposition of the Spanish colonial territories in the Pacific.
Opinion in "the city" seemed unanimous in demanding either
British or American control. This underlined the second of
Britain's interests—the strategic. Her chief aim in the Far East
was to prevent an extension of Russian and German influence
in China and thus the limitation of equal opportunity for
trade. While the American people, President, and government
were making up their minds to engage upon further imperial
adventures, Britain in Salisbury's phrase was seeking in the
lease of Wei-Hai-Wei "cartographic consolation" for Germany's
occupation of Kiaochow. She was at the same time endeavouring to plan future opposition to any extension of Russian power
beyond Port Arthur which had so recently been seized, and to
combat undue pressure from Russia upon the Tsungli Yamen
to accept Russian rather than British loans. The imminent
victory of the United States brought England a new problem,
that of keeping Germany or any other European power out of
the Philippines; and German manoeuvres to gain territorially
from the war were to create very real difficulties for Britain and
America if not for Spain.

Salisbury was well aware of Germany's interest in the disposition of the Philippines, if not of her actual intentions. In May the North Borneo Company had reported rumours of German designs on the Sulu Archipelago.[68] On 11 May Hatzfeldt (the German ambassador in London) had endeavoured to discover Salisbury's attitude to the fate of Spain's territories, as he suspected some understanding between America and England. Salisbury expressed the view that America did not intend to give away the Philippines and would resent any interference in the matter of their disposition.[69] In June came Wolff's warning that "something was going on with Germany," that Radowitz, the German ambassador at Madrid, had "from his first arrival had his mind directed to the Philippine Islands."[70] When Wolff questioned the Spanish Minister for Foreign Affairs, any understanding with Germany was denied, but suspicion remained, for America informed England that Germany had made a formal request to her for one of the Philippine Islands.[71]

This suspicion was well founded, for Germany's policy although fluctuating in intensity was to watch carefully for an opportunity to extend her territorial possessions and to strength her strategic position in the Far East. When Prince Henry and the German consul in Manila cabled that the Philippine insurgents might welcome a protectorate under Germany, Bülow carefully considered the possibilities. His view was that England's attitude was crucial. If England acquiesced then the United States could keep the Philippines without any difficulty, whereas if England objected, it would be very difficult for the United States to maintain control. Any such action by Germany might well unite America and Britain in opposition to Germany. In order to avoid this possibility, in Bülow's opinion, Hatzfeldt in London should be directed to discover Lord Salisbury's attitude. With this view the Kaiser agreed, provided that the Philippines were not acquired by any foreign power without Germany's obtaining some equivalent compensation.[72] Salisbury's discouraging reply has already been quoted. In the face of this and the unreliability of France and Russia,[73] the Kaiser and Bülow decided merely to send Von Diederichs and his naval force to observe and to protect German interests. While at Manila Von Diederichs refused to take any initiative in placing Manila under a neutral occupation and the Foreign Office approved his decision. The ill-feeling caused by the behaviour of the German admiral has already been dealt with.

In July the Kaiser once more sent the embassies into a flurry of activity. Holleben was informed that "Seine Majestät der Kaiser erachtet es für eine Hauptaufgabe der deutschen Politik, keine infolge des spanisch-amerikanischen Konflikts sich etwa bietende Gelegenheit zur Erwerbung maritimer Stützpunkte in Ostasien unbenutzt zu lassen."[74]

When because of their assessment of the opposition to German aims both Holleben in Washington and Hatzfeldt in London counselled the German Foreign Office to seek to win the support of American opinion by working through White, the United States ambassador at Berlin, their advice was followed. On 10 July Baron Richthofen in Berlin saw White and suggested that Germany should have Samoa (as compensation for Hawaii), the Carolines, and one or two positions in the Philippine or Sulu Archipelagos. White seemed favourable to a general settlement of Pacific problems but could not be at all definite because of his complete ignorance of the intentions of the American executive and Congress. However, with the hardening of American opinion in favour of annexation German hopes of any great concession in the Philippine Archipelago itself disappeared. In London Hatzfeldt saw Hay, who was excessively cold toward any suggestions of the type made to Henry White. Holleben also reported from Washington that McKinley did not reveal any such degree of friendliness as did Henry White. By the time the armistice was signed (12 August) Germany had given up hope of acquiring "maritime fulcra" in the Philippines and turned instead to a plan to purchase whatever islands the peace left to Spain.[75]

Japan and Russia were also interested. On 13 July, having

heard rumours of Germany's acquiring some Spanish islands (the Sulu Archipelago) the Japanese ambassador saw Salisbury to discuss with him the question of peace in the Pacific and especially the future fate of the Philippines. He informed Salisbury on a later occasion that Japan

> would take no umbrage at the retention of the Islands by the Americans, and of course could take no exception to their retention by Spain. But if they were transferred to any European Power, especially any continental Power—and this qualification he emphasised once or twice—the proposal would be regarded with much aversion by Japan.[76]

Sir Ernest Satow, the British ambassador in Japan, reported that the same matter had been raised in the Japanese Diet on 25 May, but the Minister for Foreign Affairs had refused to reply to what he termed a hypothetical question.[77]

As Russia's greatest rival in Asia was England, her chief interest in the Philippines was that they should not go to England. In her attempt to wean the United States from the moral support lent to England's China policy, Russia "promised the United States preferential tariffs in China if they would throw in their lot with Russia."[78] By a press campaign in Washington[79] and by ambassadorial messages Russia let it be known in European capitals that she preferred the pre-war status quo in the Philippines. However, as this was impossible she would agree to the Philippines being retained by the United States, but she would not admit the cession of any portion of the archipelago to any other power without consulting her own interests.[80]

These were the interests and pressures that were concerned with the Philippine question as such, and that were operating upon and within the cabinet. However, it was not in the light of these considerations alone that decisions were made, for at the Foreign Office a view of the Far Eastern situation as a whole governed official actions taken in any part of it. In this particular instance cabinet policy toward the Philippine issue had in fact been almost predetermined by decisions already taken over the problems of China—an area far more important to England's trading and strategic interests than the Philippines. Moreover, these same decisions, together with America's refusal in March to co-operate with Great Britian in stronger measures to prevent further encroachments upon China's territorial and administrative independence, determined Britain's attitude to the United States at this time. A brief sketch of British Far Eastern policy as a whole will show how this came to be.[81]

From the 1850's, successive British governments had been under constant pressure from commercial and financial houses interested in the Far East[82] to give greater support to their efforts to expand the China trade. Their demands took two forms. The first type, to which the consent of the Foreign Office was more readily forthcoming, was for support for particular projects such as railway, postal, or telegraph concessions, loans or mining investments. For these requests Foreign Office aid was often most helpful, the most successful period being from 1897 to 1898, when practically the full programme of such demands listed by the China Association in 1896 was supported successfully by diplomatic pressure at Peking.[83] In fact so great were the concessions won that Salisbury forbade the publication of a catalogue of successes forwarded from Peking by Sir Claude MacDonald, British ambassador in China, on the grounds that it would only cause trouble with Russia if the whole were known.[84]

Other demands were urged upon the Foreign Office, both as individual projects and on occasion, as in 1869 and 1898, as fully developed programmes designed ultimately to make China another India. Frustrated by China's reluctance to abolish all barriers in the way of the industrial and commercial revolution the Western trading interests wished to force upon her, British merchants sought the aid of their government to bend China to their will. They demanded that more ports should be opened to them, that China's rivers should be opened to steam navigation, and that railways should be constructed in order to open the vast inland markets to their trade. To these were added demands that Westerners should be free to reside and to trade in the interior, that foreign goods should be immune from tax, and that these rights and respect for the British flag should be enforced. These demands were submitted repetitively to Palmerston in 1839, to Lord Elgin in 1858, to the Earl of Clarendon in 1868-69, and in an extreme form to Lord Salisbury in 1898-99.

In the late 1890's Britain's predominance in China was challenged by Russia in Mongolia, by Germany's colonial ambitions in Shantung, and by France in the south. The tariff policies of these European rivals made it evident that any territory brought under their control in the Far East would be guarded as a preserve for their nationals, while the pressure they brought to bear upon the Tsungli Yamen made it equally evident, at least to the merchants in the United Kingdom, that they intended the partition of China, at best into spheres of influence, at worst into territorial dependencies.[85] In either case British trade would be excluded from areas under foreign influence—the open door would be closed.

In the face of these threats, the press and the Opposition in parliament urged the more active assertion of Britain's rights and influence as against her rivals, and the adoption of a policy designed to ensure predominantly British control of any area in China where British trade was paramount. The most influential organizations of Far Eastern traders went further still. The China Association, supported by the Associated Chambers of Commerce and by affiliated bodies throughout England and Scotland, urged the effective enforcement of treaty rights and active opposition to Russian and French encroachments, and demanded that fiscal and administrative reforms should be imposed upon the inefficient Chinese. It was argued that, for this policy to succeed, the Chinese government must be "re-animated" under British guidance operating at Peking, and finally that British officers should carry out the military reorganization of the country. This programme culminated in

1899 in a demand for the "effective occupation" of the Yangtse region (defined as stretching from Chusan to Burma as well as including all provinces bordering the river). It was urged finally that throughout all China "a measure of control corresponding to the preponderance of British interests should be retained *at all hazards.*"[86]

This agitation was carried out by private discussion with the permanent officials of the Foreign Office, by constant attack upon the Government in parliament both by Government and Opposition interests on behalf of the China Association's programme, by memorials from the China Committees as well as the London Committees of the Association, and by a press campaign so virulent that Salisbury characterized it as "insane" upon the subject.[87] In addition, Lord Charles Beresford, M.P. and champion of the mercantile interests, ostensibly[88] at the request of the Associated Chambers of Commerce went off upon his tour of investigation of the China situation. Before he departed, he discussed with Lord Salisbury[89] possible methods of obtaining the desired reform and rehabilitation of China, arguing that sea power was no longer sufficient, that land forces were necessary to combat Russia, and that the best source of such a land force was a Chinese army trained, advised, and led by British officers.[90] This policy he urged upon the Tsungli Yamen, as well as upon Salisbury.[91] Having met Yuan-Shih-Kai and having compared the man and his army with the existing Chinese government, he revealed the extent of his ambition by advising Salisbury in all seriousness that by using Yuan-Shih-Kai all of China could be taken over in the British interest. The note is worth quoting in full. It was forwarded to the Foreign Office by Sir Claude MacDonald.

Please wire to Foreign Office: Minutely inspected 7,000 troops of Chinese General Yuan-Shih-Kai near Tientsin. Field exercise splendid. Only even and disciplined force in China, anti-Russian, pro-English. If trouble, or strong action determined in China, I could reach Peking one day with Yuan-Shih-Kai force. Mutual confidence, friendship. Through Yuan-Shih-Kai I could maintain order, support dynasty, control government, which would have to act under Sir C. MacDonald's orders. Will you authorize me when the time comes? Perfectly possible probably without a shot. Yuan-Shih-Kai's force complete master of situation if used.[92]

This advice was given both to serve his own vast ambition and in the hope that the Foreign Office would take the "strong action" desired by the China Association to protect British commercial interests.

The sum of the criticisms from the press, parliament, and pressure groups was to demand that British treaty rights in China should be effectively enforced, that any further increase in the territorial or political influence of other European powers should be prevented, and that the Yangtse Valley should be effectively occupied as a last ditch insurance against the extension of the exclusive commercial policies of Russia or Germany.

In 1898 government policy in the face of this pressure was based upon two principles. The first was that the existing and potential China trade and investments were insufficient to justify the use of armed force against European rivals, who threatened them or stood in the way of their extension.[93] The second was that Great Britain was no longer capable by herself of ensuring the political and territorial stability of the Far East. It was neatly summed up by Salisbury in his ironic reply to Beresford's suggestion quoted above. "At the beginning of the century the idea would have been attractive. But now to attempt to assume the Government of China in defiance of the mass of Chinese and of all the European powers besides would be too exhausting for England."[94]

The first of these principles had been made clear to the Foreign Office by the Board of Trade as early as 1869 and had been adhered to consistently since then. The second principle governed Britain's search for allies following upon the demonstration of the dangers of isolation provided by Europe's reaction to the Boer War. It also inspired the attempt begun in January

1898 to reach an accommodation of the difficulties with Russia which finally broke down when Port Arthur was seized. It caused the approach to America (March 1898) which followed the failure with Russia, and it was the reason for the return to agreement with Russia which was forced upon Britain by America's refusal to co-operate. The policy based upon these principles which guided the Foreign Office through the difficult period 1898-99 and after was clearly defined by cabinet at its first meeting after the election and was outlined to parliament by Balfour in January and again in April. It was this definition that governed Britain's attitude towards the disposition of the Philippines.

The twin problems which concerned all those interested in either the China or the Philippine trade were the protection of British commercial interests and the extent to which territorial control was a necessary method of ensuring their security. To both of these questions Balfour addressed himself,[95] repeating the principles decided upon by cabinet in January. "Territorial expansion by itself and for itself in the Far East is an unmixed evil . . . and . . . unless the acquisition of territory was required for a military or naval base was, if possible, to be avoided." Secondly he laid it down that British interests were not territorial but commercial. In those areas under the direct control of the Chinese government these commercial interests had been successfully fostered by British pressure to acquire further privileges such as the opening of new treaty ports and the agreement by which China undertook not in any way to alienate the Yangtse Kiang region. In those areas where the Chinese government was subject to the dominating influence of Russia or Germany, assurances had been sought, and received, from those governments that there would be no interference with the freedom of trade. Moreover, as a reinsurance against this possibility, Wei-Hai-Wei had been occupied to counter "the constant menace to the capital of China" inherent in Russian occupation of Port Arthur. Wei-Hai-Wei was the one port in the Gulf of Pechili which the cabinet believed would balance the possession of Port Arthur. Cabinet policy in brief was that there would be no acquisition of territory in the Far East unless it became necessary as a counterpoise or balance to some such encroachment by Britain's European rivals. As Salisbury expressed it in a minute to MacDonald in China before the decision to lease Wei-Hai-Wei had been taken: "The present policy of Her Majesty's Government in China is to discourage the alienation of Chinese territory. It is therefore premature to discuss the lease of Wei-Hai-Wei unless action of other powers materially alters the position."[96] It was with great reluctance that the government accepted the fact that open trade was so threatened that it was necessary to retreat to a policy of spheres of interest, or rather as Salisbury preferred to put it, to a "partition of preponderance."

In the light of all these considerations which had to be taken into account when assessing the Philippine situation, it is evident that cabinet's decision was practically predetermined. To begin with, the China situation was so much more important to the British government than the fate of the Philippines. This was so because the value of the China trade was so much greater than the sum total of British commercial interests in the Spanish colonies, and the pressure upon the government over the China issue was immeasurably greater than the representations concerning the fate of the islands. Moreover, many of the more powerful commercial interests, such as the Hong Kong and Shanghai Banking Corporation, concerned in the Philippines, had very much more at stake in China than in the islands. Finally, Britain's European rivals were not established in the Philippines as they were on the mainland of Asia, and what was more important, none of them was in a position to challenge the will of the United States concerning the disposition of the islands. On the mainland they might ignore diplomatic platitudes, but a United States fleet and land force were in complete command at Manila. It was logical therefore that Britain's territorial and traditional policy geared to the realities of the China situation would not be overturned or modified in the interests of a side issue such as the fate of the Spanish colonies.

In this situation the basic principles of the China policy could be applied almost as a formula. Trade and investments would be protected but there would be no attempt to acquire territorial concessions unless it became necessary to establish bases as a counter to any concessions won by Germany or Russia to further their effort to enforce an exclusive trading and investment policy. Such a necessity could only arise if America decided neither to keep the islands herself nor to permit them to remain under Spanish sovereignty. The President, the Secretary of State, and past action by the United States in the Pacific area, all assured Salisbury, Balfour, and Chamberlain that American territorial control would be used to secure "open trade," rather than to limit it by the application of those restrictive American tariffs which protected the internal markets of the United States;[97] furthermore the United Kingdom press seemed agreed that high United States colonial tariffs because applied equally to all nations were not incompatible with the "Open Door."[98] Therefore any territorial adjustment following the war would not be against English interests provided that the United States controlled the territories lost to Spain. Obviously then there was only one policy open to cabinet, and that was to favour the retention of the Philippines by the United States. This would ensure the commercial policy desired in the area by Britain; it would prevent the disposition of the islands from becoming an occasion for European rivalry for concessions and counter-concessions; it would write finis to German ambitions in the area; and above all it would involve the United States territorially, and thus permanently, in an area close to that in which Britain had in the past sought her diplomatic co-operation.

This was in fact precisely the policy decided upon. It was stated quite carefully by Salisbury, who wrote to Sir Ernest

Satow (the British ambassador to Japan) in July 1898, in these terms:

> The Japanese Ambassador asked me whether Her Majesty's Government had any view with respect to the disposal of the Philippines or whether they were absolutely indifferent. I said that so long as the Spaniards or the Americans kept them in their possession, I did not think that Her Majesty's Government would consider that any case had arisen calling for an expression of opinion on their part. But if directly or indirectly the withdrawal of them from the dominion of Spain was to involve their transfer to any European power, I thought that a different set of considerations would arise and that I could not pledge Her Majesty's Government to inaction in the matter.[99]

In the same month Hay was informed that Britain preferred the United States to keep the Philippines, but if they did not intend this, then the British insisted upon first option to purchase them.[100]

All this has gone merely to demonstrate that every consideration suggested that the United Kingdom's interests would best be served by an extension of American power into Asia and by American acquisition of the Philippines. One question however is still at issue. Did the United Kingdom use this occasion as an opportunity to encourage, or to entice, or to involve the United States in territorial commitments in the Far East? Was it once again used as the occasion to call the New World into existence to redress the balance of the Old? Contrary to the belief of the governments and writers referred to at the beginning of this chapter there is no evidence that during the Spanish-American War the Foreign Office took any positive and official action after March 1898[101] to do this. No effort was made to entice the United States into international rivalry in Asia or to induce her to annex the Philippines, or, as will be seen in chapter four, to influence the United States towards the open door policy.

Arguments used to support the view that England actively

"encouraged the United States to follow up Dewey's victory by annexing the whole archipelago,"[102] and thus to embark upon imperialist expansion, are usually based upon three types of evidence. They begin by making the assumption that every advantage to Great Britain's economic and security interests would follow upon an extension into the Far East of America's territorial sovereignty and hence of her naval and military power. This assumption, based upon an appreciation of Britain's difficulties in Asia and upon her search for co-operation with the United States, has been shown to be soundly based in fact. From what has been said earlier it is clear that it summarized the beliefs and hopes of all parties in parliament and that cabinet was unanimous about the matter even though the degree of support within it varied between enthusiasm and mere acquiescence. It certainly was in accord with Lord Salisbury's view that permanent interests could only be ensured by territorial commitments.

From this beginning, the argument then proceeds to prove beyond any shadow of doubt that public opinion in Great Britain outside court circles was almost unanimous in its support for the United States action against Spain in both the Caribbean and the Pacific. That this was the case has been proven conclusively and repetitively on many occasions.[103] Leaders and articles from all the major newspapers and journals practically without exception were in favour of America's actions. Addresses were received by the government from numerous political associations in support of Anglo-American friendship. The Fourth of July was widely celebrated in England and was made an occasion for political gestures in the interests of Anglo-Saxon unity. Both the non-conformist and established churches, leaders and laity alike, vied with one another in expressions of Anglo-Americanism. Prominent men in all walks of life and from all classes spoke so often and so favourably of this ideal that it seemed they were determined not to be outdone one by the other in expressions of the fashionable sentiment. Traditional functions in Britain, such as Lord Mayoral balls and banquets and military and naval reviews, were throughout 1898 made the occasion for highlighting the Stars and Stripes and for allegorical representations of a close Anglo-American association. Finally there was formed the Anglo-American League under the sponsorship of leading citizens throughout the United Kingdom and dedicated to securing cordial transatlantic co-operation.

Even in the United States itself the traditional Anglophobia seemed for the time being to be in abeyance. Observers were surprised to see Queen Victoria's birthday celebrated in the United States, the same friendliness being manifest for more obvious reasons at innumerable Chambers of Commerce dinners and functions. There was even an Anglo-American Committee as a modified counterpart of the British Anglo-American League. These outbursts of comradely gestures were a great surprise to the British ambassador even though they did not in any way overcome either his scepticism or his hard-headed appreciation of the volatile nature of American public opinion. After some months of silence occasioned by illness, Pauncefote wrote in a private letter to Salisbury[104] to acquaint his Prime Minister with the current scene:

The most astonishing feature of the present time is the sudden transition of this country from Anglophobia to the most exuberant affection for England and "Britishers" in general. I am overwhelmed with addresses in prose and in verse in the form of music or drawings or illustrated buttons with flags intertwined, commemorative of the supposed Anglo-American "Alliance." How long the fit will last no wise man would venture to predict, but it will certainly have an excellent effect in the future relations of the two countries and we must seize the opportune moment to "straighten out" as they call it, all our Canadian difficulties.

Rumours of an alliance between the two traditional Anglo-Saxon enemies spread throughout the European chancellories and embassies and were of course induced by the volume as well as the effusiveness of the public expressions of Anglo-

American accord. Reference has been made to the difficulties this caused with Spain, particularly after the notable speeches by Chamberlain and Richard Olney.

Having emphasized the fact that British interests would be served by America's acquisition of the Philippines, and having elaborated the unanimity of public opinion, the argument then proceeds to silhouette against this background, and thus to exaggerate in importance, the rather meagre evidence thought to show that attempts were made by cabinet or Foreign Office or embassy officials to encourage the United States to act as Britain desired. It is customary to mention the well known enthusiasm of Balfour and Chamberlain for the acquisition of allies and particularly for American friendship and co-operation and to quote Henry Adams' references to Ambassador Hay's dinners and the lively discussions which took place there concerning the balance of power in Asia as it would be affected by the American operations in the Philippines. It is then pointed out that Hay was urged by Cecil Spring Rice, a member of the British embassy in Germany, to take Hawaii and that Hay was assured by Salisbury that Britain would not object if America annexed the Philippines. There is frequently also in this context reference to the popular rumour that Chamberlain, either while in England or while visiting America in 1898, advised the American executive to annex Spain's Pacific territories. From all this the inference is drawn that the United Kingdom actively encouraged and put positive pressure upon the American government to adopt those policies best suited to British interests.

There are two basic fallacies in this type of argument. The first is the assumption that policy was synonymous with what public opinion thought it was or ought to be. The second is the further assumption that positive diplomatic pressure is always the method best suited to achieve diplomatic ends. Nothing is clearer than that the British cabinet would have welcomed a solid American territorial commitment in the Far East and that public opinion in England would support this.

However it is equally clear that cabinet took no positive action whatever to involve or entice or encourage the United States into territorial expansion. The negative policy followed by the United Kingdom during the war can be demonstrated conclusively from a résumé of official action from the files of the Foreign Office and from the memoirs and letters of those concerned. What is more, the reasons for this negative policy are readily apparent and are convincing.

To begin with, the English government as well as the national press were confident that the United States would successfully destroy Spanish power in both the Atlantic and the Pacific. Reluctant as many were to see this happen it was regarded as inevitable once war broke out. In these circumstances the British and for that matter all other European powers with colonial interests were concerned to assure for themselves the maximum benefit attainable from any transfer in sovereignty over Spain's former colonies. But Salisbury and the cabinet were well aware of the danger involved in any British action which was either designed to influence the United States or which could be construed as such by any group in the United States. Certainly all were intent to capitalize upon the current friendly mood of officials in the United States and to prevent any revival of the active anti-British policy expressed so violently by Secretary Olney during the Venezuelan dispute and incipient in United States-Canadian difficulties and in the isthmian question.

When Salisbury regretfully informed Queen Victoria that nothing could be done to prevent the outbreak of war he explained that "even the very temperate and guarded note which was addressed by the Powers to the United States Government was very much resented by a large portion of the community as an undue interference, and had no other effect than to harden the war feeling."[105] Pauncefote constantly referred to the malignity of the Irish and German voting blocs and declared them to be eager to capitalize upon any event to prevent Anglo-American accord. So virulent was the hatred of these professional "tail-twisters" that any policy espoused by Republicans or Democrats which could be shown to have originated in England or currently to serve English interests was in danger of defeat, even though its adoption might be demonstrably in the interests of the United States. This was stated almost in so many words by Lord Herschell, the Lord High Chancellor of England and Britain's chairman of the Joint High Commission appointed in May 1898 to settle Canadian-American difficulties. Early in the New Year, as the British parliament was soon to meet, Pauncefote felt it wise to telegraph Lord Herschell's views. This he did[106] three days before the United States Senate ratified the peace treaty with Spain. Herschell (and Pauncefote seemed to agree with him) reported that "without there being any change in the general sentiment towards England, there seems to be a widespread disposition to regard her as desirous of close relations with the United States only to serve her own ends." This he was convinced was an interpretation of British policy spread by the American opponents of territorial expansion. Herschell believed that it might endanger the treaty under negotiation by the High Commission if all that could be represented as concessions by America could be assailed as having been yielded "only for expansionist reasons and to suit the wishes of England." Hence any enthusiastic references to the friendship of the two countries might be prejudicial to a satisfactory settlement. This of course refers to a matter other than, though contemporary with, the Spanish-American War, but it illustrates the constant danger of which the British were very conscious, of providing either the German or Irish tail-twisters with an opportunity to pursue their anti-British campaign. It was to this danger that Pauncefote so frequently referred and about which Hay when Secretary of State so bitterly complained.[107] As the danger was always more acute during election campaigns, it was incumbent upon the British to be most circumspect during the tense months preceding the elections of November 1898 in the United States.

Again, having been rebuffed by the United States in March 1898 and having returned to direct agreement with Russia on the principle of partition not of territory but of "preponderance," the Foreign Office in the early period of the war was more concerned with the renewal of negotiations with Russia and Germany, and particularly with the effort to achieve an accommodation of her difficulties with France. It was not until the question of the disposal of Spanish territory was raised by the calling of the peace conference that the interest of the United Kingdom once more reverted to American policy. It was most unlikely in these circumstances that England would add to her troubles by antagonizing the United States by any attempt to influence opinion in the legislature or the executive. Such an action would be bound to compromise the British and was in fact unthinkable, given the deep-seated convictions of Chamberlain and Balfour that friendship with the United States must at all costs be maintained.

The correspondence between Cecil Spring Rice and John Hay is sometimes used as evidence of British attempts to encourage the expansion of the United States. In April 1898[108] Rice wrote to Hay concerning American policy towards Hawaii. He pointed out that Germany had intervened after the event in both the Sino-Japanese and the Turko-Greek Wars and in each case had won concessions for herself, and he therefore once more put to Hay, as he had on previous occasions, the argument that it was vitally important if Hawaii was "to be annexed *without* compensation, to annex it now." Samoa was the compensation Rice thought Germany would demand. Again on 16 July 1898,[109] he wrote from Berlin to reassure Hay that Germany had no thought of war or of the use of force against the United States but to warn him that the Kaiser meant to obtain a coaling station in the Philippines. But this can hardly be looked upon as British pressure upon the American executive. Rice was writing in a private capacity. He was second secretary in the Berlin embassy and had no instructions from either his ambassador, Sir Frank Lascelles, or from any member of the cabinet. He was in the habit of writing frequently to the many American friends he had made during his early service in Washington where he had been such a popular figure in society.[110] He wrote often to Theodore Roosevelt, to Henry Cabot Lodge, to Henry Adams, and others. In 1897 his letters to Roosevelt abound with references to one of his favourite themes, the common inheritance of the English speaking races and America's role of increasing importance in the partnership and her increasing influence in the world as a whole. His letters ranged over most subjects and many individuals in the diplomatic calendar, and in November 1897 he discussed the German attitude to the Cuban affair, pointing out the many "strong factors" which suggested German sympathy for Spain, but correctly prophesying Germany's war-time policy. There was no mention of the Philippines at all. His letter to Hay of 30 April 1898, urging annexation of Hawaii, continued a conversation which had taken place in London in September 1897 and can in no way be interpreted as an attempt to persuade the United States into the first stages of a policy of expansion in the Pacific in British interests. But even if this is not admitted, the significant point is that Spring Rice could write so freely about these topics because he knew he was writing to an already convinced audience who needed no urging to let their views be heard in Washington. As Hay explained to Spring Rice, he passed on the substance of his letter to the President for the very reason that "it jumped so precisely with my own view." Similar conviction appeared in Cabot Lodge's reply to Spring Rice's letter of congratulation upon the annexation of Hawaii,[111] and particularly in his comments to Hay early in 1898 upon America's China policy. "If I had my way I should be glad to have the United States say to England that we would stand by her in her declaration that the ports of China must be opened to all nations equally or none. . . ."[112] But certainly neither Lodge nor Hay was converted to his conception of what United States foreign policy should be by any letters from Spring Rice.

The official correspondence between the Foreign Office and the State Department and between the statesmen actually engaged in formulating policy is a much more reliable guide to the facts of diplomacy than the personal letters of Spring Rice, who was not involved in any direct way at all. British policy immediately prior to and in the early period of the war was formal and correct, even if on Salisbury's part faintly disapproving. When Henry White asked Salisbury his views on the Cuban trouble he was told that Her Majesty's government's interests were purely commercial; and as early as June 1896 he could say to White: "It is no affair of ours, we are friendly to Spain and should be sorry to see her humiliated, but we do not consider that we have anything to say in the matter whatever may be the course the United States may decide to pursue."[113] The only matter upon which the United States was questioned was her attitude to the neutrality regulations and the Declaration of Paris to which the United States was not a party. After being assured that all American action would be in accordance with the treaty, no further question was put to the American government until the first enquiry concerning probable peace terms made in May 1898. The alarm occasioned by Wolff's pro-Spanish activities and the refusal to risk offending the United States by offers of mediation were friendly in intent but as has been shown this policy was not motivated by any attempt to persuade the Americans into action against Spain in the Pacific or anywhere else. The same must be admitted about Britain's friendly neutrality as administered in Hong Kong.

The first sign of British interest in the possibilities posed by the prospect of peace was on 7 May when Chamberlain asked Hay whether the evacuation of Cuba would be the sole condition of peace. Hay being "wholly without information" cabled Washington[114] and received a reply from Secretary of State Day on 3 June. At that date, the President's aim was to acquire title to Cuba until a stable government could be established, to acquire Puerto Rico in lieu of a cash indemnity, and to obtain a port in the Philippines, as well as an island in the Ladrone group as a coaling station. These were the current views of the President but it was pointed out that they might well change if the war was prolonged. Salisbury was informed of these terms by Hay on 6 June, but he had already received the substance of the information from Pauncefote two days earlier. It will be remembered that this information seemed to Pauncefote to suggest that the occasion would be opportune to initiate peace negotiations, but Salisbury would do no more than to forward the information to the Austrian government in case they wished to take the lead in any move for peace. Salisbury himself would not take any initiative at all, and so well aware were the British officials of the necessity not to appear to intervene or to seek territory that Rumbold was, as has been shown, very reluctant even to carry out his instructions.[115]

By 14 June, entirely upon the initiative of the United States executive, and without any prompting whatever from external sources, the President had extended his conception of what would be regarded as an acceptable basis for peace. This according to Secretary Day was brought about by the changing nature of the war and the dangers involved in the spread of insurgent activity. When informed of this development Hay saw Salisbury and the question of the fate of the Philippines as a whole was discussed. The result of the interview was that Hay cabled to Washington that no objection would be likely if the United States obtained a permanent foothold in the Philippines. On 27 July Hay once again sought Salisbury's opinion about the peace proposals suggested in Washington and the next day cabled his report. The significant section reads: "I may add that the British Government prefer to have us retain the Philippine Islands or failing that insist on option to purchase in case of future sale."[116] It is significant then that the first suggestion concerning the retention of the Philippines came from America and it was not until after the question of their fate was raised that Salisbury let his attitude be known. And surely his policy cannot be described as "positive pressure" or encouragement. On the contrary it presented the executive with an alternative in the event that they wished to be rid of any imperialist embarrassment. By 27 July Salisbury's expression of opinion to Hay had become a settled policy which was made known to other states in the more cautious and non-committal statement to Satow concerning the fate of the islands.[117]

The armistice between America and Spain was signed on 12 August 1898. The peace conference met in Paris in October of the same year, the peace treaty being ratified by the Senate on 6 February 1899. Throughout this period there is still no evidence of any attempt by the United Kingdom to influence the American legislature, executive or peace commissioners. This is equally true of the crucial period between 16 September when McKinley delivered his first instructions to the peace commissioners and 26 October when he expanded these instructions by the direction that the United States could not be satisfied with one island (Luzon) only, but must choose between annexing either the whole of the island group or none at all.

If Britain had wished secretly to urge upon the United States executive any particular policy concerning the Philippines the occasion was provided in August when in an interview with A. J. Balfour, Mr. F. W. Holls, a personal emissary of Mr. McKinley, introduced the question of the disposal of the Philippines. Balfour's memorandum of the interview reads as follows.

Mr. F. W. Holls* (* of Algonah, Yonkers on the Hudson) with whom I had some slight previous acquaintance and who has been sent by Mr. McKinley to Berlin on some special business connected with the international relations of Germany and the United States, called on me this afternoon. He informed me that what he was going to say must be regarded as quite unofficial, but that he had received authority from Washington to say it. He begged however that if anything were mentioned to Mr. Hay implying a knowledge of what he was about to communicate, care should be taken to prevent the Ambassador from thinking that negotiations were being carried on behind his back. The substance of his communication was as follows:—

Germany had made a formal request to the United States for one of the Philippines, and according to her usual agreeable methods had promised that if this were conceded, no more should be heard of the perpetual little diplomatic difficulties which were always cropping up between her and the U.S. America had replied that nothing would be done until the peace negotiations at Paris had begun, or, (as I *think* he said) were concluded; and that even then *nothing could be done which was not thoroughly agreeable to Great Britain*. He suggested that this veto of Great Britain's might be used as a lever to make Germany come to terms with us and the United States in China. If I agreed in that view and desired to act on it the first move should come from us and we should inform Germany that if she made a satisfactory arrangement in the Far East we should use our good offices at Washington to get her an island in the Philippines.

I asked Mr. Holls whether if we took this course it could under any circumstances give offence in Washington. He said that although he could not undertake that such representations would be successful, he could answer for it that they would be well received. He incidentally mentioned that the Russians had recently approached the U.S. Government and promised them preferential tariffs in China if they would throw in their lot with Russia.[118]

This was in fact the prelude to a rather amateurish attempt to offer England some form of quid pro quo for a revision or abrogation of the Clayton-Bulwer Treaty, which would give the United States freedom in international law to do what the executive intended to do in any case, namely to build and to maintain sole control of a canal across the isthmus linking North and South America. Balfour of course refused to indicate any official reaction to this, the main point of the communication. But if the cabinet had felt strongly over the question of the fate of the Spanish Pacific possessions, and if it had been desired to put a British case secretly but effectively to the President, or to convince him of the necessity for territorial annexation by the United States, then surely this occasion would have been regarded as a golden opportunity. As it happened the matter was not even commented upon either by Balfour to Holls, or by Balfour in the usual form of a private minute to members of cabinet, or by any of the Foreign Office officials who handled the document.

Joseph Chamberlain visited the United States during this crucial period in the formation of American colonial policy. Given his avowed pro-American sentiments and actions, this visit understandably was made the occasion in the United States and in Spain for many rumours as to its purpose. The common belief spread by press reports was that Chamberlain had advised America to annex the Philippines. Wolff in Madrid cabled that the Spanish Foreign Minister had been reliably informed that Chamberlain had in fact advised annexation and he enlarged upon the concern this had caused the Queen Regent and the government. The Spanish ambassador wrote to Sanderson at the Foreign Office for confirmation. Sanderson's reply is instructive. He explained that Chamberlain had gone to the States for a holiday seeking rest. He had taken no cypher with him and the Colonial Office had not heard a thing from him. Sanderson himself did not know Chamberlain's address and wrote to Pauncefote in an endeavour to contact him. He added that Lord Salisbury was convinced that the press reports were unreliable and that Chamberlain would not have in fact said anything to give offence. The visit, according to the Prime Minister, had no political object whatever.[119] It is of course most unlikely that Chamberlain did not in any way mention or discuss the war with members of his wife's family or with close acquaintances in the United States, but it is equally certain that he would be careful not to intrude political advice in any way upon the public scene or upon the executive especially as the American elections were to be held in November. When shown by Salisbury Wolff's version of Spanish fears and beliefs, Chamberlain cabled a categorical denial. "I did not see nor did I have any communication direct or indirect with any member of the United States Government, and I declined to the reporters to offer any advice as to the way in which the United States Government should deal with the Philippines. Signed C. 10/11."[120]

This carefully negative policy was followed continuously. In September, when the peace commissioners were passing through England on their way to Paris, Henry White requested that Salisbury should receive them in order that they might pay their respects and emphasize the excellent understanding existing at the time between the two countries. The request was refused, and the reasons were thought to be so obvious that they were not enumerated. With the world suspicious of British aims, with Germany, Russia, France, and Japan watching carefully to guard their interests, and with the American elections only a few weeks away, no risks could be taken. White was downcast but saw that it was better that the reception should not take place—they were of course promised a hearty welcome if they returned through England.[121]

During October there was a complete lull in official consideration of the peace question. However, Wolff reported from Spain that Russia had made it clear that she preferred the status quo in the Philippines but as it was realized that this was impossible the alternative was that they should go to the United States but to no one else. This it will be noted was essentially the British view. Wolff's plaintive queries from Madrid continued to plague the Foreign Office and to elicit rather tart replies which accurately summed up the situation. Sanderson in a private telegram to Wolff said bluntly: "We have no news about the Philippines. United States have not in any way confided to us their views and Monson gets no information in Paris [where the peace commissioners were meeting]. United States Government have carefully avoided communicating with us."[122]

That this was in fact the case and not just a statement induced by suspicion of Wolff's Spanish sympathies is confirmed by a private report from Pauncefote two days later. He explained that he had not written during the last few months because there had been a complete lull in the discussion of Anglo-American questions, because of America's preoccupation with the war. He had seen Mr. Hay several times but found him "very reticent" about the peace commission and the "Expansionist policy." He tried to draw Hay into discussion about the future commercial policy in the Philippines if they were annexed by saying that if this policy were to be the same as for Puerto Rico "the acquisition of the Philippines by the United States would hardly be hailed with satisfaction by other nations," but that if Manila were to be made a free port like Hong Kong this would give fresh impetus to trade in China and would induce great prosperity. Hay replied cautiously that it was impossible to predict future policy, but his personal view was that the Puerto Rican regulations would not be applied to such a distant possession as the Philippines, that was of course in the event of annexation.[123]

It was perhaps very fitting that this period of negative relationship between the Anglo-Saxon powers should end with Wolff receiving a final rebuke and Pauncefote sounding a final warning. In January 1899 Wolff enquired whether he should report to the Foreign Office some suggestions concerning the future government of the Philippines and Cuba, suggestions which he had received from several Spaniards who did not wish their names known. Salisbury minuted succinctly: "I think you had much better let the matter alone—it does not concern us."[124] It obviously was of concern to England but it was Salisbury's concern also to keep a still tongue and await the American decision. Once more a letter from Pauncefote confirmed the accuracy of Salisbury's reading of the situation and reflected the fear that for Britishers to advise or to suggest or to interfere in any way might well serve to prevent the achievement of that expansion of the United States into the

Far East so desired by most members of the cabinet. This letter was the one referred to earlier which conveyed Lord Herschell's warning of the use which could be made by the anti-expansionists of any statement which could be shown to prove that to suit her own ends England was encouraging the United States into overseas adventures.[125]

The negative policy pursued by Britain is then clearly demonstrated from the above résumé. In sum total it amounted to two basic principles. The first was merely to let the United States know that no objection would be made if the Philippines were to become American but that if this were not possible then England insisted upon first option to purchase them. This was in fact little different from the attitude of Russia and Japan, each of whom would have preferred the islands to remain Spanish, but as this was impossible they were prepared to recognize American sovereignty. The chief difference was that British policy provided the United States with an alternative to annexation, an alternative which would relieve the executive of any responsibility for an imperialist experiment if this were not desired. The second principle was to stand clear and permit the expansionist mood of the United States executive to take its own course uncomplicated by any charge that Britain was manoeuvring its neighbour into international policies to secure British rather than American interests.

The essence of the whole matter is this. Between March 1897, when Secretary of State Sherman refused point blank to do anything to extend the limits of the territories of the United States, and December 1898 internal United States business and political[126] influences had brought the United States policy in the Pacific to a point where it was roughly parallel to that of the United Kingdom's Asian policy in March 1898. In this process neither the United States expansionists—Lodge, Mahan, and Roosevelt—nor their party throughout Congress and the executive, needed any prompting from the British Foreign Office or British commercial interests to urge action upon

McKinley. In formulating their policy in the Pacific, American officials made their own decisions in their own time and in response to pressures from within the United States.[127] Despite the intensity of the British need for allies, and the deep-rooted and continuing British hope for active co-operation with the United States, the policy of the United Kingdom remained formal and correct and cannot in any way be designated an effort to embroil the United States in the Far East.

Notes

1. FO72/2062, Barclay to F.O., 3 May 1898, and cuttings from the Spanish newspaper *Imparcial* enclosed with the despatch.

2. Wolff reported the Spanish reaction to Chamberlain's speech in FO72/2068, Telegram No. 106, 15 May 1898, and Telegram No. 125, 25 May 1898.

3. FO72/2064, Wolff to F.O., Telegram No. 189, 10 June 1898.

4. *Ibid.*, Telegram No. 192, 12 June 1898.

5. *Ibid.*

6. FO72/2068, Wolff to F.O., Telegram No. 167, Very Secret, 14 June 1898.

7. *Hansard*, LVIII, May-June 1898, 1310.

8. The French government used similar language in the Chamber of Deputies. Reported by Martin Gosselin from Paris, FO27/3394, Telegram No. 156, 17 March 1898.

9. FO72/2068, Wolff to F.O., Telegram No. 131, 27 May 1898.

10. FO5/2364, Salisbury to Pauncefote, Telegram No. 100, 10 May 1898.

11. FO5/2365, Pauncefote to F.O., Telegram No. 68, 16 May 1898.

12. FO72/2067, Salisbury to Wolff, Telegram No. 89, 16 July 1898.

13. FO27/3400, Monson to F.O., Telegram No. 94, 8 June 1898.

14. This appeared in the same article that charged Pauncefote with initiating a second plan for collective action against the United States to prevent the outbreak of war. See above, chap. i.

15. FO5/2364, Salisbury to Pauncefote, Telegram No. 100, 10 May 1898.

16. FO5/2365, Pauncefote to F.O., Telegram No. 82, 11 June 1898.

17. *Ibid.*

18. Dennett, *op. cit.*, p. 190.

19. The section in brackets was Salisbury's second thought to replace the phrase "not to neglect any opportunity for promoting peace." FO5/2365, Pauncefote to F.O., Telegram No. 79, 4 June 1898, Salisbury's Minute.

20. Dennis, *op. cit.*, p. 79. This is not referenced and no record appeared in the Austrian file, neither is there any reference in the Salisbury Papers.

If true, Salisbury probably took the step because of the threat implicit in Mr. Day's statement.

21. FO5/2262, Private Minutes by Rosebery on 25 March 1895 and by Kimberley on 26 March 1895.

22. Salisbury to Hicks Beach, 2 January 1896, Hicks Beach Papers, quoted by J. A. S. Grenville, "Great Britain and the Isthmian Canal," *American Historical Review*, LXI, No. 1 (October 1955), 51.

23. FO5/2290, Private Letter Pauncefote to Bertie, 26 June 1896, prompted by Olney's note of 22 June 1896, re Venezuela.

24. Salisbury Papers, Vol. CXXXIV, Salisbury to Wolff, 17 July 1899.

25. See Salisbury's comment in Gooch and Temperley, *op. cit.*, II, 68: "Count Hatzfeldt [the German ambassador in London] speaks of our isolation as constituting a serious danger for us. Have we ever felt that danger practically . . . ? It would hardly be wise to incur novel and most onerous obligations in order to guard against a danger in whose existence we have no historical reason for believing."

26. *Die Grosse Politik*, Band XV, Nr. 4155, Telegram of 8 July from Hatzfeldt. "Aus allen Ausserungen Lord Salisburys über die Amerikaner habe ich bis jetzt den Eindruck, dass er nur sehr geringes Vertrauen in ihre Freundschaft für England setzt, und es scheint mir daher nicht wahrscheinlich, dass er weittragende politische Pläne verfolgen wird, deren Verwirklichung zum grössten Teil von dieser Freundschaft abhängen würde." See also Dennis, *op. cit.*, p. 85: ". . . privately Lord Salisbury was sceptical concerning American friendship for England."

27. Dugdale, *op. cit.*, p. 225.

28. *Times* (London), 10 November 1898, p. 8, speech at Lord Mayor's Banquet.

29. Olcott, *op. cit.*, II, 135.

30. A. Nevins, *Henry White: Thirty Years of American Diplomacy* (New York and London: Harper & Bros., 1930), p. 140.

31. *Ibid.*, p. 165, White to Hay, 2 November.

32. Drummond Wolff to Salisbury, Gooch and Temperley, *op. cit.*, II No. 300, 253. See above, chap. ii, for the dispute over Gibraltar.

33. FO72/2068, Wolff to F.O., 19 May 1898, and Telegram No. 169 of 15 June 1898.

34. Queen Regent to Queen Victoria, Buckle, *op. cit.*, III, 268.

35. FO72/2068, Wolff to F.O., Telegram No. 167, 14 June 1898.

36. FO7/1276, Rumbold to F.O., Telegram No. 23, 7 June 1898.

37. *Ibid.*, Salisbury to Rumbold, Telegram No. 86, 8 June 1898.

38. *Ibid.*, Rumbold to Salisbury, Telegram No. 25, 10 June 1898.

39. FO115/1075, Copy Telegram No. 83, Madrid to F.O., 10 April 1898.

40. R. H. Heindel, *The American Impact on Great Britain, 1898-1914* (Philadelphia: University of Pennsylvania Press, 1940).

41. Gelber, *op. cit.*

42. *Ibid.*, p. 1.

43. *Ibid.*, p. 8.

44. *Ibid.*, p. 17.

45. Shippee, *op. cit.*, p. 763, translating Kaiser's comment on Holleben's

letter to Hohenlohe, 28 April 1898; *Die Grosse Politik*, Band XV, Nr. 4143.

46. *Boston Herald*, reprinted in Paris edition of *New York Herald* of 20 November. Republished in Spain, this became a source of protest by Spain to the British ambassador in Madrid. FO72/2066, Despatch No. 407 of 22 November 1898.

47. Gwynn, *op. cit.*, pp. 246-47.

48. *Ibid.*, p. 249.

49. H. Adams, *The Education of Henry Adams: An Autobiography* (Boston: Merrymount Press, 1918), pp. 363-64.

50. FO5/2264, Kimberley to Pauncefote, Telegram No. 18, 23 April 1895.

51. Dugdale, *op. cit.*, p. 253.

52. FO5/2364, F.O. to Pauncefote, Telegram No. 18, 7 March 1898.

53. *Ibid.*, Telegram No. 21, 15 March.

54. FO5/2361, Pauncefote to F.O., Telegram No. 13, Confidential, 18 March, and Despatch No. 70, 17 March 1898.

55. *Ibid.*, Despatch No. 70, 17 March 1898.

56. See p. 3.

57. FO72/2084; see below, n. 67.

58. See chap. ii, sec. 1.

59. E.g. *Times* (London), 24 May 1898.

60. FO115/1077, Consul at Manila to F.O., 20 August 1898. There is no comment in Chamberlain's reports to the Admiralty.

61. FO72/2084, Note to Villiers, 3 May 1898.

62. *Ibid.*

63. FO72/2085, 11 June and 15 June, Minutes reporting action.

64. Sanderson told the Japanese that it was most improbable that Spain would risk ceding territory to anyone other than the United States unless for a price, and Germany had nothing to offer as she had no intention of becoming involved with the United States.

65. FO72/2085, Memorial from the British Empire League, 15 June 1898.

66. Letter from Andrew Clarke, Agent-General for Victoria, in *ibid.* There is no mention in the Victorian Parliamentary Debates or press of any such interest on the part of the government.

67. FO72/2084. This memorial also pointed out that a large proportion of imports claimed as Spanish were actually on British account.

68. See p. 120.

69. *Die Grosse Politik*, Band XV, Nr. 4146, n. 2. On Germany's policy generally, see Shippee, *op. cit.*

70. FO72/2068, Wolff to F.O., Nos. 173, 175, 176, 16-18 June 1898.

71. FO5/2378, Memorandum from Balfour, 16 August 1898.

72. *Die Grosse Politik*, Band XV, Nr. 4146. Shippee, *op. cit.*, p. 765, n. 29.

73. See above, chap. i, sec. 2.

74. *Die Grosse Politik*, Band XV, Nr. 4151.

75. In February 1899 Germany purchased from Spain the Carolines, the Pelew, and the remainder of the Marianne Islands. J. F. Rippy, *Latin America in World Politics* (New York: A. A. Knopf & Co., 1931), pp. 173-77.

76. FO115/1077, Salisbury to Satow, Telegram No. 59, 27 July 1898.

77. *Ibid.*, Satow to Salisbury, Telegram No. 97, 6 June 1898.

78. FO5/2378, Memorandum from Balfour to F.O., 16 August 1898.

79. FO5/2362, Pauncefote to F.O., Despatch No. 217, 27 June 1898. See also *New York Times*, 23 June 1898, and *New York Tribune*, 24 June 1898.

80. FO72/2066, Wolff reporting the Russian ambassador to Spain. Wolff to F.O., Telegram No. 350, 2 October 1898.

81. The most detailed study in existence of the development of Britain's China policy is N. A. Pelcovits, *Old China Hands and the Foreign Office* (New York: King's Crown Press, 1948).

82. These firms worked through the China Association and the Associated Chambers of Commerce. See *ibid.*

83. See the China Association Letter to Lord Salisbury, 2 November 1896, in *ibid.*, pp. 200-201.

84. FO17/1337, Minute by Salisbury on a letter from MacDonald to Beresford enclosed in a private letter to Bertie at the F.O., 27 November 1898.

85. E.g. see the opinions of Sir William Harcourt and the Lord President of the Council, *Hansard*, 1898, LVI, 5 April, 239-51 and 166.

86. Quoted Pelcovits, *op. cit.*, p. 229. Author's italics.

87. FO17/1339, Salisbury to MacDonald, Telegram No. 310, Secret, 22 October 1898.

88. See p. 180.

89. FO17/1337, Beresford to MacDonald, 27 November 1898.

90. A draft scheme for the reorganization of the Chinese army by British officers was actually prepared by Sir John Ardagh, the Director-General of Military Intelligence, on 16 June 1898. The report was forwarded to Sir Claude MacDonald in China and discussed at length by Lieutenant-Colonel G. F. Browne, military attaché in China. *Ibid.*, F.O., to MacDonald, Despatch No. 100, 22 June 1898; also MacDonald to F.O., Despatch No. 214, 28 October 1898.

91. FO17/1341, MacDonald to F.O. at request of Beresford, 23 October 1898.

92. *Ibid.*, Telegram No. 332, Sir Claude MacDonald to F.O. at request of Lord Charles Beresford, 7 November 1898.

93. This is the central thesis elaborated by Pelcovits, i.e. that the British government refused to attempt to make China another India, "when the Board of Trade announced to the rest of Whitehall that the China trade would never be worth the expense of war or sovereignty." Pelcovits, *op. cit.*, Preface.

94. FO17/1339, Salisbury to MacDonald, Telegram No. 313, 8 November 1898.

95. *Hansard*, 1898, LVI, 5 April, 223-29.

96. FO17/1340, F.O. to MacDonald, Secret, 25 February 1898.

97. E.g. *Foreign Relations of the United States, 1898*, Instructions to Peace Commissioners, 16 September 1898. See pp. 907-8 for McKinley's views.

98. E.g. *Times* (London), 28 November 1898.

99. FO115/1077, Salisbury to Satow, Despatch No. 59, 27 July 1898.

100. Hay to Secretary of State, quoted Dennett, *op. cit.*, p. 191.

101. The approach of December 1898—January 1899 was merely for conjoint action to prevent France from extending her concessions in Shanghai. The general argument developed from here on is supported by J. A. S. Grenville. See his reference to an early article by the present author in Grenville, *op. cit.*, p. 51, n. 7.

102. Campbell, Jr., *op. cit.*, p. 41.

103. See particularly Reuter, *op. cit.*, Campbell, Jr., *op. cit.*, Gelber, *op. cit.*, Heindel, *op. cit.*, and A. E. Campbell, *Great Britain and the United States 1895-1903* (London: Longmans, Green & Co., 1960), chap. v.

104. Salisbury Papers, Vol. CXXXIX, America From and To 1895-98, No. 72, Pauncefote to Salisbury, 26 May 1898.

105. 22 April 1898. Buckle, *op. cit.*, III, 224.

106. Salisbury Papers, Vol. CXL, America From and To 1899-1900, No. 162, Pauncefote to Salisbury, 3 February 1899.

107. See p. 167.

108. Gwynn, *op. cit.*, I, 246-47.

109. *Ibid.*, p. 251.

110. See *ibid.*, pp. 51-55 for an interesting summary of Spring Rice's American experiences.

111. *Ibid.*, pp. 250-51.

112. A. W. Griswold, *The Far Eastern Policy of the United States* (New York: Harcourt Brace & Co., 1938), p. 52 quoting from Nevins, *op. cit.*, p. 166.

113. White to Olney, 17 June 1896. Text in James, *op. cit.*, p. 244.

114. Dennett, *op. cit.*, p. 190.

115. See p. 112.

116. Dennett, *op. cit.*, p. 191.

117. See p. 133.

118. FO5/2378, Memorandum in Balfour's handwriting dated F.O. 16 August 1898.

119. FO72/2083, copy of Sanderson's letter 25 September 1898. This lack of news at the Colonial Office was a fact and was not a fabrication to placate Wolff and Spain. This is quite apparent from a survey of Colonial Office files for the period concerned.

120. Salisbury Papers, Vol. CXXXIII, No. 54.

121. *Ibid.*, Vol. CXL, America From and To 1898-1900, No. 64, Henry White to Salisbury.

122. FO72/2067, Sanderson to Wolff, Private, 9 November 1898.

123. Salisbury Papers, Vol. CXXXIX, America From and To 1895-98, No. 75, Pauncefote to Salisbury, 11 November 1898.

124. *Ibid.*, Vol. CXXXIV, No. 1, Wolff to Salisbury, 12 January 1899.

125. See p. 138.

126. J. W. Pratt, "The 'Large Policy' of 1898," *Mississippi Valley Historical Review*, XIX (1932), 219-42.

127. C. S. Campbell, Jr., *Special Business Interests and the Open Door Policy* (New Haven, Conn.: Yale University Press, 1951).

Diplomacy After the War

IV

IT is a difficult task to assess the importance of the Spanish-American War in post-war Anglo-American relations. In the past, great claims have been made for it, but in such a manner as to claim all and yet in the same breath to claim nothing. For example, Allen agreed with Gelber that the period saw the development of an understanding between England and America which must because of its after-effects "take first rank" among "the decisive events of modern history."[1] Nevertheless, Allen qualified this assessment by adding that "the understanding hardly reached the stage of positive co-operation, let alone of actual alliance."[2] Similarly Gelber emphasized the "deep and historic significance" of the Anglo-American rapprochement in which the year 1898 was "a turning point," yet pointed out that "international affairs could not wait upon the sluggish evolution of American politics, finance and statesmanship,"[3] and as a result of America's refusal to co-operate in March 1898, Great Britain had to seek elsewhere for methods of stabilizing the Far East. A third assessment of the quality of the Anglo-American relationship during and immediately after 1898 is provided by Griswold,[4] who implied that Great Britain played an important part in influencing the formation of America's post-war policy in the Far East, just as she did in the formation of America's policy toward the Philippines.

These seeming contradictions have arisen, I believe, because of a failure to distinguish sufficiently between the effects of the war upon public opinion in England and its effects upon opinion in the United States and, further, because of a failure to distinguish accurately between expressions of public opinion and actual diplomatic negotiations. The first point can be demonstrated from known and published material and therefore will be dealt with very briefly. The second point can be demonstrated from a more detailed examination of Anglo-American diplomacy after 1898.

I

It must be admitted immediately that during the war English and American expressions of public opinion achieved an unprecedented degree of cordiality. The first highlight was Hay's speech at the Lord Mayor's Banquet in April, in which he developed the theme that "the good understanding between us is based on something deeper than expediency. All who think cannot but see there is a sanction like that of religion which binds us in partnership in the serious work of the world. . . . We are joint ministers in the same sacred mission of freedom and progress, charged with duties we cannot evade by the imposition of irresistible hands."[5] [*sic*]. This was followed by Chamberlain's great Birmingham speech of 13 May in which he startled the world by saying "I go even so far as to say that terrible as war may be, even war itself would be cheaply purchased if, in a great and noble cause, the Stars and Stripes and the Union Jack would wave together over an Anglo-Saxon alliance."[6] Even Richard Olney, the former Secretary of State, renowned for his bitterness toward England over the Venezuelan dispute, published his remarkable article on "The International Isolation of the United States."[7] Only his own words can do justice to the revolution in his attitude.

There is a patriotism of race as well as of country—and the Anglo-American is as little likely to be indifferent to the one as to the other. Family quarrels there have been heretofore and doubtless will be again, and the two peoples, at the safe distance which the broad Atlantic interposes, take with each other liberties of speech which only the fondest and dearest relatives indulge in. Nevertheless, that they would be found standing together against any alien foe by whom either was menaced with destruction or irreparable calamity, it is not permissible to doubt. Nothing less could be expected of the close community between them in origin, speech, thought, literature, institutions, ideals—in the kind and degree of the civilization enjoyed by both.[8]

Sometimes coloured by a cynical appreciation of Britain's needs, sometimes by a realistic awareness of the similarity of Anglo-American interests in the Far East, these sentiments were reflected in most of the leading papers and journals on both sides of the Atlantic. This has been conclusively demonstrated in the surveys of public opinion carried out by Reuter and by Heindel.[9] They have shown that the period of the war, particularly for England and to a lesser extent for America, was an occasion for an extensive exercise in mutually effusive expressions of goodwill. This was due in the first place to a coincidence in time between America's experiment in imperialism and Britain's realization of the dangers involved in an isolation no longer glorious. It was due to a mutual sense of isolation, to a common fear and suspicion of Germany, and to a confused yet widespread and sincere belief in an identity of economic interests in the Far East. It was due also to Britain's friendly neutrality, to the myth of her assistance in Manila Bay, and to the determined efforts of Balfour, Chamberlain, Hay, and Pauncefote.

The effect of this war-time exercise was lasting in England. The public became convinced of the desirability of a policy upon which the cabinet had already acted and upon which it was to continue to act, namely that friendly relations between America and Britain were necessary to British security. The best example of this is the popular support in England for active co-operation with America in maintaining the open door in the Far East,[10] and the use by Chamberlain of the catch-cry of co-operation with America in the elections of 1900.[11] However, in America no such lasting effects were obvious. In fact by the time of the Boer War, much of American public opinion was positively hostile to Britain's African policy. But even while American public opinion was still predominantly friendly, that is in the period immediately after the Spanish-American War, there remained enough of the traditional American Anglophobia and it remained so latently powerful that it was in fact a deterrent to any effective co-operation between the powers. In fact in the opinion of Hay (now Secretary of State) it was even a positive hindrance to the adoption of policies most suited to America's needs, if it could be shown by his political opponents that such policies were those followed by England. This Anglophobia had been used very effectively by Cleveland and Olney as well as by Cleveland's Republican opponents, and both Hay and Pauncefote found it severely restricted their actions. It may have been, as Allen[12] claims, drained of much of its poison by the Spanish-American War, but it still remained a potent force in American politics to be used, particularly at election times, by those either opposed to Anglo-American co-operation, or by those prepared to use it merely as a weapon of party politics. Its presence was known and feared by those in the executive whose conviction it was that Britain and America should deal harmoniously together. Hay, writing to Henry White in 1899, could say of the Democrats: "All their State conventions put the Anti-English plank in their platform to curry favour with the Irish (whom they want to keep) and the Germans (whom they want to seduce). It is too disgusting to have to deal with such sordid liars."[13]

One reason why Pauncefote was so successful an ambassador in the very difficult Washington post was his ability accurately and realistically to assess both the value of American expressions of goodwill and the latent dangers of Anglophobia. He was always sceptical of sentimental effusions but welcomed them as an aid to agreement over vital issues. More than this, after the passage of time had soothed the indignation aroused in his mind by America's attack upon Spain he even came to believe that there was a degree of sincerity in American expressions of goodwill; but he never let this blind him to the political capital which would be manufactured by the opponents of Anglo-American accord from any public expressions of friendship. His scepticism of war-time friendship was most marked in May 1898. He reported to Salisbury "the most astonishing feature" of the transition from Anglophobia to "the most exuberant affection for England and 'Britishers' in general" but added "how long the fit will last no wise man would venture to predict." However he believed that while it lasted it would have an excellent effect upon the future relations between the two countries and would help in a settlement of the Canadian difficulties.[14]

In February 1899 he warned the Foreign Office of Lord Herschell's opinion that any enthusiastic reference to the friendship between England and the United States would be used in America by the anti-expansionists and would endanger the success of the Joint High Commission sitting in Washington.[15] In November 1899 the extremely hostile reaction to Chamberlain's speech at Leicester and a careful reporting of this by the *Times* confirmed the accuracy of Pauncefote's and Herschell's fears.[16] This outcry completely justified Pauncefote's caution in concealing his assistance to John Hay in January 1899 in the first draft convention dealing with the attempted modification of the Clayton-Bulwer Treaty which stood in the way of America's intention to construct and defend an isthmian canal.

Not until 1901 was his full contribution made known to the Foreign Office and Pauncefote had specifically suggested to Lord Lansdowne that the part he played in the draft, even though it had been at Hay's request, should remain secret because of the opposition to Hay as an Anglophile.[17] By January 1900 Pauncefote had come to believe to a degree in the sincerity of the friendship for England on the part of some of the United States executive but he never permitted this to blind him to the limitations imposed upon it by the opponents of England and by the tactics of party conflicts in America. In the midst of the Boer troubles he reported to the Foreign Office that "the general sentiment and attitude of the nation" concerning the war in South Africa "is as reasonable and friendly as can be expected given the agitation kept up against us by the Irish, Germans, Dutch and others." There were great entertainments at the White House and a very "marked warmth and friendliness" by the President and all the cabinet to Pauncefote personally. He commented that this was "evidentally intended to show their desire to maintain and promote the Entente Cordiale and the 'Unwritten Treaty' which undoubtedly exists in spite of the outcry about the word alliance." However having reported this, the good side of the question, he felt bound again to sound the warning that it was necessary to remember that this was the presidential year and that the government would not lay itself open to any charge of Anglophilia.[18]

These twin themes of friendship at the executive level and nevertheless an inability to co-operate actively in diplomatic ventures were a constant feature of Pauncefote's letters to his Prime Minister. They appear again in his report that Holleben (the German ambassador) endeavoured to win the United States to Germany's side over the Samoan affair but that he "met with nothing but snubs." Similarly Count Arturo Cassini (the Russian ambassador) "much to the amusement of Mr. Hay" ridiculed the "open door" and "spheres of influence" which he affected not to comprehend. But in the same letter Pauncefote closed with the glum statement that the United States would not back up China in rejecting Italy's claim to San Mun Bay.

"The United States intends to keep out of the China question unless their treaty rights are threatened. They have enough on their hands at Manila."[19]

The depth of his concern with and fear of this Anglophobia was effectively demonstrated in a trivial incident in 1900, and it is the very triviality of the affair which lends great significance to the importance attached to it in America. In January 1899, on behalf of Sir F. Mowate of the Pacific Cable Company, Pauncefote was instructed by Salisbury[20] to "sound Mr. Hay" as to the possibility of the sale or exchange of some island in the Hawaiian group suitable for a cable station. The object was to ensure exclusive control of a cable line across the Pacific. Pauncefote's reply, sent after "many private and confidential communications with Mr. Hay," is worth quoting in full:

Mr. Hay after consulting his colleagues very secretly, assures me that any cession of an American Island by way of sale or exchange would require the assent of two-thirds of the Senate which it is hopeless to expect in the present conditions of politics in this country. He believes that the Senate would not even sanction a *lease*. But the Executive has power independently of Congress to grant any public Company landing privileges for cables, and the United States Government would favourably consider any application for such landing privileges in Necker Island under conditions which would practically be a lease of that Island which is little better than a barren rock. If that idea were entertained the quid pro quo would be the laying of a connecting cable with Honolulu and of a cable between Fiji and Samoa. It is useless however to go further into the matter until I learn whether mere landing rights on Necker Island are worth having. If so the conditions of such a grant and the consideration for it can be discussed later on. The present administration are very nervous in view of the coming Presidential election and the Anti-British agitation which is being fomented by the Irish and German voters and they would not dare to grant even *landing rights* on Necker Island to a British Company until *after* the election.[21]

If it is in the field of practical peace-time politics that the quality of Anglo-American understanding should be tested then this incident is surely instructive. It demonstrates quite clearly the friendly attitude toward Britain at work in the American executive led by Hay, and with equal clarity it reveals the limitation imposed upon the executive by the continuing existence in the United States of an Anglophobia capable of stultifying any practical understanding between England and America.

II

An even more accurate estimate of the nature of any understanding which might have existed between England and America can be obtained by an examination of the actual diplomatic relations between the two countries quite separately from public opinion. This can be done at two levels, firstly in the attempts to settle the issues in the American hemisphere still in dispute and which involved only America and Britain or British imperial interests, and secondly in the general international situation in the Far East.

The details of the Venezuelan dispute, of the problem of the Alaskan boundary and the questions which formed the agenda of the Joint High Commission which met first in August 1898, and of the isthmian canal problem, have been exhaustively presented and studied for many years and the facts are too well known to warrant repetition.[22] However the effect of the Spanish-American War upon the attempts to settle these difficulties has not been placed in its true perspective. If the war was such a watershed in British-American affairs surely its effects should have been most marked during the period 1898 to 1899 when feeling between the two nations was at its friendliest. The crucial test is to discover whether this friendship initiated, facilitated, accelerated, or determined in any way the nature of the settlement of the issues at stake. Without recapitulating the details, several pertinent facets of these very controversial negotiations when brought together will place the effects of the Spanish-American War upon Anglo-American relations in their proper perspective.

It is evident to begin with that apart from the canal question the attempts to negotiate agreements over outstanding issues were not initiated by the war-time rapprochement at all. In fact, of course, the rapprochement began in 1896 over the Venezuelan affair and not over the Spanish-American War. At a time when Britain was isolated and threatened with the hostility of the great European powers, Germany's reaction to the Jameson Raid and the Kaiser's telegram to Kruger in January 1896 underlined the urgency of Britain's need to settle peaceably her dispute with the United States. By February 1897 before the Spanish-American War broke out, the Treaty of Washington was signed, thus prescribing the conditions of the arbitration which brought in the award of October 1899. The intention at the executive level to settle, and to settle amicably, any outstanding differences was evident again in the Olney-Pauncefote convention of arbitration of January 1897, which was supported by the British parliament but rejected by the United States Senate. Similarly the Joint High Commission which began its controversial career in August 1898—the month of the armistice between Spain and America—was not in any way an outcome of the war-time relationship. All the issues involved antedated the war. The North Atlantic fisheries, the fur seals dispute both in the Behring Sea and concerning pelagic sealing, the question of commercial reciprocity and the American tariff, and above all the Canadian boundary dispute, had embittered relations between Canada, the United Kingdom, and the United States for many years. The only thing added by the war was the problem of the effect of the American tariff upon Canadian traders and shipping interests if it were applied to the former Spanish territories in the Caribbean and the Pacific.

Just as the substance of the difficulties antedated the war, so did the preliminary negotiations leading to the establishment of the Joint High Commission. The 1893 agreement which had terminated the Behring Sea sealing dispute was initially for five years and was due to be reviewed automatically in August 1898. However, Senator John W. Foster, the spokesman for the North American Commercial Company, raised the issue in 1897 in a different and more difficult form by proposing that all pelagic sealing should be prohibited in a determined attempt to prevent the destruction of the seal herds. An unsuccessful conference on this subject between the United Kingdom, Canada, and the United States met in October 1897. Mr. Foster then proposed that a commission should be established to attempt a settlement of all outstanding Anglo-American problems. This was dependent upon Britain's accepting his suggestion that a conference of naturalists should be convened to make recommendations which should be binding for the amendment of the sealing agreements. Pauncefote advised against this and Salisbury agreed with him. Their opposition was because of the difficulty of dealing with the very able but very pugnacious and uncompromising Senator Foster. The actual suggestion for the Joint High Commisison as finally established was made by President McKinley in a discussion with Pauncefote on 10 March 1898, five weeks before the outbreak of war.

The isthmian canal question had been the subject of the Clayton-Bulwer Treaty in 1850, and in August 1898 notice was served upon the British government that the question of its revision was soon to be raised by the President. The discussion was initiated in an atmosphere of goodwill but in such a way as to make clear that the United States intended to build the canal and to control it. Mr. Holls informed Balfour on 16 August 1898 that President McKinley would probably raise the matter in his next presidential message. This in fact happened on 5 December 1898. Balfour's memorandum of the relevant part of the interview with Holls reads as follows:

It appears that the United States government are contemplating, as a national undertaking, the construction of an inter-oceanic canal. They have not yet decided whether it is to be at Panama or Nicaragua but they are determined that in either event it shall belong to them and their idea is that whatever be the state through which it is constructed a strip of land 40 miles wide running on each side of it is to be bought by the United States and become part of their territory.[23]

In these circumstances it is hardly possible to see the improvement in relations between the two countries during the Spanish-American War as the chief reason for the attempts to settle all differences, but it might well be surmised that the more favourable atmosphere in which these attempts were made might have facilitated agreement. It was for this, it will be remembered, that Pauncefote hoped when commenting to Salisbury upon the extraordinary development of a public opinion favourable to Great Britain.[24] But even this was not to be. By February 1899 the Joint High Commission had been adjourned without having reached any decision, for although near a agreement on some minor issues the Canadian boundary problem was as far from solution as ever, drifting until the final settlement in 1903. In the same month, February 1899, negotiations on another most important matter at issue between the two friendly countries collapsed because of America's refusal to relate the adjustment of the Clayton-Bulwer Treaty to any other issue and Britain's refusal to adjust unless agreement could be reached on those other issues.

Many things contributed to these notable failures. The increased self-confidence and the freedom of manoeuvre afforded the United States by the armistice in August 1898 (the victory had been conclusive and overwhelming and the need for support had greatly decreased); the play of special interests in the United States and Canada; the unilateralism so apparent in the United States, and her determination to solve all issues not by compromise but entirely to suit the congressional conception of national needs; Salisbury's refusal to negotiate under pressure; the skill and the single-mindedness of Senator Foster leading to heated clashes with Lord Herschell; all these things go to explain why friendship at the personal level in the United States executive and the British cabinet was quite insufficient to achieve agreement. But this is merely another way of stating the problem in its true light, namely that international disputes between friendly countries, and in particular these disputes between America and Britain, are and were settled upon a basis of hardheaded realistic appreciation of the national interests and not upon sentimental effusions of international fellowship. In the positive sense the desire to foster friendly relations with the United States was certainly the aim of British statesmen and in the negative sense the intention of settling differences and disputes by peaceful methods rather than by war was widespread in the United States legislature and executive. But in no case was "friendship" an element weighed against national interest and valued as such in the diplomatic bargaining during and immediately following the Spanish-American War.

Despite Mr. Hay's urgency in presenting to the British government the draft conventions for the revision of the Clayton-Bulwer Treaty, and despite, if not because of, the latent hostility of congressional bills dealing with the canal problem, Lord Salisbury refused to be hurried or rushed into any action. The matter was referred in the usual way to Intelligence, to the Admiralty, to the Board of Trade, and to Canada for comment before it was raised at cabinet level. Although the Board of Trade was reasonably disposed, the opposition of strategic considerations and Canada's interests is clear in Salisbury's reply to Hay.

The Cabinet to whom I submitted question of the Clayton-Bulwer Treaty felt that the force of the U.S. navy would in war be doubled by the project. They are adverse to obstructing what may be of value to commerce, but they fear that if they yield a point so entirely to the advantage of the United States without some diminution at least of the causes which might bring the two countries into conflict there would be a serious dissatisfaction here.[25]

Just as the United Kingdom was endeavouring to preserve its vital interests and those of its empire by refusing to retreat from a position entirely justified in international law, without receiving due compensation elsewhere, so the United States was determined not to be forced into any position where such a bargain might appear logical. For this reason they steadfastly refused to deal with any question in association with that of the canal or the Canadian boundary. The breakdown of February 1899 was inevitable. Further proof of the hard-headedness of the canal negotiations lies of course in the fact that they were not renewed until the Boer War and the united hostility of the European powers recreated in a more dangerous way the situation of 1896. This forced the United Kingdom again to agree to a settlement upon American terms. It was this threat to Britain's security that forced cabinet's retreat from the demand for a settlement on the basis of a fair compromise to a position where it had to bring pressure to bear upon Canada to agree both to the settlement of the boundary question and to withdraw her insistence that the boundary should be settled in conjunction with that of the isthmian canal. This process was greatly facilitated by Lansdowne's appointment to the Foreign Office in succession to Salisbury.

The hard-headed intention of American leaders, other than Mr. Hay, to settle affairs in their own way, in their own interests, and without considerations of friendship, shows in both great and small issues. Campbell has shown that for reasons of local politics it was necessary for the American representatives of the Joint High Commission to oppose any settlement of the fisheries dispute, which was opposed by the New England fishing interests centred in Boston, Massachusetts. Lord Herschell commented to Lord Salisbury that it "seemed strange that it should be regarded as more important to conciliate a single town in one of the States than, at the risk of giving offence to the inhabitants of that town, to ensure a satisfactory settlement with Great Britain." He added that it was not what he had been led to expect "when assured of the very strong amicable sentiment which now animated the people of the United States."[26] At the other extreme the hostile activities of the Senate in threatening unilateral abrogation of the Clayton-Bulwer Treaty and in amending and reamending a draft treaty submitted to it provide excellent examples of the hard-headed realism which determined America's action. Finally, in the boundary question, President Theodore Roosevelt's intention to run the boundary desired by the United States and to defend it despite what the British wished is hardly an example of international action based upon friendship.

It would appear then that the practical effect of the Spanish-American War upon the development of the rapprochement between the Anglo-Saxon powers has been greatly exaggerated. All the great issues between the two existed before the war. The British decision to seek American co-operation and to seek a settlement of disputes was the result of the threat inherent in the Venezuelan crisis and the evidence it provided of the dangers of isolation. The friendship and goodwill so effusively expressed during the war were quite ineffective in achieving any settlement, or in preventing the breakdown of negotiations between the two nations. Finally, the British capitulation to American demands was a reflection of the degree of Britain's need, of the strength of European threats to her security during the Boer War, and of the strength of America's determination if necessary to determine the issues in her favour by unilateral action. Hay could complain bitterly and truly in reply to charges that he was acting in England's interests: "All I have ever done with England is to have wrung great concessions out of her with no compensation."[27] The history of the negotiations and the nature of the settlement of the disputes demonstrate once again that the basic condition of Anglo-American understanding was the accommodation of Britain's international commitments to suit the unilateralism of the United States Senate.

III

In the international scene as a whole, the most notable and the most controversial issue upon which to test the nature of Britain's relationship with the United States in the immediate post-war situation is in the Far East. What was the nature of the relationship between the two powers in the diplomatic issues involved in the formulation and despatch of, as well as the response to, the open door notes? Both nations were involved territorially in the Far East, both were known opponents of any territorial partition of China, and of any restriction upon foreign trade with her. Did these common interests together with the recent war-time friendship lead to the adoption of a co-operative policy in the Far East, and more specifically, did the British executive seek to influence the United States to adopt this policy?[28] These questions have puzzled diplomatic historians[29] for many years, for the relevant documents were not published in the *British Documents on the Origins of the World War 1898-1914*, despite the fact that these do include a great number of other papers referring to the Far East. In the absence of this definitive official Foreign Office and cabinet material a wide variety of interpretations have appeared, each suggesting a different degree of collaboration or understanding, and each assuming a different channel through which British influence upon the United States executive was exerted. As the Salisbury Papers in addition to the relevant British archival material have become available it is possible to assess this variety of opinion with greater accuracy.

The September open door note was drawn up and submitted to the European powers by Secretary of State Hay. Since 1928 it has been known that this note was drawn up upon the advice of W. W. Rockhill, a personal friend of Hay and one who had previously spent many years in China as diplomat and student. Rockhill's advice, however, was based upon that which he himself received from a friend, Alfred Hippesley,[30] who was visiting Rockhill in the United States at this time. Hippesley was an Englishman working in the Chinese Customs service under Sir Robert Hart and the September note bears a striking resemblance to Hippesley's letter to Rockhill. This sequence of advice from Hippesley to Rokhill to Hay led Fairbank to conclude that "in its origins the Open Door was an Anglo-American defensive measure in power politics. . . ."[31] The implication of the whole of the argument is that the British government played some active part in the process by which Hay received the expert advice that decided his action. Fairbank argued: "It has never been adequately emphasized that Hippesley was not an isolated individual. He had been one of the closest co-workers and assistants of Robert Hart. . . . It should be borne in mind that the Maritime Customs was the mechanism which fostered the British commercial interest in China."[32] The proof of this British Customs influence in Fairbank's view is that the first note was concerned primarily with the Customs problem and did not refer to the integrity of China or to measures to prevent the extension of spheres of influence; it referred largely to the tariff, to reduced freight charges, and to port dues. Not until July 1900, in an effort to prevent any further Russian encroachment, did Hay's supplementary note raise the question of the integrity of China.

Another English proponent of the open door was Lord Charles Beresford, "a quasi-official British propagandist who circled the globe in 1899 urging a joint Anglo-American policy in the Orient."[33] Griswold described the tour as "one long after-dinner speech in favour of the Open Door."[34] Beresford had interviewed Hay before leaving London and wrote to him from China telling him of the enthusiasm of Americans resident in China for the open door. The United States consul-general in Hong Kong wrote Hay that Beresford's chief hope was to "enlist the sympathies" of the United States in the cause of the open door and his speeches to American Chambers of Commerce and to the American Asiatic Association as well as his book[35] bear out this assertion.

The third individual proponent of the open door, who was subject to British influence and most influential in the development of the United States policy, was of course John Hay. As United States ambassador in England and as Secretary of State he was an enthusiastic Anglophile, perfectly at home in English society and in the English diplomatic circle. Friendly with Balfour and Salisbury and an intimate of Chamberlain's, he was a strong supporter of cabinet's attempt to reach an accord with the United States not only upon all outstanding disputes between the two powers but in international action. When Secretary of State he summed up his own policy in these terms: "As long as I stay here, no action shall be taken contrary to my conviction that the one indispensable feature of our foreign policy should be a friendly understanding with England."[36] Typical of his friendly attitude and of his accord with British estimates of the Far Eastern situation was his personal letter to President McKinley[37] in June 1898 (after his return from Egypt), in which he again raised the subject of Pauncefote's proposal of 8 March that the United States should stand with Great Britain to prevent any partition of China. His letter urged McKinley to reconsider the previous refusal.

Those who see British influence behind the American enunciation of the open door doctrine highlight the activities of Hippesley and Beresford and the importance of Hay's English experience, by placing them against a background designed to reveal a consistent pattern of "unremitting pressure"[38] brought to bear by Britain upon America in order to influence her to adopt those policies most suited to British needs. It is pointed out that the open door was traditionally Britain's Far Eastern policy. In 1898, it had for so long been Britain's policy that it could be referred to in parliament by Balfour as "that phrase that has been quoted and requoted *ad nauseam.*"[39] It is recalled that in March 1898 Britain formally sought the collaboration of the United States in maintaining China against the aggression of the other European powers. The investigations of public opinion made by Reuter, Heindel, and Vaghts are used to show the growth of a public opinion in favour of Anglo-American collaboration and even of an Anglo-American alliance. "Concurrently [with this development of opinion] the open door policy was proclaimed so loudly and so consistently by Cabinet officers, members of parliament and journalists as to suggest the desire to impress it on other countries than England."[40] Although it is admitted that the requests were refused, it is emphasized that even as late as December 1898 MacDonald in China and in January 1899 Pauncefote in Washington sought the "conjoint action" of the United States with England to prevent the French attempt to enlarge their Shanghai concession.[41] It is argued that Hay had an intimate knowledge of British policy, that he realized that Great Britain might leave the United States a free hand in the New World in return for co-operation in Asia, and that he endeavoured to take advantage of this to aid him in his efforts to secure the revision of the Clayton-Bulwer Treaty and hence the control of the future isthmian canal. This point gains added significance if it is considered in relation to the claim that Britain found the open door notes extremely gratifying[42] and "that they undoubtedly helped Hay in adjusting the Isthmian question and the Alaskan boundary disputes."

It is argued further that although there is no evidence of a diplomatic bargain the net result of this phase of Anglo-American relations was "that Britain got out of the Caribbean and the United States got into Asia."[43] The final touch to this background picture is the continual suggestion that British officials sought, in the minds of the United States executive, to sow distrust of other European powers.[44] Spring Rice for instance, working through Hay,[45] fed the growing suspicion of Germany, and Foreign Office officials sought frequently to warn the United States Secretary of State against France and particularly against Russia. Furthermore, Britain's "sedulous courting of American favour" during the war with Spain is said to have convinced the Americans that British and American interests in the Far East were identical and that Germany and Russia were the common enemy.

If this method is adopted of drawing into one sequence or pattern all the varieties of official action, of pressure group activity, and of the public expression of popular ideas, it does give the impression of unremitting pressure upon the United States. However, to highlight the Beresford and Hippesley stories in this way is to throw them completely out of focus. It is to suggest a unity of effort and an inter-relationship which just did not exist. It is to suggest also a cumulative effect that has been grossly exaggerated.

The first and basic fallacy in this line of argument is the assumption that the United States needed any conversion to the open door doctrine. It was almost as much a tradition with the United States traders and government as it was with the British government that trade privileges should be shared equally by all Western nationals trading in China.[46] This was the inevitable corollary of the refusal by the United States to take "ulterior" measures to ensure that equal participation in the China trade which was the constant demand of United States merchants and of their government.[47] In 1844, with the Treaty of Whanghea, the successful conclusion of most favoured nation agreements with China safeguarded by treaty that equality of trading rights which was the essence of what was later formulated as the open door doctrine. The only difference between the United States and Britain was that when it was within her power, and necessary in the pursuit of her interests, the United Kingdom either alone or in co-operation with other European powers was prepared to use force to achieve her ends. The policy of the United States on the other hand alterternated between blunt refusal to co-operate (as in the 1857 attempt by Britain and France to obtain the co-operation of the United States in a joint attempt at treaty reform) and the active cooperation of the sixties when Seward was Secretary of State. However, the United States was consistent in that whether in isolated or co-operative action most favoured nation treatment and hence equality of trading rights and privileges were always demanded. This was pointed out many years ago by Dennett, who argued the thesis that "in the nineteenth century, the issue in American policy in Asia was not the open door. That was never a question. The real issue was whether the United States should follow an isolated or cooperative policy to make sure of the open door."[48] This being so, the only way in which England could influence American policy in 1898 was in the clearer formulation of the open door as a code of commercial conduct, in extending it to protect China's territorial and administrative integrity, and in leading the United States once more into a co-operative effort to support or enforce this policy. The question thus becomes, did the British Foreign Office attempt this?

That the United Kingdom desired co-operation with the United States is quite certain, the clearest evidence being the formal approach made to the Secretary of State in March 1898; but it is equally certain that neither Beresford nor Hippesley was acting on behalf of the Foreign Office. That they were so acting, and that they were pressing the United States to accept a policy designed by the British Foreign Office, is the second false assumption commonly accepted. As very little has hitherto been known of Beresford's famous tour of China, Japan, and the United States, it will be necessary to examine in some detail the nature of his relationship with the Foreign Office and the Chambers of Commerce.

There is no question about Beresford's views on the open door and the desirability of Anglo-American co-operation, or if possible and necessary Anglo-American-Japanese-German co-operation in keeping the "door" open. His constant demands in parliament for stronger action in defence of British interests in China against the sphere of influence policies of Russia, France, and Germany, the repetitive theme of his speeches to and interviews with consuls, ambassadors, merchant deputations, and traders' associations throughout China and Japan, were merely the prelude to his lecturing on the same theme throughout the United States. His report to his sponsors, the Chambers of Commerce, took the form of a book, *The Break-up of China*. It repeated his demands for action and his pleas for Anglo-American co-operation in preserving for the world and for England the vast commercial opportunities of the Chinese market.[49] The question at issue is whether or not Beresford was, as he constantly asserted, making his investigation merely as a representative of the Chambers of Commerce or whether he was in some way a "quasi-official" agent of the British Foreign Office seeking to influence American opinion to serve the interests of British policy.

There would seem to be reasonable grounds for the traditional and contemporary view that Beresford was something more than a private personage representing solely the Chambers of Commerce and interested only in furthering British trade in China and in doing his private and unofficial best to spread the doctrine of the open door and of British-American collaboration. A strong, even headstrong, personality, he was a personage to be reckoned with and had a very close association with the "establishment" in England. He was a member of parliament, on two occasions holdings seats for Salisbury's party. He was a friend of Disraeli and Lord Randolph Churchill, and was a former aide-de-camp to and close friend of the Prince of Wales. The Prince's influence with Salisbury, while insufficient to win high political office for Beresford, was sufficient to have him appointed the Fourth Naval Lord under Lord George Hamilton. He was commended in parliament and decorated for his naval services in Egypt and the Mediterranean and was promoted rear-admiral in September 1897. Beresford had as far as is known never been a member of the Chambers of Commerce, certainly he had never been a member of the executive committee nor had he held any office in the organization.[50] It seems very odd that a man with such a background should be chosen to conduct an investigation for an organization solely concerned with the propagation of trade. The appointment of the president, Sir Stafford Northcote, or one of the executive council would have appeared much more logical.

There was some suspicion and confusion about Beresford's "unofficial" status in the minds of foreign officials even at the time of his tour. At the instance of the Tsungli Yamen, the Chinese minister in London questioned Lord Salisbury about the matter, saying that the Yamen had written to him claiming that Beresford had shown them credentials from Lord Salisbury himself.[51] The British ambassador, MacDonald, having enquired into the matter, explained that Lord Charles had in fact represented himself to Prince Ching and the Yamen as unofficial, but in order to impress upon them the importance of his mission, he had shown them letters from the Prime Minister and cabinet members—personal and private letters—referring to such delicate and controversial questions as the control of the Chinese waterways. This of course had put a somewhat different complexion on his mission.

The effect of these letters on Yuan-Shih-Kai is worth quoting. It will be remembered that Beresford proposed to Lord Salisbury that with the aid of Yuan and his army he could take over Peking and control the whole country. MacDonald had the story from a Swede, Munthe, "a very sensible level-headed man and pro-English who commanded Yuan's cavalry." Munthe, being "quite staggered" by the way Lord Charles had shown the letters around to "all sorts and conditions of men," let MacDonald know the story. Apparently Yuan at first treated Beresford rather curtly as being non-official for, wrote MacDonald, "if you are not an official in China you are very small beer. . . ." He went on:

When however these letters were translated he (Yuan) thought Lord Charles had been sent on a secret and special mission from H.M.G. and at a word from me, so said the excellent Munthe, would have made a dash for the palace for he was assured that the whole might of England would have been at his back—as I didn't move he sat tight—for which I do not think we can all be sufficiently grateful. However these letters are doubtless the credentials to which the Chinese minister alluded and which so perplexed and confused the Yamen.[52]

Even MacDonald was puzzled about the status of his celebrated and somewhat troublesome visitor. When Beresford first arrived, MacDonald sent off a telegram to Mr. Bertie (his friend in the Foreign Office) saying, "Beresford is staying with me. Can I take him into general confidence? . . . I have nothing about him from anybody." Salisbury drafted the reply: "Yes. Lord C. Beresford is a very honourable and quite reliable man. It is very desirable that you should give him every information and assistance you can. But do not treat him publicly as having any commissions from H.M.G."[53] Earlier in August 1898 Mr. Goschen at the Admiralty who knew Beresford of old had written to Balfour "what is not my business. Should not MacDonald be informed before long of C. Beresfords visit? Its unofficial nature and the objects to pass in view? Some diplomats but probably not a man like MacDonald would be huffy at the interference which is certain to ensue."[54] Balfour had, however, informed MacDonald on 15 August in purely formal terms of Beresford's impending visit.

The Russians also were very much annoyed at the mission, believing that Beresford had been sent by England to spy upon their activities in China.[55] According to Satow in Japan the Russians were "very anxious about the effect of his visit to Japan supposing him to have a secret political mission."[56] One reason for this was the very marked attention paid to Beresford by the Japanese. He was received in audience by the Emperor, was shown the law courts, the prisons, and the arsenal, according to Satow seeing there more than any other man he knew. In fact, by the tone of Satow's reports of Beresford's activities in Japan, it is quite evident that although he "followed his line that he represents the Chambers of Commerce and is not in any way an emissary" he believed that there was more to the visit than was generally known.

Although it was sometimes the practice to send British officials on missions ostensibly on tasks of commercial importance only but in reality on matters involving diplomatic and international policy,[57] there is a great deal of reliable evidence to suggest that Beresford was in fact a private person who went to China representing solely the Chambers of Commerce and outside China was acting upon his own initiative. This is what he himself insisted upon in his speeches, in his book, and in his statements to the press. The *New York Times* accepted this version of his visit, saying, "Lord Charles Beresford has reached our shores in pursuance of his mission of securing the open door in China. The mission seems to be self-imposed and it does not appear that Lord Charles carries any credentials or officially represents anybody. But his mission is not less respectable on that account and his talk about it is even more interesting as being free from official reserves."[58] This was the theme Beresford emphasized throughout his tour, namely that he had no official status and was in the United States purely on his own responsibility.

Balfour, in his telegram notifying Ambassador MacDonald of the tour, was quite specific that Beresford was "proceeding to China at the request of the Associated Chambers of Commerce to make a report on the future prospects of British trade and commerce with that country . . . his visit is entirely of an unofficial nature."[59] An entry in the minute book of the executive council of the Association of British Chambers of Commerce supports this version. "The President [Sir Stafford Northcote] having heard that Lord Beresford intended to visit China during the parliamentary recess had suggested that he might report as to whether the organisation of the Chinese Civil and Miliary Administration was of a quality to ensure adequate protection to commercial men who may be disposed to embark their capital in trade enterprises in China." The president's aim was to obtain "a comprehensive report from a non-official source."[60] The executive approved the president's action. Beresford used language similar to this in his memoirs,[61] when recalling the invitation he received from Sir Stafford Northcote to go as the Chambers' representative. Again in a private letter to the Prime Minister he was quite explicit: "I quite understand that I am in no way accredited to the government [of China] or are they in any way responsible for my going out or for my actions."[62]

Finally it might well be assumed that any "real" as well as any ostensible reason for such a mission and for the choice of Beresford as "missioner" would appear in Northcote's letter offering him the position.[63] The letter used much the same language as appeared in the minutes already quoted, but added that the commissioner chosen must "be of sufficient position to warrant the expectation that he will be able to secure ready access to all sources of information." Northcote went on to say that he would like the services of an officer with naval or military experience so as to know how effective the protection of the Chinese government was. The letter concluded with a nice touch of irony by asking Beresford "whether his engagements would permit" a visit to China and whether he would furnish a report on his experience and upon any other matters he thought would be of interest and advantage to the Associated Chambers of Commerce.

To support this somewhat elaborate emphasis on the nonofficial character of the whole affair other arguments of reason can be marshalled. It must be remembered that Lord Charles Beresford, although a member of the government, was a noted and bitter critic of the government's Far Eastern policy which he declared to be completely supine in the face of continual Russian encroachment.[64] It is hardly likely in these circumstances that he would have been chosen as an emissary to lead the United States executive toward a policy desired by Britain. It is even less likely when the policy Beresford advocated is compared with that desired by the Foreign Office. He supported the open door wholeheartedly, but in face of the efforts by Russia and Germany to carve out spheres of influence it was his constant demand that Britain should follow suit at the very least in the Yangtse Valley and possibly to take over all China. His advocacy of this sort of policy brought upon him a continual barrage of criticism from Ambassador MacDonald in China. Salisbury's ironically tolerant refusal to follow his suggestion to take over Peking has already been quoted. His parliamentary speeches make it very difficult to regard him as a probable choice as an exponent of Britain's official policy, a policy of which he was one of the leading and most outspoken critics.

Until Lord Salisbury's papers were made available, the real nature of Beresford's activities remained uncertain, but the private correspondence between the two makes the complete story quite plain even if it might appear to be somewhat contradictory; for example when it appears that although Salisbury continued specifically to emphasize that Beresford must be in all ways unofficial, his expenses were in fact met out of Secret Service funds. The details of the story are not only interesting in themselves, but they throw a great deal of light upon the British government's conception of its China policy at the time, particularly as to any part America might be expected to play in it. They also solve with finality the question as to whether Beresford's activities involved any attempt by the British government to influence both the United States executive and public opinion throughout the nation.

The first thing that is clear is that the initiative for the visit to China came from Beresford and not from Salisbury or any member of the government. Beresford, recently promoted rear-admiral, found himself an admiral without a fleet and set out to find some other outlet for his restless energy. He first approached Lord Salisbury in March 1897, writing that although in his opinion it was unlikely at the moment,

possibilities may make it necessary that a British expedition should go up the Nile this Autumn. If it is a large expedition I should like to go in command of the flotilla under the General who may command the whole and I am writing to you to ask you to think of me as the future governor of the Sudan under the orders and control of Lord Cromer. I have not mentioned the matter to him as yet. The idea of conducting any administration in the East or the Nile valley has great fascination for me and without being egotistical I can point out the rapid success I had at Alexandria when governor of the town in 1882 at a moment of considerable difficulty. You may remember that all I did was conducted by civil administration and not by the aid of bayonets and bullets. Owing to my becoming an Admiral this year it is improbable that I could hope for employment afloat for three or four years if I take my turn in fairness to those senior to me and as I am now over 51 I should like to be doing something in the meantime. I thoroughly understand the Easterners, particularly those of the Nile valley . . . I am sure that the Sudan will require a man who not only has military knowledge but the art of administration by civil methods.

The story is continued in a memorandum from E. B. Barrington, Lord Salisbury's private secretary, to the Prime Minister dated 19 July 1898.

Lord Charles Beresford called on me today. Having failed to get an appointment in the Sudan he wants to go to China. After half an hour's conversation I failed to discover in what capacity but he thinks "we must have somebody on the Yangtse" to protect British interests there and he suggests himself failing a better man. He would be an official under the Chinese government like Gordon but he would go out under the aegis if not on the recommendation of H.M.G. He would drill troops and see that they were paid, British merchants who wanted concessions would come to him and he would gradually demolish the influence of the bribe taking Mandarins. He would keep the finances on a sound footing and generally imitate Lord Cromer's example in Egypt. I pointed out that our position [sic] in the two countries was not identical and asked him what would happen at York [the seat which Beresford was currently holding for the government]. He said we would lose the seat and he begged me to communicate with you.

Having obtained an interview with Lord Salisbury and discussed the matter with him, Beresford promptly went off to see Sir Stafford Northcote. The style of the argument he developed is apparent in a letter from Northcote to Salisbury which reads: "Charles Beresford tells me you strongly approve the idea of his going out to China but would like some such machinery as the Chambers of Commerce employed to approach H.M. government and suggest such a mission." Northcote went on to say that he had no doubt he could arrange this but that he would be glad to know privately if Beresford's account was an accurate reflection of Salisbury's views. In the meantime Northcote decided to call a meeting of the Chambers of Commerce in early August to consider "the promotion of British interests in China."[65]

Salisbury's reply was most instructive and is worth quoting in full.

My dear Northcote, Many thanks for your letter. What took place was this. Charles Beresford went to the Chinese minister to offer his assistance in organising the defensive forces of the Chinese empire. The minister gladly accepted his offer; but before Beresford would close he thought it better to ascertain what the government thought of it. We had some communication. My reply (in writing) was that in the first instance he must obtain the sanction of his hierarchical chief Mr. Goschen: and that if he obtained it I should view with satisfaction such an expedition on his part but I warned him that we could take no initiative in the matter or accept any responsibility. He came to see me on Friday and I repeated this. I pointed out to him that if H.M.G. appeared in the matter foreign powers would demand what they call compensation: that is some form of concession in China. It was therefore essential that when we were questioned on the matter we should be able to reply with truth that we had in no sense sent him out and were in no degree responsible for his activities.

This being promised we should observe his undertaking in the attitude of a benevolent by-stander. He suggested that he might be sent out by the Associated Chambers of Commerce or some other body which exists for similar purposes. I entirely approved of the idea; and said that if he did so we would give him any introduction or other facilities which we should naturally accord to the authority of the Associated Chambers of Commerce and to his own distinguished position. I think that there is a fair chance that he may do a greater deal of good in giving a start to the military reorganisation of the Chinese empire and perhaps carrying it to some distance—but I think he will hinder the object he has in view—and do other mischief if he mixes us up in the affair, therefore our participation is strictly limited by the boundaries I have mentioned. It will be very kind of you if you will give him a helping hand. Ever yours truly, Salisbury.

The nature of Beresford's representation to Northcote of Salisbury's view of the mission can be gauged from Northcote's cryptic reply to Salisbury's letter: "I thought C.B. might be romancing."

This exchange of personal and private letters is very revealing indeed. The initiative was entirely Beresford's. The primary object was the satisfaction of his personal ambition. He saw himself not as a "tidewater" admiral but as the Cromer of China. Salisbury's interest does not appear to have been in any way concerned with British-American relations or with the open door, but solely with the possibility of Beresford giving new life and strength to the military power of the moribund Chinese empire. This was in line with the traditional British policy[66] by which it was hoped to strengthen the administration of China sufficiently to make trading in the hinterland safe for all and thus to deprive any European power of an excuse to carve out a sphere of influence in order to protect those of their nationals who were engaged in commercial or missionary activities. To achieve this end the Prime Minister was prepared to facilitate Beresford's plan, but he was not in any way prepared to assume any responsibility for it, or for what Beresford might say or do.

It should be added that even though Salisbury might lend this limited support, the Queen certainly did not approve. When informed of the plan she wrote a hurried and forceful minute to her Chief Secretary of State for Foreign Affairs, saying: "Lord Charles Beresford should be watched and not told or shown anything as I know for a fact (the Duke of York told me) that he writes every week to the German Emperor who is better informed about our navy than I am."[67] Surprisingly enough Salisbury replied in his calm way that any "possible indiscretion" Lord Charles Beresford might commit could not do much harm as England and Germany were working together in China at the moment.

Despite Beresford's constant speech-making and despite his assiduous interviewing of the commercial organizations in China, Japan, and the United States, the Salisbury Papers emphasize the fact that his concern with trade and commerce and his obligation to the Associated Chambers of Commerce were to him very secondary matters. They merely provided the opportunity, the method, and the ostensible justification for his tour. This is obvious both from Northcote's initial reaction and from his estimate of the attitude of the executive council and members of the organization of which he was president.

After listening to Beresford's first account of his interview with Salisbury and on the assumption that Salisbury "strongly approved" of the idea, Northcote was prepared to go along with the plan and to call a meeting quickly to arrange the Chambers' participation. After checking with Salisbury, however, he wrote to give a more considered view of the matter. Having remarked that he had "thought C.B. might be romancing," he went on to express grave doubts as to whether the Chambers would agree to send Beresford as there had been the greatest difficulty in extracting approval for a few hundred pounds to finance a mission to South America and there had been profound relief within the organization when the plan for such an expedition had fallen through.

It is this belief that the Chambers would be very difficult over the approval of Beresford's idea and especially over the finance it would require, that explains two interesting facts. The first is that the Chambers as an organization were in fact not consulted about the affair until after Beresford had left.

Northcote explained to Salisbury that as Beresford wished to leave immediately, "I had to take the responsibility on my own shoulders and appoint him myself instead of appointing him as the nominee of the Chambers."[68] This action was subsequently "heartily approved" by the executive council. The second interesting fact is that the Chambers of Commerce did not finance Beresford except in a very token fashion. He was paid a total of £140 by the organization upon whose behalf he was ostensibly carrying out his exhaustive investigation, and of that amount £40 was to go towards the purchase of copies of his report, that is of his book *The Break-up of China*.[69] For the rest, his expenses, totalling £1,319/0/11, were met in the first instance by Sir Stafford Northcote, who was afterwards reimbursed by Sanderson of the Foreign Office from Secret Service funds. This had been arranged prior to Beresford's departure between Northcote and Balfour, Salisbury's nephew and First Lord of the Treasury.[70]

One of the letters from Northcote revealing this arrangement, written after Beresford's China visit, is pregnant with meaning and deserves quotation.

I can assure you I deeply regret having been mixed up in any business that has caused you annoyance and worry. . . . I would suggest that I should continue to pay his expenses, my reason being this. Should he by any possible chance be tempted to disclose the fact that they had been found for him out of S.S. I should ask your permission to repay the £750 Sanderson has recouped me— and you could then say you had found it impossible to carry out your intentions of paying his expenses considering how entirely adverse to this country's interests his action had been. The money would not be any consideration to me. I do not for a moment think C.B. would act so dishonestly but you can't tell what temper might induce him to blurt out.[71]

The Prime Minister was prepared to gamble approximately £1,200 upon the chance that Beresford might do some good in hastening the military reorganization of China but the Associated Chambers were not prepared to subsidize the venture which they did not initiate and which was presented to them as a *fait accompli*.

Beresford's preparation for his venture, together with the central emphasis of his interviews with the officials in China, add further proof to the view that trade, the open door, and the affairs of the Chambers of Commerce were secondary interests, at the most supplying the justification for the type of appointment he was seeking from the Tsungli Yamen. Most of his efforts were directed toward achieving the success of his personal project and certainly most of his letters to Salisbury were concerned to convince him of the necessity for the employment he envisaged.

He saw the Chinese ambassador to explain his mission and to seek his support in the form of introductions. He sought from Salisbury an answer to "a very pertinent question" put to him at the interview. "Suppose," asked the ambassador, "my government ask the English government for your services to help us to organise our defence in the south and perhaps in other matters and that the English government gives permission but that after such permission the Russian government object to us employing you. Will the English government stand firm and say if we want you they will not allow outside interference?" Salisbury's reply was designed to reassure him. "If any power commits an act of aggression on China because China employs in any capacity a British subject with the approval of Her Majesty's government I should certainly hold that we were bound to support China materially."[72] He saw Lord Wolseley and persuaded him to work out a complete scheme in terms of equipment and clothing "for a military force of some five to fifty thousand men."[73] He explained that he had made a tour of industrial cities in order, as he said, "to see for myself the possibilities *if* the Chinese do employ me to reorganise their forces. I am also listing prices, dimensions and dates of possible delivery of vessels if they, the Chinese, think of their fleets. But the military question is far the most important for the time being if only they will let us take it in hand."[74]

In most of his letters to Salisbury there appeared somewhere the repetitive theme, "if we can only get that military or police security in the Yangtse valley which we call our sphere of influence. . . ." He endeavoured to persuade Mr. Goschen at the Admiralty to put warships at his disposal both to give him consequence in the eyes of the Chinese and "to save expense." He sought the use of a cypher for communication with the Foreign Office but this was refused. All contacts and messages were to be sent through the ambassador. He discussed in detail with Salisbury and noted carefully all that his Prime Minister "wished done as to observations and suggestions on the waterways" and he hinted broadly "if the force of events determine you to send gunboats up to Hankow or a squadron to Nanking before or after my arrival in China it will assist me a great deal and although irresponsible [sic] I could make great capital of it."[75]

However, Beresford did not completely neglect the commercial side of his preparation although it is evident that his chief concern with it was to show how beneficial his plan for military reorganization would be for the China trade. He wrote to the German Emperor and spoke to the Japanese and American ambassadors seeking their assistance with interviews and hoping for their approval in attempting to foster friendship between the various national merchant groups. He visited the directors of most of the leading firms interested in the China trade arguing the need for security of a police or military nature. He assured Lord Salisbury that Sir Thomas Lippmann had promised him to invest £1,000,000 in China if greater security could be guaranteed. His aim always was to convince merchants of all nations of the desirability of achieving security through British influence, thus hoping to reduce any opposition to his plan. As he naïvely explained, "if we can get security, that is police, military or gunboats on the waterways, capital will surely follow from all countries and then we may be easy as other countries will help us to resist aggression while we hold the dominant position really by means of police."[76]

It was this type of comment and his inopportune speeches, particularly in Singapore, where he argued publicly the necessity for increased military and police security in inland China as a necessary condition for the future of investment of capital there, that caused Salisbury to minute even before Beresford reached China, "I am afraid C.B. is an ass."[77] As late as 27 September while on his way from Singapore to China he wrote again to Salisbury to remind him of his chief ambition. "In the event of the Chinese government asking for a British subject to reorganise their forces or administer a province in the Yangtse valley would you kindly remember that I should be very glad to devote what energy I possess to such a duty. I believe the future of our trade and commerce in China will depend upon the man who can organise and command with confidence a Chinese army in the region of the Yangtse."[78]

His primary concern with his own career rather than with British trade or the welfare of the Chambers of Commerce is illustrated also by his activities in China. He was most assiduous in interviewing consuls, speaking to Chambers of Commerce, in discussing the Far Eastern situation with representatives of the great firms and banks which controlled the China trade, in hearing their grievances and bewailing with them the closing of the open door, and preaching the doctrine of the necessity for greater security for both traders and the capital they might invest. But again, his chief concern was to convince Prince Ching and the Tsungli Yamen of the necessity for them to adopt a plan for the effective reorganization of their army by appointing a commander and officers, to be supplied by the British government upon request. His method of achieving this was to play upon China's fear of partition. In an audience with the Tsungli Yamen in October he threatened that unless the Chinese government asked for British officers to organize their army, public opinion in England would force the government to adopt the sphere of influence policy so favoured by other nations. He reported that the Yamen "appeared alarmed" and having seen the Emperor and Dowager Empress stated that a request would be sent for a British officer to commence the reorganization of the army with 1,000 Chinese and 1,000 Tartar troops from Hopeh Province under the viceroy Chang Chi Tung.[79]

Beresford was equally concerned to convince Lord Salisbury to take a much stronger line in China in support of the central government and against any encroachment by other powers, particularly by Russia. "I believe," he wrote in October, "now is the exact moment to get hold of the Chinese authority but they must be frightened insist [sic] on their having a British subject to organise their army if they do not ask for me. If they do as they promised me, the matter is simple enough, as long as a strong man with tact is sent." He assured Salisbury that Russia could do absolutely nothing. Britain and Japan could push her out of Manchuria easily. France was a threat to smile at and "we could laugh at Russia with a well-organised *Chinese* army officered by British officers, worked by Mandarins and these worked [sic] by a strong-minded officer." This together with the suggested quadruple alliance between Britain, Germany, Japan, and the United States would keep the open door open and be a perfect counter to Russia, whom he reported to be arming furiously in Manchuria.

With a Chinese army such as I suggest we could be strong long before Russia. There is no chance of war over my proposal, the Chinese can ask for whom they like to organise if *only* they know we will stick to them if we begin the organisation. The basis of all reform must be law and order combined with a show of strength. If we can only get the military under our control I am certain all else will follow.[80]

This theme was repeated time and again in letters to Salisbury throughout October, November, and December. Early in November he summarized his views saying that the only possible solution to the China problem was to have a Chinese army officered by British but nominally under Chinese control. There were only two ways in which this could be done, by preserving the integrity of China who would herself ask for a British subject to organize the whole of her forces, or by England's assuming control of the Yangtse Valley and organizing her own Chinese army. The first was the better but the second would still be successful in preserving the open door provided that a commercial alliance between Japan, Germany, and America was made with England, based upon the continuance of the open door.[81] On 7 November, he went further and sought Salisbury's approval to take over Peking, using Yuan-Shih-Kai's army, and in a later letter justifying this plan he wrote:

I most respectfully suggest to you that (1) if the Chinese do not ask for a man to organise their forces they should be made to ask for me—a couple of cruisers at Nanking would bring that about as they would believe that China is about to be split up. (2) That when they do ask for a man it should be clearly represented that as England has undertaken the matter her honour demands that it should be done properly and no interference with the individual sent will be brooked.[82]

In December he sent to Salisbury a letter of eighteen typed pages outlining his preparations with the Chinese to take over their army. He had been in communication with Prince Ching and the Yamen, he had pointed out to them that the plan did not mean merely the use of a few drill sergeants, but assumed that he would accept responsibility for reorganizing the whole army and this without interference. He advocated what he called a "sugar and bamboo policy." "No people could be so easily managed as these Chinese if only they are seized with a firm and unmistakable grip." He was confident he could begin without imposing any additional financial burden upon England but the full reorganization would need to be financed by a loan.

By 20 December he could report that he had all the southern

viceroys agreeable to his plan, he had inspected all the Yangtse forts and arsenals, the military and naval schools, and ships of war. He had seen all the mandarins save two and claimed to have made the way perfectly "smooth and clear." As he wrote to Northcote on 22 December, "all is arranged and all that is wanted is a little pressure (to save their faces) from England." "Now is the time and if they won't ask we should make them" was his phrase to Salisbury. He had "everything ready to act at once without extra finance," he had chosen his agents in the south and in the north who were ready to take over and put the arsenals in order, and he claimed that all the viceroys would support him. He was bitterly disappointed at the lack of support from London, claiming that before he left England he had outlined and obtained a general approval for all that he had accomplished. He could only conclude that Salisbury had changed his mind.[83] But enough has been said to show where Beresford's real interests lay and to show how far removed his views were from the American conception of the open door and the integrity of China.

The Salisbury Papers also make it clear that there was no mention of America in any of the plans concerted in London before Beresford left. The plan was directed solely to China. He saw Hay before he left and discussed with him the problem of maintaining the open door but there was no mention of extending his visit to the United States. There is no suggestion anywhere that he was even to go to the United States, let alone to endeavour to influence their policy. That part of his tour was planned again on his own initiative and after being in China for some time. It was the result of his view of his own importance and influence and of suggestions made to him in China by Americans. In October he discussed trading policy with E. H. Conger, the American ambassador, and received an encouraging reply from him. "The interests of your country and mine lie along the same line as far as this country [China] is concerned: both need the doors kept open and in my judgment an understanding can and should be reached by a sufficient number of great powers interested absolutely to secure this end but without making a general alliance for other purposes."[84] This was in reply to Beresford's talk of the possibility of the quadruple commercial alliance mentioned above. But Conger was far ahead of the executive in his conception of the desirability of any such alliance.

Beresford explained the extension of his visit to Japan and America as being in response to an invitation by Japan and to pressure from Americans.

All the American officials and otherwise who have met me have asked me to go home across America. They are complimentary and say that if I will go and make a speech or two in America and see the President and warmly support the now suggested Anglo-American alliance it will do an infinity of good; unless you would rather that I did not do this I will go home that way and do all I can to cement the new friendly feeling that is growing up between us and the U.S.[85]

He added that he intended to "wake them up to the necessity of the open door for America as well as for the United Kingdom."

Here was no Foreign Office plan; on the contrary, by the time the suggestion was made Beresford was heartily disapproved of by Northcote, by Salisbury, by the cabinet, and in particular by MacDonald in China. He had become a positive embarrassment through his persistent and vociferous advocacy of a policy in China of which the Foreign Office specifically disapproved. They had approved, as part of Britain's traditional China policy, the initial suggestion to rehabilitate China's military system but they were both amused and appalled at Beresford's grandiose plans to take over all China or at least the Yangtse Valley and to keep the doors open everywhere by his quadruple commercial alliance.

In fact, given the opinion of Beresford's acumen formed in the embassies and in the government in response to his activities in China, it is quite inconceivable that his original commission to China which was, it will be remembered, limited to the question of the military reorganization of the country, would have been extended to include a public relations tour of the United States, or even as has been suggested a tour designed to influence public opinion within the executive of the United States. It will be remembered that before his arrival in China, Lord Salisbury had reached the conclusion that Beresford was an ass. Both Northcote and Barrington, who knew Salisbury's mind on the subject, could treat the plan for a commercial alliance with something approaching amused derision.[86] Even Beresford realized that Salisbury thought his famous plan for a "dash to the palace" to be a "huge joke."[87] Northcote felt himself obliged to apologize for and to express his deep regret that he had been associated with Beresford's tour which had caused Salisbury so much "annoyance and worry," and as has been shown he was prepared to pay Beresford's expenses himself.[88]

All the advice received from China revealed that the men on the spot felt that Beresford's plan could not possibly succeed and in particular they were extremely exasperated with Beresford's ineptitude as a representative. Before Beresford left for China, Sir John Ardagh, the Director-General of Military Intelligence, had set forth a draft scheme for the reorganization of the Chinese army by British officers and it was sent to the Peking embassy for comment. The reply was drafted by Lieutenant-Colonel G. F. Browne, the military attaché, and was approved by MacDonald. It agreed that Sir John Ardagh's plan would be effective if the Chinese could be persuaded to accept it. However this was thought to be most unlikely for two reasons. One was the venality and corruption of Chinese officials which would inevitably neutralize any plan directed against their interests. But the more important reason stemmed from the nature of the Chinese state, in particular from the fact that an alien dynasty occupied the throne. The Manchus permitted the Chinese to administer the country according to Chinese custom but the Tartar army was held in reserve and jealously watched over the loyalty of Chinese officials. Any trained Chinese army would be regarded as a danger to the state and the present rulers believed that the British would use it to that end:

> . . . so formidable would be the opposition to any reform that it is well nigh hopeless to expect that the existing government will ever consent to complete control of the military force passing into foreign hands and without complete control, financial and adminis-trative, the best officers our service can produce are doomed to humiliation and failure.[89]

MacDonald supported this view, arguing strongly that the Chinese would do no more than nominally accept the scheme, that they would not voluntarily put themselves under any out-side control, and that they did not trust Britain's motives. In a later comment he was prepared to state that it was impossible for England to organize the entire military force of China be-cause of the opposition of both China and the European pow-ers, and because the task would be beyond the strength of the United Kingdom even if there were no opposition offered to it at all.[90] Salisbury's conversion to this view (he had never be-lieved very strongly in the chances of Beresford's success) is shown by his minute to the effect that MacDonald's comments were too sensible to be repressed and that the whole should be printed for the cabinet, the Queen, and the Prince of Wales.[91]

Official comments upon Beresford's activities in China are a salutary corrective to his own enthusiastic evaluation of his services and reveal how unlikely it is that Beresford's intention to come home via the United States would have received official recognition. When MacDonald forwarded Beresford's telegram seeking Salisbury's authority for his "dash to the palace," he added a footnote: "I think it would be wiser if Lord C. Beres-ford confined himself to trade and commerce. Under any cir-cumstances if strong action were determined on, for which I see no immediate necessity, Admiral Seymour would be in charge." So much was this the view in London and so low had opinion of Beresford become, that even a senior clerk could risk minuting "but L.C.B. knows nothing about trade and commerce either and the utility of his presence in China in any capacity seems open to doubt." A further minute made it clear that Beresford's conception of the high quality of Yuan-Shih-Kai's army was entirely opposed to the estimate of it reported to Intelligence by a Captain Waigate.[92]

In the eyes of the Foreign Office, the embassies, and cabinet officials, it was Beresford's capacity completely to misinterpret the international situation in China, just as he had failed to understand the attitude of the viceroys, that destroyed any belief in his usefulness. Justifying his plan to use Yuan-Shih-Kai's army to take over Peking, he argued to MacDonald that he would merely have arranged to do just what the Russians were in fact doing; "everything is apparently being done by the Chinese but the Russians are pulling the strings."[93] MacDonald forwarded this letter together with his reply to it to the Foreign Office. He explained to Bertie that in case questions were asked in the House the truth had better be known. The "gallant Admiral" was the "best of good fellows" but "some of the grumblers at the Treaty Ports may have got hold of him and primed him with 'bunders' the local name for yarns." His reply to Beresford was sufficiently frank: "You say 'everything is being done by the Chinese but the Russians are really pulling the strings.' I recognise in this the 'gup' of the Treaty Ports. I beg of you, as what the French would call *'un homme sérieux'* not to go home primed with stuff of this kind." He then proceeded to give facts and figures concerning investment facilities, railway and mining concessions to disprove Beresford's belief that the English trader was being neglected. He went on, "There is another and more personal way of looking at it. You have stayed in this house and can certify (I hope) that I am not a born idiot which, if I allowed the Russians to pull the strings, as they are made out to do, I certainly should be." MacDonald's comment, with which Salisbury entirely agreed,[94] was not printed for the cabinet in case the extent of British concessions should be made public and become a cause of conflict between England and Russia. But other similar comments were printed for cabinet, notably Lieutenant-Colonel Browne's comments upon Lord Charles's "dash to the palace," as MacDonald had labelled the episode. MacDonald in forwarding these fully agreed with Browne and emphasized the truth of those which referred to Beresford's lack of reticence:

Possibly this may read as though I have bitter feelings toward Lord Charles Beresford, but such is not the case. No one can help being captivated by his open hearty manner but one has a right to expect an *ordinary* share of discretion and *some* reticence from a man holding a public position and carrying weight in the country at home. One cannot be too thankful that his coup was declined. I cannot imagine any undertaking involving greater risks. No good could have come of it and where it would have ended none can hazard a guess. The first element was secrecy yet it would have been almost impossible to have withdrawn a force of 75,000 men from Hsiao Chan, ferry it across the river and entrain it for Peking without news reaching the capital. But even suppose they had seized the palace, troops would have been moved in from the Hunting Park and when the two conspirators would have been caught in a trap you would have had to negotiate to save their heads which it would be impossible to deny they richly deserved to lose.[95]

In fact throughout the whole period, the only good word spoken for Beresford's efforts was by Satow from Japan where Beresford's speeches and activities facilitated Satow's efforts in cementing good relations between England and Japan. But even Satow was horrified at Beresford's suggestion, made in a public speech in Japan, that all four members of the proposed quadruple "commercial" alliance, Britain, Germany, Japan, and the United States, should have a part in the military reorganization of China. Satow "ventured the opinion" to Salisbury that "who controls the army, controls China and if you have separate armies you have spheres of influence."[96]

Most certainly opinions of Beresford in England were such that his activities abroad and his return home were awaited with some trepidation. Every effort was made by Salisbury and Northcote to prevent Beresford's disagreement with Salisbury's policy from taking a more virulent and public form. Northcote begged him not to be interviewed before seeing Salisbury upon his return, pointing out to him "that the question of co-operation with other powers in the Far East had not escaped Lord Salisbury's attention but that the question of alliance is not one that is determined by English, American or German men of business, but by Cabinets."[97]

The final touch to this picture of the government's view of Beresford's activities in China in 1898 is supplied in the following incident. In August 1899 the question arose of Beresford's further career in the navy. He wanted to go afloat, and there were only two vacanies, as second in command in either the China station or the Mediterranean. Mr. Goschen, who regarded Beresford as a great troublemaker, preferred him in China where he would cause less difficulty in the navy. But he feared that Salisbury might not want him in China "because of his reckless talk." "Shallow as he is, he is a personage to contend with for he has secured the ears of the press and of the national public to a considerable extent." The content of Salisbury's remarks, although not documented, can be gauged from Goschen's comment, "after what you told me as to your view of Charles Beresford being sent to China I will drop the idea at once."[98]

It is quite apparent that the traditional view of Beresford's relationship with the British government and of his activities in China and America is without foundation. Although he went to China with official approval and although his expenses were met by Secret Service funds, he was in fact unofficial and cabinet accepted no responsibility at all for him or for his actions. His connection with the Chambers of Commerce was purely a convenient subterfuge. He was concerned primarily with his own career and with an attempt to make that career in the military rehabilitation of China. Any concern he showed for the fate of British commerce or with the open door was a very secondary matter. The actions and the policies he advocated in China were opposed both to the British cabinet's and to America's conception of preserving China from partition. Finally, his visit to the United States was not a part of the original plan and was entirely the result of his own estimate of the value of his activities.

Neither does there seem to be any relationship between Beresford and Hippesley, for Hippesley would certainly not have approved of any extension of a sphere of influence policy in the style of Beresford's advice to the Foreign Office; he specifically disagreed with that section of Beresford's book dealing with the military reconstruction of China.[99]

The most that can be said of Beresford's role was that, despite the suspicion of him as an Englishman, he may have assisted the development of a climate of opinion in favour of the open door note that was being so effectively created in the United States by interested pressure groups. He was certainly not the exponent of Britain's official policy, a policy of which he was one of the leading and most outspoken critics.

It is equally certain that Hippesley was not acting upon any official or unofficial brief from the British Foreign Office. He was an Englishman in the service of the Chinese Maritime Customs, his advice to Rockhill was in accord with that adopted by Sir Robert Hart, and the first open door note does in fact bear a striking similarity to the letter to Rockhill in which Hippesley outlined his recommendations.[100] However, all the evidence seems to show that Hippesley was acting purely in a private capacity. In doing so he was motivated by his concern for China's administrative and territorial integrity and his advice reflected the policy of his superior in the Chinese Maritime Customs. However there is nothing to connect his initiative or his advice with the British government.[101]

The evidence for this view as against Fairbank's interpretation seems quite conclusive. For Hippesley to have acted at the behest of the Foreign Office would presuppose an elaborate and subtle plan. This would have been to employ one who had not been in England for thirty years and whose wife was an American with relatives in Baltimore, thus providing a plausible reason for a visit to permit consultation with Rockhill with whom Hippesley had been friendly in China some years earlier. Hippesley's task would then have been subtly to lead Rockhill and through Rockhill, Hay, to adopt an economic foreign policy in British interests. The credibility of such a plan does not bear close examination.

In the first place it is inconceivable that cabinet would have resorted to this type of subtlety when Pauncefote was such a trusted and successful ambassador and so close a friend of Hay. It is inconceivable also that Pauncefote would not have at the least been instructed to endeavour to influence Hay to adopt the open door policy. Yet neither the private correspondence between Salisbury and Pauncefote nor the official files[102] in the Foreign Office mention any such instruction. Pauncefote was not even consulted when Joseph Choate delivered the first note, and the inefficient drafting, of which the Foreign Office officials complained, does not suggest any such secret assistance by Pauncefote as in the case of the canal treaty. In the second place, as Varg has shown, "Rockhill had no desire to rake England's chestnuts out of the fire," for he condemned England as being "as great an offender in China as Russia itself."[103]

In the third place, although Fairbank's claim that the Chinese Maritime Customs "was the mechanism which fostered the British commercial interest in China" is true, it is not the whole story. The primary aim of the Maritime Customs as administered by Sir Robert Hart was to collect efficiently and honestly the Chinese customs duty which had been instituted by the powers to provide the Chinese government with a permanent income from its foreign trade, an income which could be used to finance an efficient administration within China. Fairbank's suggestion that Hippesley devised a policy specifically in the interests of the Chinese Customs might be true, and it is accepted by Kennan. But even here there is a doubt for, as Varg has shown,[104] the Hippesley-Rockhill correspondence reveals that the section of the note suggesting that all customs should be collected by Chinese officials was included not by Hippesley but by Rockhill as a means of preserving the administrative integrity of China within those spheres of influence that already existed. Furthermore, it has been pointed out by Kennan[105] that at this time, and over the particular issue of the administration of the Customs, the British Foreign Office and Sir Robert Hart were at odds. This point is corroborated by the fact that Bertie in the Foreign Office specifically raised the question of the effect of the notes upon customs collection in Kowloon.[106] It would be hard to credit that the Foreign Office in these circumstances would choose for its agent the second officer of an independent organization with whose policy the Foreign Office did not agree.

Finally there is no shred of evidence in the official and private records of any connection between Hippesley and either the Foreign Office or Her Majesty's Customs. Wherever Customs dealt with a matter affecting foreign policy, or a matter thought for any reason to be of interest to the Foreign Office, the relevant papers were forwarded for information, or at the very least a full report was rendered. But in the voluminous files in the Foreign Office[107] of correspondence concerning the appointment of a successor to Sir Robert Hart there is no suggestion at any time that Hippesley visited the United States on furlough at the instance of the government or that there was any connection whatever between his action in America and the policies of the Foreign or Customs Offices. In the long controversy as to whether Sir Robert Bredon or Hippesley should succeed to Hart's position in China, the key document is a lengthy detailed memorandum drawn up for the information of cabinet, in which there is a complete summary of Hippesley's career and of his official connection with the British government and with the Chinese Customs. In this there is no mention whatever of the open door. It is at least probable that if Hippesley had successfully carried out such a coup as to lead the United States Secretary of State to the pronouncement of a policy to serve Britain's interests, his skill and success would have been indicated in this biographical record. To complete the case a thorough examination of all the Hippesley-Rockhill correspondence led Rockhill's biographer to conclude that "Hippesley was in no sense an emissary of the British government."[108] In fact it can be said that the only thing Hippesley and Beresford had in common was their advocacy of policies of which the Foreign Office disapproved.[109]

In the generally accepted explanation of British influence upon the United States at this time then, the first weakness is the false assumption that the United States needed to be converted to the open door policy. The second is the unfounded belief that both Beresford and Hippesley were in some way acting on behalf of the United Kingdom in an attempt to lead the American executive to adopt a co-operative policy in the Far East. The third chief weakness now to be demonstrated is that the effect of Anglo-American friendship operating in the United States executive through Hay has been greatly exaggerated. Given his ignorance of Far Eastern affairs, John Hay's English friendships and experience had certainly convinced him of the suitability of the open door policy for American needs; but it was not Hay's conviction nor was it his initiative that led the United States to the formulation and adoption of the open door. When he became Secretary of State, Hay, although convinced of the value of the open door policy, did not attempt to formulate America's Far Eastern policy in these terms. Preoccupied with other affairs he left the matter to his Far Eastern adviser, Rockhill, and was not even responsible for the formula within which the United States returned to a co-operative policy in China.

Hay was renowned as an Anglophile and was quite frank about it in his letters, but he was under no illusions as to the fate of any policy thought by Congress or the public to be English in origin. In 1898 he was convinced that Britain's Far

Eastern policy favoured American economic interests in China, and when he heard of McKinley's refusal to act in response to the British suggestion in March for a co-operative effort, he wrote to him urging a reconsideration of the decision. There is no evidence of any British initiative in this matter. Hay was not even forewarned of the intended approach by the British Foreign Office, nor was his aid sought; in fact he was on holiday in Egypt at the time. He was convinced of the importance of the open door and when he became Secretary of State it is likely he sought Rockhill's advice in formulating a Far Eastern policy in accord with that conviction. But there is no evidence of any sustained effort on his part to lead the United States executive along English paths nor of any Foreign Office efforts to persuade him to do so. His reply to Rockhill's suggestion for some such action as that later taken reveals both his agreement with Rockhill and some of the reasons for his inaction. "I am fully awake to the great importance of what you say, and am more than ready to act. But the senseless prejudices in certain quarters of the 'Senate and people' compel us to move with great caution."[110]

The same fear of the effect of anti-British feeling appeared in Rockhill's reply to Hippesley's suggestions. He was quite in favour of some declaration by the United States designed to assist in maintaining the open door, but pointed out his fear

that home politics and next year's elections will interfere with this for it might be interpreted by a large part of the voting population of the United States, especially the Irish and the Germans, as an adoption of the policy advocated by England, and any leaning towards England on the part of the administration would at this time be dangerous and might lose the President his nomination. . . . I consequently fear that he will do absolutely nothing either on the lines you indicate, and which are clearly those most beneficial to our interest in China, or in any other which will commit us.[111]

It is this hesitation upon the part of the executive to take the plunge into Far Eastern affairs, to annex the Philippines, to intervene in China, or to risk any appearance of following an English line, that provides the key to the problem of assessing Hay's influence. The simple fact is that any return to a policy of intervention or co-operation in international politics on the Asiatic mainland had to wait upon the development of an opinion in the country, in the Senate, and in the executive favourable to such a venture. In this task, the leaders were those pressure groups studied so fully by Campbell[112] and particularly those voluble exponents of the "large policy," the "expansionists of 1898," Henry Cabot Lodge, A. T. Mahan, and Theodore Roosevelt. As Griswold put it: "The annexation of the Philippines and the desire for a more spirited defence of American rights and interests in China were co-products of the same thing—the impulse toward expansion which had lately taken so decisive a stride."[113]

The debate over the annexation of the Philippines and the decision to annex them accustomed the nation and the Senate to the idea of Far Eastern intervention. This was accompanied by an increase in pressure group activity which sought the protection of American rights in China, which in turn received the strongest support from Dr. Jacob Gould Schurman, McKinley's personal adviser on the Far East and president of the United States-Philippines Commission. Upon his return to America from the Far East, Schurman reported to the press his evaluation of the Far Eastern situation.[114] In his opinion, the great question in the Orient was neither Formosa nor the Philippines but China. China was the "one over-shadowing question." China should be maintained in its independence but its doors should be kept open. Economically and politically this would mean as much to America as to England and Japan. Finally, a reassurance from Russia in the Ukase of 16 August (the day after the press published Schurman's opinion) in which Talienwan was declared a free port, convinced the President that some such action as that proposed by Hay and his advisers should be taken; it should be taken for the protection of American interests, and the Czar's Ukase made it apparent that this action could be taken without involving the United States in hostile negotiations with European powers. McKinley realized also that this action, if taken, would placate those economic interests which had for so long and with such insistence sought to convince the executive of the necessity for such a policy.

Before summing up, a fourth and basically important point must be made, namely that when the open door notes were forwarded to the European powers, they embodied a policy which, though not actually opposed to, was nevertheless different from, that being followed by the British Foreign Office. Although known for many years, the significance of this has escaped those who emphasize the effect of English activities and ideas upon American Far Eastern policy. It has too often been assumed that the policy of the British Foreign Office when America issued the open door notes was still the same as in March 1898 when Britain sought the co-operation of the United States. The notes were in accord with British policy in that they sought to protect an equality of commercial opportunity within the existing spheres of influence and because they could perhaps act as a brake upon further foreign (particularly Russian) encroachments in China. However, in other ways the notes and Britain's contemporary policy were not in accord. In the first place, the Foreign Office was not happy that the policy of the notes should apply to British leased territories in China or any of Britain's colonial possessions in the area. It was only under pressure from the State Department that Britain finally agreed and then with two provisos: that Kowloon be exempted from the leased territories mentioned, and that Britain's adherence should be dependent upon a similar agreement and its observance by all other powers.[115] So that in this case, far from the State Department running in British leading reins, it was the British Foreign Office which reluctantly agreed to America's representations. The second difference was that Britain was no longer willing to agree that equality of opportunity within spheres of influence should apply to investment concessions. This was made quite clear by the Duke of Devonshire in a statement to parliament,[116] and was quite evident in official agreements such as the Scott-Muraviev agreement of 1899 with Russia.

It should be apparent then that neither Beresford nor Hippesley was an agent of the Foreign Office or even of the Customs Office. Beresford was primarily concerned with his attempt to take over the military reorganization of China, and only secondarily with the interests of British trade. Salisbury's initial hope that he might do some good in the military sense was rapidly replaced by fear of the harm he would do in sharpening the conflict in the Far East between England and Russia. Hippesley, while as far as is known acting upon his own initiative, supported a policy in the interests of the Chinese Maritime Customs. Beresford and Hippesley advocated policies which were opposed both to each other and to that being followed by the Foreign Office.

Hay and Rockhill, within the United States executive, were in favour of the open door policy but were not acting upon Foreign Office advice or in response to any Foreign Office initiative. Rockhill saw the United Kingdom as being as grave an offender against China as any other power. Hay was forced to wait upon the slow development of internal United States policy until he could move in the direction plotted for him by Rockhill and Hippesley. In this matter, as throughout his period as Secretary of State, far from being aided by any American friendship for Britain he was continually hampered by the anti-British prejudices in the country and the fear that any policy which could be labelled as pro-British was bound to be overturned in the Senate. When he did move, Britain's response was hesitant and her acceptance limited by the exclusion of specific territories and by the condition that her acceptance depended upon the observance of the notes by all other powers. This hesitancy was because England's policy as it had developed since March 1898 was now in essentials so far removed from that adopted by the United States that Britain could no longer wholeheartedly support a policy she herself had proposed as the basis of a co-operative Anglo-American policy in the Far East.

The conclusion to be drawn from these facts is surely this: that despite Hay's presence as Secretary of State, despite England's sedulous courting of the United States during the Spanish-American War, and despite the effusive expressions of American goodwill during that war, Anglo-American friendship was entirely inadequate as a basis for co-operative diplomatic action in the Far East. On the contrary, as Hay fully realized, suspicion of Britain's motives remained such an explosive issue in United States national politics that it was a positive deterrent to the acceptance of any such policy.

Notes

1. Gelber, *op. cit.*, p. 1. H. C. Allen, *Great Britain and the United States: A History of Anglo-American Relations 1783-1952* (London: Odhams Press, 1954), p. 556.

2. Allen, *loc. cit.*

3. Gelber, *op. cit.*, p. 14.

4. Griswold, *op. cit.*

5. *New York Times*, 21 April 1898.

6. *Times* (London), 14 May 1898, and quoted in most text-books.

7. Olney, *op. cit.*

8. *Ibid.*, p. 588.

9. Reuter, *op. cit.* Heindel, *op. cit.* The surveys of American and English press by these two authors are complementary one to the other, even though they disagree to a limited extent in the conclusions they draw from their material.

10. See pp. 168-204.

11. Garvin, *op. cit.*, p. 598.

12. Allen, *op. cit.*, pp. 565-69.

13. Quoted R. B. Mowat, *The Diplomatic Relations of Great Britain and the United States* (London: Arnold & Co., 1925), p. 131.

14. See p. 135.

15. See p. 138.

16. Grenville, *op. cit.*, p. 50 and n. 4.

17. The details of this negotiation are most thoroughly and excellently revealed and assessed by Grenville, *op. cit.*

18. Salisbury Papers, Vol. CXL, America From and To 1899-1900, No. 24, Pauncefote to Salisbury, 19 January 1900.

19. *Ibid.*, unbound, Pauncefote to Salisbury, undated.

20. FO5/2425, Salisbury to Pauncefote, Private and Confidential, 4 January 1900.

21. FO5/2426, Pauncefote to Salisbury, 16 February 1900; the italics are Pauncefote's.

22. See Campbell, Jr., *Anglo-American Understanding 1898-1903*, Bemis, *op. cit.*, Bailey, *op. cit.*, Grenville, *op. cit.*, Langer, *op. cit.*

23. FO5/2378, Mr. Balfour's memorandum, 16 August 1898.

24. See p. 135.

25. FO55/392 [*sic*], Salisbury to Pauncefote, 2 February 1899, quoted Grenville, *op. cit.*, p. 59.

26. FO5/2421, Herschell to Salisbury, 25 November 1898, quoted Campbell, Jr., *Anglo-American Understanding 1898-1903*, p. 95.

27. Hay to Foster, 23 June 1900. W. R. Thayer, *The life and Letters of John Hay* (Boston and New York: Houghton, 1915), II, 234-35.

28. That this was the case is argued by Griswold, *op. cit.*, pp. 46-49, 54.

29. Bemis, *op. cit.*, p. 484, n. 3.

30. This was revealed by Dennis, *op. cit.*, and Dennett, *op. cit.*, chap. xxiv. The correspondence is published in Griswold, *op. cit.*

31. J. K. Fairbank, *The United States and China* (Cambridge, Mass.: Harvard University Press, 1951), pp. 320-21, and in the 1961 edition pp. 254-256.

32. *Ibid.*

33. Bemis, *op. cit.*, p. 484, n. 1.

34. Griswold, *op. cit.*, pp. 48-49.

35. Lord Charles Beresford, *The Break-up of China* (London: Harper & Bros., 1899).

36. Quoting letter Hay to White, 24 September 1899. Dennett, *op. cit.*, p. 221.

37. Quoted Griswold, *op. cit.*, p. 51.

38. *Ibid.*, p. 50.

39. *Hansard*, 1898, LXIV, 827.

40. Griswold, *op. cit.*, p. 48. See n. 3 for a list of these speeches.

41. *Foreign Relations of the United States, 1899*, pp. 143-45.

42. Nevins, *op. cit.*, p. 167, and Bemis, *op. cit.*, pp. 484-85.

43. Dennett, quoted in Bemis, *op. cit.*, p. 485. The only actual evidence of anything approaching the conception of a diplomatic bargain was McKinley's suggestion through Holls that American policy in the Philippines would take account of Great Britain's interests as against Germany in return for the modification of the Clayton-Bulwer Treaty. Balfour's rejection has been quoted. In fact Britain did not recognize the need to abandon supremacy in the Caribbean until after Lansdowne succeeded Salisbury at the Foreign Office and until January 1901 preceding the signing of the Olney-Pauncefote treaty concerning the canal. See Grenville, *op. cit.*, pp. 63-69.

44. Langer, *op. cit.*, II, 519.

45. Hay to Lodge, 27 July 1898. "I have been under great obligation the last few months to Spring Rice who knows Germany as few men do and has kept me wonderfully au courant of facts and opinions there. Voilà

l'ennemi in the present crisis." See Griswold, *op. cit.*, p. 21, and Dennis, *op. cit.*, p. 78.

46. Cf. T. Dennett, *Americans in Eastern Asia* (New York: Macmillan & Co., 1922). "One frequently meets the assumption that the Open Door policy was invented by John Hay and first applied in 1899. The Open Door policy is as old as our relations with Asia. It was pronounced in China as early as 1842 and the spirit of the policy is as old as the Declaration of Independence. The policy was not limited to China. It was enunciated on the coast of Africa in 1832 and was repeated in Japan and Korea many times before 1899," p. 111. Again, "The oldest economic foreign policy of the United States in foreign affairs was the demand for most favoured nation treatment for her merchants," p. 215.

47. Cf. Secretary of State Daniel Webster's instructions to Caleb Cushing, 1842: "Finally you will signify in decided terms and a positive manner that the Government of the United States would find it impossible to remain on terms of friendship and regard for the Emperor, if greater privileges or commercial facilities should be allowed to the subjects of any other Government than shall be granted to the citizens of the United States." Quoted P. H. Clyde, *The Far East* (3rd ed.; Englewood Cliffs, N.J.: Prentice-Hall, 1958), p. 130.

48. Dennett, *Americans in Eastern Asia*, p. ix.

49. See Griswold, *op. cit.*, pp. 48-49; Campbell, Jr., *Special Business Interests and the Open Door Policy*, pp. 44, 164-65; Beresford, *op. cit.*; and *Hansard*, 1898, LVI, 4-29 April, 283, 287, 1644-47, for examples of Beresford's speeches on the subject of the open door and the aggression of European powers especially Russia and China.

50. Beresford's name does not appear as an ordinary member or as a member of the executive in any of the letter books or minutes of the executive council of the Association of British Chambers of Commerce. These documents were very kindly made available to the author by the president and secretary of the Chambers in 1959. Beresford was, however, made an honorary member of the Chambers for 1899.

51. Salisbury Papers, Vol. CVI, No. 26, Salisbury to MacDonald, 26 October 1898.

52. *Ibid.*, China and Siam From and To 1895-1900, No. 15, MacDonald to E. Barrington, Christmas Day 1898.

53. *Ibid.*, MacDonald to Bertie, 18 October 1898.

54. *Ibid.*, Goschen to Balfour, 25 August 1898.

55. *Ibid.*, undated memorandum from Barrington to Salisbury.

56. *Ibid.*, Vol. CXXVI, Japan To and From 1895-1900, No. 56, Satow to Salisbury, 25 January 1899, Private.

57. E.g. FO17/1339, Balfour to MacDonald, Telegram No. 308, 18 October 1898.

58. *New York Times*, 23 February 1899. See also Campbell, Jr., *Anglo-American Understanding 1898-1903*, p. 164, n. 33.

59. FO17/1339, Balfour to MacDonald, Telegram No. 242, 15 August 1898.

60. Minute Book of the Executive Council of the Association of British

Chambers of Commerce, undated but covering the monthly meetings 15 August 1895 to 12 February 1907 inclusive, save for some omissions.

61. Lord Charles Beresford, *The Memoirs of Admiral Lord Charles Beresford* (London: Methuen & Co. Ltd., 1914), II, 424.

62. Salisbury Papers, unbound, 4 August 1898.

63. *Ibid.*, unbound; the letter to Beresford dated 1898 was enclosed with a letter to Lord Salisbury dated 3 August 1898.

64. E.g. *Hansard*, 1898, LVI, 4 April, 283, 284, 287.

65. Salisbury Papers, unbound, Northcote to Salisbury, 23 July 1898.

66. As a matter of fact Beresford himself had been considered as early as 1895 as the naval officer best suited to go to China to reorganize the Chinese fleet. "Much the best man to go would be Charlie Beresford *but* the Admiralty are rather in a fix about him as owing to his fighting 'my Lords' any overtures on their part might be *misconstrued* by him into a desire to get rid of him. Could Lord Salisbury or the Foreign Office approach him delicately on the subject? If the importance of the job (and of the man undertaking it) be properly placed to him it is possible he might accept it say for three years but we cannot move as far as he is concerned, you know what a ticklish man he is. Of course Admiralty would be pleased for him to go. If not we will get somebody else at once." Salisbury minuted on the bottom of this Admiralty memorandum: "I am afraid that reasons of a very similar character would prevent me from undertaking the negotiation." Salisbury Papers, Admiralty and War Office From and To 1895-1900, Lambton to Barrington, 30 November 1895.

67. *Ibid.*, The Queen From and To 1895-1900, 24 October 1898.

68. *Ibid.*, unbound, Northcote to Salisbury, 3 August 1898.

69. This amount was not paid until June 1899. See the Letter Book of the Executive Council of the Association of British Chambers of Commerce 1899, Letter No. 429. Beresford very kindly presented the Chambers with a copy of one of his books.

70. Salisbury Papers, unbound, Northcote to Salisbury, 13 March 1899 and 3 August 1898: "I had a talk with Jim yesterday and he will tell you how matters have been arranged financially for the present."

71. *Ibid.*, 26 February 1899.

72. *Ibid.*, Beresford to Salisbury, 9 August 1898 and Salisbury to Beresford, 11 August 1898.

73. *Ibid.*, Beresford to Salisbury, 14 August 1898.

74. *Ibid.*

75. *Ibid.*, 23 August 1898.

76. *Ibid.*

77. *Ibid.*, undated note from Barrington to Salisbury.

78. *Ibid.*, Beresford to Salisbury from S.S. "Parramatta," 27 September 1898.

79. FO17/1341, MacDonald to F.O., 23 October 1898 at request of Lord Charles Beresford, See also FO17/1337, MacDonald to F.O., 20 October 1898.

80. Salisbury Papers, Lord Charles Beresford, Beresford to Salisbury, 30 October 1898 from Tientsin.

81. *Ibid.*, 2 November 1898.

82. *Ibid.*, 15 November, at sea, Kiaochow–Shanghai.

83. *Ibid.*, 26 December 1898. These opinions were also forwarded officially (and very much more succinctly) through the British ambassador, who commented: "The statements of the Yangtse Viceroys to his Lordship are no more to be relied upon than the statements made to him by the Central Government. If there is any objection they know he is unofficial and temporary and they will say and promise anything to induce him to leave their particular jurisdiction and go to the next." FO17/1341, MacDonald to F.O., 15 December 1898 enclosing and commenting upon Beresford's telegram No. 352 dated Chinkiang, 12 December 1898.

84. Salisbury Papers, Lord Charles Beresford, Conger to Beresford, 31 October 1898.

85. *Ibid.*, Beresford to Salisbury, 18 November 1898 and 10 January 1899.

86. Northcote forwarded to Lord Salisbury a letter he had received from Beresford outlining his plans and hopes with the comment "the following may amuse you, especially the writer's views that he may be wanted to proceed to Japan to conclude a commercial alliance. I confess I think his report to the Chambers of Commerce will be a curiosity." *Ibid.*, Northcote to Salisbury, 11 December 1898.

87. FO17/1337, Beresford to MacDonald, enclosed in a letter from MacDonald to Bertie at the Foreign Office, 27 November 1898.

88. See p. 184.

89. FO17/1337, MacDonald to F.O., Despatch No. 214, 28 October 1898.

90. FO17/1341, MacDonald to F.O., Telegram No. 352, 15 December 1898, forwarding Beresford's telegram from Chinkiang of 12 December 1898.

91. FO17/1337, MacDonald to F.O., Despatch No. 214, 28 October 1898.

92. FO17/1341, MacDonald to F.O., 7 November 1898.

93. FO17/1337, Beresford to MacDonald from Chefoo, 12 November 1898, enclosed in MacDonald to Bertie of 27 November 1898.

94. *Ibid.*

95. *Ibid.*, MacDonald to Bertie enclosing a letter from Lieutenant-Colonel Browne to MacDonald from Chefoo, dated 15 December 1898.

96. Salisbury Papers, Vol. CXXVI, Japan To and From 1895-1900, No. 56, Satow to Salisbury, 25 January 1899.

97. *Ibid.*, Lord Charles Beresford, Northcote to Salisbury, 26 February 1899.

98. *Ibid.*, unbound, Goshen to Salisbury, 23 August 1899.

99. "Rockhill and Hippesley approached the problem of formulating a policy for the United States with primary interest in staving off the threatened partition of China." P. A. Varg, *Open Door Diplomat* (Urbana: University of Illinois Press, 1952), p. 24, on the authority of Hippesley to Rockhill, 25 July 1899, in Rockhill Papers. Hippesley's attitude to Beres-ford is well summed up in a letter to Rockhill: "I suggest negotiations be opened before Beresford arrives, for, bluff, garrulous, and unrestrained by any sense of responsibility as he is, and already committed to impossible

proposals, he will, I fear, do more harm than good by his speeches."
Griswold, *op. cit.*, p. 71.

100. Griswold, *op. cit.*, pp. 475-500.

101. Whether or not Hippesley was in any way acting upon Sir Robert Hart's orders is another matter. It is not indicated in the Hippesley-Rockhill correspondence, and there is no suggestion of it in Stanley F. Wright's exhaustive biography of Sir Robert Hart, *Hart and the Chinese Customs* (Belfast: Queen's University, 1950).

102. FO5/2408.

103. Quoted Varg, *op. cit.*, p. 29.

104. *Ibid.*, p. 31.

105. G. F. Kennan, *American Foreign Policy, 1900-1950* (Chicago: University of Chicago Press, 1951), p. 36. Kennan points out that this matter of the collection of the customs had been in dispute in Kowloon and that the first section of the note seems directed against the British.

106. FO5/2408, Minute by Bertie to Salisbury, 30 September 1899.

107. FO17/1769 is the case volume dealing with the appointment of Hart's successor, covering the problem from 1898 to 1905.

108. Varg, *op. cit.*, p. 29.

109. See above, n. 99.

110. Quoted Griswold, *op. cit.*, p. 67.

111. *Ibid.*, p. 87.

112. Campbell, Jr., *Special Business Interests and the Open Door Policy.*

113. Griswold, *op. cit.*, p. 26.

114. *Ibid.*, p. 70, and *New York Times*, 16 August 1899.

115. See above, n. 106. The discussion in the Foreign Office over the difficulties that could arise through adherence to the open door notes suggests very plainly that they were not of official British origin.

116. G. P. Hudson, *The Far East in World Politics* (Oxford: Clarendon Press, 1937), p. 113.

Conclusion

IT IS PERHAPS unnecessary to restate the conclusions reached in each section of the argument in this diplomatic history, but one or two points might well be made in retrospect. In the past, judgments concerning the nature of Anglo-American relations during and immediately after the Spanish-American War have been based chiefly upon examinations of public opinion. Conversely, when the available diplomatic documents have been used in conjunction with studies of public opinion, there has frequently been a failure to distinguish adequately between actual diplomatic action and what public opinion thought such action was or should have been. It is hoped that the preceding analysis provides a more accurate and a more complete assessment of the quality of friendship existing between the powers and of the effect of the war upon the Anglo-American diplomatic relationship.

In the first place the diplomatic record has borne out the belief engendered by public expressions of opinion on both sides of the Atlantic, that England showed marked consideration for American interests during the period of the war. This attitude was not in any way affected by America's refusal to co-operate actively with Great Britain in stabilizing the Far East. Before the outbreak of war cabinet made it quite apparent that Britain would not participate in any diplomatic action unless previously assured that such an action would be acceptable to the United States. Pressure from Spain and Austria was quite insufficient to alter this determination and Balfour even rejected the move sponsored by Pauncefote, Britain's experienced and trusted ambassador at Washington.

In guiding Britain's neutrality during the war the same policy persisted. In Spain and Egypt, as at Singapore and Hong Kong, the niceties of international law were frequently accommodated to Britain's purpose of demonstrating her friendly attitude towards the United States. If, as in the Philippines and Canada, British action remained within the law, part of the reason was that American interests were thus best served. During the peace negotiations Britain made it clear that no objection would be raised if the United States decided to annex the Philippines; it was made equally clear that if the Senate decided against annexation, Britain should be given first option to purchase the islands. She then held aloof, merely watching carefully to see that the situation did not become an occasion for the territorial aggrandisement of other European powers. During the war Britain had been forced, as a consequence of America's refusal to co-operate, to seek other methods of ensuring the Far Eastern settlement. Nevertheless, when in 1899 and 1900 by her elaboration of the open door notes America finally reached a point where she could seek Britain's co-operation in a policy from which Britain had been forced to depart, Salisbury and cabinet made every effort to co-operate within the limits of existing commitments to other European powers.

The second point that has appeared in the preceding pages is that Britain's policy has frequently been misrepresented. In the negotiations arising out of plans for a great power mediation the British ambassador in Washington was far more active than the Foreign Office could have wished and certainly far more active than they knew, lending his support to Austria's last-minute effort to prevent the outbreak of war. It thus appears that although England and the powers refrained from any intervention, Pauncefote, looked upon as the champion of Anglo-American friendship and co-operation, was in fact more opposed to American policy at this period than has ever been realized.

It has also been demonstrated that America was not indebted to England's restraint for the neutrality of the powers, nor was England's restraint decisive in preventing any last-minute intervention. Moreover, the type of intervention actually planned had nothing of the dramatic character with which it had previously been invested. In Balfour's terms it was no more than an academic gesture. It was chiefly to the rivalries and ambitions of the European powers that America owed her freedom of action. During the war Britain's naval force in the Philippines was concerned with observing the quality of American naval tactics and gunfire and was not in any way expecting or prepared to meet a clash with Germany in the interests of Anglo-American friendship. During the peace negotiations Britain did not, as has so frequently been claimed, bring any positive pressure to bear upon the United States in order to persuade the American executive to annex Spain's Pacific empire. After the war, this negative policy was continued and no attempt was made to capitalize upon wartime friendship by attempting to lead American Far Eastern policy into the service of British interests.

It has been shown, also, that the quality of Anglo-American friendship and the effect of the Spanish-American War upon Anglo-American relations have both been greatly exaggerated. Throughout the whole period the initiative toward co-operation and the concessions that were necessary to its continuance were, in both cases, British rather than American.

In fact one of the reasons that Britain's policy after March 1898 remained carefully negative was cabinet's understanding that any attempt to induce the American executive to adopt policies favoured by England would be very likely to produce the opposite result. This was because cabinet was well aware of the continuing Anglophobia always latent in American politics. After the war as before it, America continued her unilateral way, expecting and receiving those concessions which were, as in the Venezuelan and isthmian canal disputes, the measure of Britain's need and of her determination to achieve an Anglo-American entente.

Similarly in the history of Anglo-American diplomatic relations, as distinct from the development of English public opinion, the Spanish-American War was not a crucial event, for war-time friendship was quite inadequate as a basis either for the settlement of outstanding differences or for the development of a co-operative policy. Under threat from the European powers, Britain had begun her rapprochement with America as early as 1896, long before the Spanish-American War. By 1901, in the face of further European threats, she had, in the Olney-Pauncefote treaty which solved the isthmian canal dispute, abandoned any pretensions to supremacy in the American hemisphere. In the meantime the request for active co-operation had been made in March 1898. The rejection by America of this request for co-operation was the really crucial event in the history of Anglo-American diplomacy and indeed in the history of the Far East, for after this the paths of British and American Far Eastern policies diverged. Britain, left isolated in the Far East, was forced to make some practical arrangement with her European rivals. The result was the understanding with France and Russia, the reluctant acceptance of a spheres of influence policy, and ultimately the Anglo-Japanese Alliance. Meantime America, preoccupied with the disposal of Spain's colonies and with domestic elections, remained unconcerned with the problem of the Far East as a whole. When Hay was finally permitted by the slow development of American opinion to return to the larger issues, it was merely to seek British co-operation in a policy she herself had first devised but from which cabinet had departed because of the impossibility of maintaining it without active American participation.

At the turn of the century, as so often in the future, there were two basic conditions for Anglo-American co-operation in international affairs. The first was that Britain should wait upon the slow development of United States opinion and policy and then endeavour to accommodate to America's unilateral decisions British international commitments made during this waiting period. The second was that Britain should resign from any attempt to maintain in the American hemisphere those policies which the United States regarded as being in any way inimical to her national interests.

Bibliography

Primary Sources: Unpublished

Foreign Office (FO) correspondence, together with relevant documents from the Customs Office, the Colonial Office, the Admiralty, and the War Office, referring to the Spanish-American War, are collected in the Public Record Office, London, in the files listed below.

FO5, United States of America, Vols. 2262-2571 inclusive.
   The case volume dealing with the proposed mediation by the great powers is FO5/2517, containing all the relevant papers from the Austrian, German, Russian, French, Spanish, and American embassies. As the papers relating to the dispute between Britain and Germany in 1902 are collected in this volume, the German files are not included.
FO7, Austria, Vols. 1252-76 (1898).
FO17, China, Vols. 1332-44 (1898).
FO27, France, Vols. 3382-3400 (1898).
FO72, Spain, Vols. 2062-99 (1898-99).
FO115, Japan, Vols. 1075-77 (1898).
The Papers of the Third Marquess of Salisbury. (MSS in Christchurch College Library, Oxford).
The Private Papers of Lord Lansdowne and Sir Thomas Sanderson 1898-1905, General, Vol. XXXI. (MSS in the Foreign Office Library, London).

The Letter Books and Minute Books of the Executive Council of the Association of British Chambers of Commerce.

Primary Sources: Published

House Documents, 55th Congress, 3rd Session, 1898-99. Vol. I, No. 1, Vol. II, No. 3, Vol. XII, No. 3, 1898. Washington: Government Printing Office, 1901.

Foreign Relations of the United States. 1896, 1897, 1898, 1899. Washington: Government Printing Office, 1897-1901.

GOOCH, G. P., and TEMPERLEY, H. W. (eds.). *British Documents on the Origins of the World War, 1898-1914.* Vols. I and II. London: H.M.S.O., 1926-38.

Hansard, The Parliamentary Debates of the United Kingdom of Great Britain and Ireland, 1898, 1899, 1902. London: H.M.S.O., 1898-1902.

LEPSIUS, JOHANNES, et al. (eds.). *Die Grosse Politik der Europäischen Kabinette 1871-1914.* Band XV. Berlin, 1924.

Secondary Sources

A. BIOGRAPHIES AND LETTERS

ADAMS, H. *The Education of Henry Adams: An Autobiography.* Boston: Merrymount Press, 1918.

BERESFORD, Lord Charles. *The Memoirs of Admiral Lord Charles Beresford.* 2 vols. London: Methuen & Co. Ltd., 1914.

BUCKLE, G. E. (ed.). *The Letters of Queen Victoria.* Series III, 1886-1901. 3 vols. London: Murray & Co., 1930-32.

BÜLOW. *Memoirs of Prince von Bülow.* Translated by F. A. Voigt and G. Dunlop. 4 vols. London: Putnam, 1931-32.

DENNETT, T. *John Hay.* New York: Dodd Mead & Co., 1933.

DEWEY, G. *Autobiography of George Dewey.* New York: C. Scribner & Sons, 1913.

DUGDALE, B. E. C. *Arthur James Balfour.* Vol. I. London: Hutchinson & Co., 1936.

GARDINER, A. W. *The Life of Sir William Harcourt.* London: Constable & Co. Ltd., 1923.

GARVIN, J. L. *The Life of Joseph Chamberlain.* 3 vols. London: Macmillan & Co., 1932-34.

GWYNN, S. (ed.). *The Letters and Friendships of Sir Cecil Spring Rice: A Record.* 2 vols. London: Constable & Co. Ltd., 1930.

JAMES, H. *Richard Olney and his Public Service.* Boston and New York: Houghton Mifflin & Co., 1923.

MOWAT, R. B. *Life of Lord Pauncefote, First Ambassador to the United States.* London: Houghton, 1929.

NEVINS, A. *Henry White: Thirty Years of American Diplomacy.* New York and London: Harper & Bros., 1930.

NEWTON, T. W. L. *Lord Lansdowne: A Biography.* London: Macmillan & Co., 1929.

Bibliography

OLCOTT, C. *The Life of William McKinley.* 2 vols. New York: Houghton Mifflin & Co., 1916.

THAYER, W. R. *The Life and Letters of John Hay.* 2 vols. Boston and New York: Houghton, 1915.

VARG, P. A. *Open Door Diplomat: The Life of W. W. Rockhill.* Urbana: University of Illinois Press, 1952.

WOLFF, H. D. *Rambling Recollections.* London: Macmillan & Co., 1908.

WRIGHT, S. F. *Hart and the Chinese Customs.* Belfast: Queen's University, 1950.

B. GENERAL WORKS

ALLEN, H. C. *Great Britain and the United States: A History of Anglo-American Relations 1783-1952.* London: Odhams Press, 1954.

BEMIS, S. F. *A Diplomatic History of the United States.* 3rd ed. New York: Holt & Co., 1950.

BENTON, E. J. *International Law and the Diplomacy of the Spanish-American War.* Baltimore: Johns Hopkins Press, 1908.

BERESFORD, Lord Charles. *The Break-up of China.* London: Harper & Bros., 1899.

BERTRAND, L., and PETRIE, C. *The History of Spain.* London: Appleton Century & Co., 1945.

BREBNER, J. B. *North Atlantic Triangle.* London: Ryerson Press, 1946.

CAMPBELL, A. E. *Great Britain and the United States 1895-1903.* London: Longmans, Green & Co., 1960.

CAMPBELL, Jr., C. S. *Special Business Interests and the Open Door Policy.* New Haven, Conn.: Yale University Press, 1951.

———. *Anglo-American Understanding 1898-1903.* Baltimore: Johns Hopkins Press, 1957.

CLYDE, P. H. *The Far East.* 3rd ed. Englewood Cliffs, N.J.: Prentice-Hall, 1958.

DENNETT, T. *Americans in Eastern Asia.* New York: Macmillan & Co., 1922.

DENNIS, A. L. P. *Adventures in American Diplomacy, 1896-1906.* New York: Dutton & Co., 1928.

ENSOR, R. C. K. *England 1870-1914.* London: Oxford University Press, 1936.

FAIRBANK, J. K. *The United States and China.* Cambridge, Mass.: Harvard University Press, 1951 and 1961.

FERRARA, O. *The Last Spanish War.* Translated by William E. Shea. London: Williams & Norgate, 1937.

GELBER, L. M. *The Rise of Anglo-American Friendship.* London and New York: Oxford University Press, 1938.

GRISWOLD, A. W. *The Far Eastern Policy of the United States.* New York: Harcourt Brace & Co., 1938.

HEINDEL, R. H. *The American Impact on Great Britain, 1898-1914.* Philadelphia: University of Pennsylvania Press, 1940.

HUDSON, G. P. *The Far East in World Politics.* Oxford: Clarendon Press, 1937.
KENNAN, G. F. *American Foreign Policy, 1900-1950.* Chicago: University of Chicago Press, 1951.
LANGER, W. L. *The Diplomacy of Imperialism.* 2nd ed. New York: A. A. Knopf, 1951.
LODGE, H. C. *The War with Spain.* New York: Harper & Bros., 1899.
MILLIS, W. *The Martial Spirit: A Study of Our War with Spain.* Boston & New York: Houghton Mifflin Co., 1931.
MORSE, H. B., and McNAIR, H. F. *Far Eastern International Relations.* Boston and New York: Houghton, 1931.
MOWAT, R. B. *The American Entente.* London: Oxford University Press, 1939.
————. *The Diplomatic Relations of Great Britain and the United States.* London: Arnold & Co., 1925.
NEWTON, A. P. *A Hundred Years of the British Empire.* London: Methuen & Co. Ltd., 1940.
PELCOVITS, N. A. *Old China Hands and the Foreign Office.* New York: King's Crown Press, 1948.
REUTER, B. A. *Anglo-American Relations During the Spanish-American War.* New York: Macmillan & Co., 1924.
RIPPY, J. F. *Latin America in World Politics.* New York: A. A. Knopf & Co., 1931.
SAVAGE, C. *The Policy of the United States Towards Maritime Commerce in War.* Vol. I, 1776-1914. Washington: United States Government Printing Office, 1934.
SMALLEY, G. W. *Anglo-American Memories.* 2nd series. London: Duckworth & Co., 1912.
SMITH, G. *The Treaty of Washington, 1871.* Cornell: Cornell University Press, 1941.
WILSON, H. B. *American Ambassadors to England, 1785-1928.* London: John Murray & Co., 1928.
WILSON, H. W. *The Downfall of Spain: Naval History of the Spanish-American War.* London: Low, Marston & Co., 1900.

C. ARTICLES

BAILEY, T. A. "Dewey and the Germans in Manila Bay," *American Historical Review,* XLV, No. 1 (October 1939), 59-81.
GRENVILLE, J. A. S. "Great Britain and the Isthmian Canal," *American Historical Review,* LXI, No. 1 (October 1955), 48-69.
NEALE, R. G. "Anglo-American Relations During the Spanish-American War: Some Problems," *Historical Studies Australia and New Zealand,* VI, No. 21 (1953), 72-89.
PRATT, J. W. "The 'Large Policy' of 1898," *Mississippi Valley Historical Review,* XIX (1932), 219-42.
OLNEY, R. "The International Isolation of the United States," *Atlantic Monthly,* LXXXI, No. 487 (May 1898), 577-88.

SHIPPEE, L. B. "Germany and the Spanish-American War," *American Historical Review*, XXX, No. 4 (July 1925), 754-77.

D. NEWSPAPERS

As explained in the Preface, no survey of public opinion was made, and these papers listed, except those in the Foreign Office files, were used only to check material used in the existing public opinion surveys.

ENGLISH: *Times* (London), 1898, 1902.
AMERICAN: *New York Times,* 1898, 1902.
　　　　　　New York Tribune, 1898, 1902.
　　　　　　New York Herald, 1898, 1902.
INCLUDED IN FOREIGN OFFICE FILES:
Singapore Free Press, 2 May 1898.
China Mail, 4 May 1898.

Index